THE AUTHORS:

Roy Lewis, Commonwealth correspondent of *The Times* (London), has been visiting Africa since 1952. His books include *Sierra Leone: A Modern Portrait; The English Middle Classes* (with Angus Maude); *The Boss* (with Rosemary Stewart); and *The Visitor's Book* (with Harry Ballam).

Yvonne Foy, a librarian and bibliographer, lived in Central Africa for many years.

PAINTING AFRICA
WHITE

Endpaper : Print of 1806 showing Dixcove, a British settlement on the Gold Coast (The United Africa Company Limited).

PAINTING AFRICA WHITE

WHITE

The Human Side of British Colonialism

Roy Lewis

and

Yvonne Foy

UNIVERSE BOOKS

New York

Published in the United States of America in
1971 by Universe Books
381 Park Avenue South, New York, N.Y. 10016

Published in Great Britain under
the title *The British in Africa*

Library of Congress Catalog Card Number:
75-148053

ISBN 0-87663-144-8

Printed in Great Britain

CONTENTS

ILLUSTRATIONS

EARLY SETTLERS (*between pp. 14 and 15*)

Title-page of *New Voyage to Guinea*, 1735, by John Atkins (British Museum)

George Cruikshank's cartoon, 'A strong proof of the Flourishing State of the Country' (Africana Museum, Johannesburg)

George Cruikshank's cartoon, 'All among the Hottentots capering ashore' (Africana Museum, Johannesburg)

Thomas Baines, Landing of the 1820 Settlers in Algoa Bay (The William Fehr Collection)

C. Vandenberg, Algoa Bay in 1820 (The William Fehr Collection)

TRANSPORT (*between pp. 30 and 31*)

Thomas Baines, *The Victoria Falls* (Courtauld Institute of Art)

Livingstone's *Ma Robert* (Mansell Collection)

White girl in rickshaw (British Museum)

Missionary in West Africa (Church Missionary Society)

Army & Navy price list, March 1911 (Army & Navy Stores)

Goldfields coach at the Royal Hotel, Potchefstroom, South Africa (Royal Commonwealth Society)

On trek in South Africa (Africana Museum, Johannesburg)

A carriage full to the Transvaal Goldfields (Radio Times Hulton Picture Library)

Carts going to the Transvaal Goldfields (Radio Times Hulton Picture Library)

Iron girder railway bridge over the Kumayli torrent (British Museum)

The trouble in the Transvaal (Radio Times Hulton Picture Library)

An armoured train by R.S.S. Baden-Powell (British Museum)

Traction engine in Matabeleland (Rhodes Museum, Bishop's Stortford)

Early English car in Khartoum (Werner Forman)

A car at Dodowah, Gold Coast (Royal Commonwealth Society)

Morning market, Kimberley, 1888 (State Information Office, Pretoria)
The new Primrose gold-mine (Radio Times Hulton Picture Library)
Gold-mining in South Africa, 1888 (Royal Commonwealth Society)
Cockney Liz's billiard saloon, Barberton (Radio Times Hulton Picture Library)
A bull dance in a Barberton canteen (Radio Times Hulton Picture Library)
A night's lodging in a Barberton hotel (Radio Times Hulton Picture Library)
A trading hulk in Nigeria (The United Africa Company Limited)
Shop in Freetown, Sierra Leone (The United Africa Company Limited)

SOCIAL LIFE (*between pp. 174 and 175*)

Lady Anne Barnard (The William Fehr Collection)
Sir Charles D'Oyly's Personages at the Cape (Africana Museum, Johannesburg)
T. W. Bowler, Sunday Concert in Cape Town (The William Fehr Collection)
Mrs Harkness's sitting room at Fort Murray (Africana Museum, Johannesburg)
At the Club, Port Elizabeth, 1867 (Radio Times Hulton Picture Library)
Tennis courts at Simonstown, *c.* 1885 (Royal Commonwealth Society)
Opening meet of the Salisbury hounds (British Museum)
Polo at Maseru (British Museum)

GOVERNMENT AND ARMY (*between pp. 190 and 191*)

Cartoon by I'ons of Sir Andries Stockenström (Africana Museum, Johannesburg)
Arrival of the Governor at Cape Coast Castle during the Ashanti War (Radio Times Hulton Picture Library)
Opening of the first Cape Parliament (Radio Times Hulton Picture Library)
Grand Palaver in the Gold Coast (Radio Times Hulton Picture Library)
Carved wooden panel on the palace doors of the Ogogo of Ikere Ekiti, now in the British Museum (Werner Forman)
Group at Government House, Entebbe (Royal Commonwealth Society)
Garden party at Freetown, Sierra Leone (Royal Commonwealth Society)
Departure of Governor from Freetown, Sierra Leone (Royal Commonwealth Society)
Visit of the Prince of Wales to Lagos, Nigeria (The United Africa Company Limited)
Defeat of the Ashantis, July 1824 (Radio Times Hulton Picture Library)
Ambushed by Kaffirs (The William Fehr Collection)
Kaffir women advancing as a screen to their men (Radio Times Hulton Picture Library)
Kaffirs bush-fighting (Radio Times Hulton Picture Library)
Landing troops on the Gold Coast, Ashanti War (Radio Times Hulton Picture Library)
The kings' slaughtering place, Kumassi (Radio Times Hulton Picture Library)

ILLUSTRATIONS

Awaiting Zulu impi at Greytown (Radio Times Hulton Picture Library)

Bringing Sekukuni to Pretoria (Africana Museum, Johannesburg)

The Queen's envoys in Bulawayo from Central African Archives (Rhodes Museum, Bishop's Stortford)

Wagon laager in the Matabele Wars (Rhodes Museum, Bishop's Stortford)

Seven pounders and barbed wire (Radio Times Hulton Picture Library)

Children chasing a shell by R.S.S. Baden-Powell (British Museum)

Field Hospital at Paareberg Drift (Radio Times Hulton Picture Library)

First Welsh Regiment in camp (Radio Times Hulton Picture Library)

Endpaper Print of 1806 ohowing Dixcove, a Diitish settlement on the Gold Coast (The United Africa Company Limited).

ACKNOWLEDGEMENT

The authors and publishers would like to thank all those mentioned above who have lent illustrations for the book. The photographs from the British Museum, the Army & Navy Stores, the Royal Commonwealth Society and the Royal Geographical Society were taken by John Freeman. The authors also wish to thank Mr D.H. Simpson, Librarian of the Royal Commonwealth Society Library; Rhodes House Library, Oxford; the Church Missionary Society and the International African Institute for help in their researches.

Picture research by Pat Hodgson and Kathy Henderson.

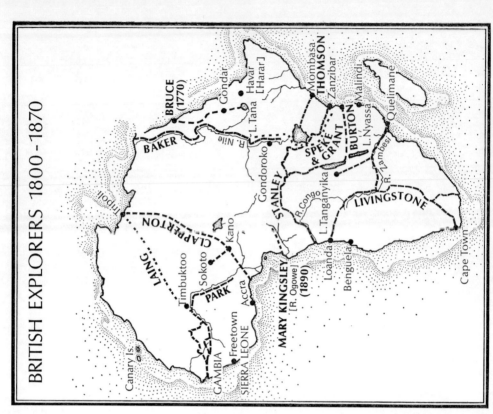

BRITISH EXPLORERS 1800-1870

BRUCE (1770)
Gondar
L. Tana
Havar [Harar]
Mombasa
THOMSON
Zanzibar
Malindi
Quelimane
BAKER
R. Nile
Gondoroko
SPEKE & GRANT
BURTON
L. Nyassa
STANLEY
R. Zambesi
R. Congo
L. Tanganyika
LIVINGSTONE
Tripoli
CLAPPERTON
Kano
LAING
Timbuktoo
Sokoto
PARK
Accra
Loanda
Benguela
MARY KINGSLEY [R. Ogowe] (1890)
Canary Is.
Freetown
SIERRA LEONE
GAMBIA
Cape Town

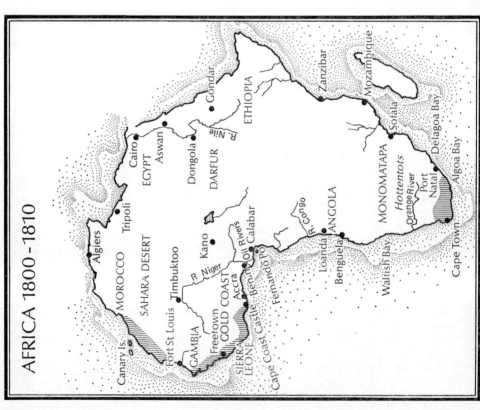

AFRICA 1800-1810

Algiers
Tripoli
MOROCCO
Cairo
EGYPT
Aswan
Dongola
DARFUR
Gondar
ETHIOPIA
R. Nile
Zanzibar
Mozambique
Sofala
MONOMATAPA
Hottentots
Orange River
Port Natal
Delagoa Bay
Algoa Bay
SAHARA DESERT
Timbuktoo
R. Niger
Kano
R. Congo
Loanda
ANGOLA
Benguela
Walfish Bay
Fort St Louis
GAMBIA
Freetown
SIERRA LEONE
GOLD COAST
Accra
Cape Coast Castle
Benin
Oil Rivers
Calabar
Fernando Po
Canary Is.
Cape Town

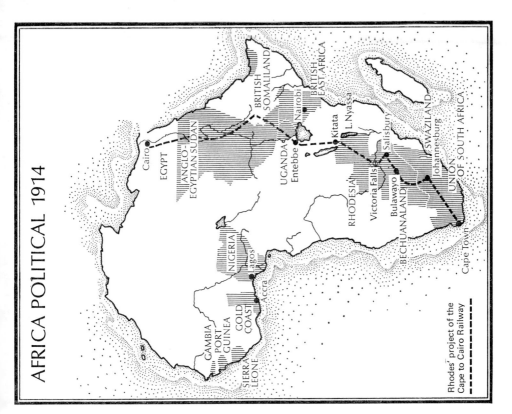

AFRICA POLITICAL 1914

Cairo

EGYPT

ANGLO-EGYPTIAN SUDAN

BRITISH SOMALILAND

BRITISH EAST AFRICA

Nairobi

UGANDA

Entebbe

Kitata

L. Nyassa

Salisbury

SWAZILAND

Johannesburg

RHODESIA

Victoria Falls

Bulawayo

BECHUANALAND

UNION OF SOUTH AFRICA

Cape Town

NIGERIA

Lagos

Accra

GAMBIA

PORT GUINEA

GOLD COAST

SIERRA LEONE

Rhodes' project of the
Cape to Cairo Railway ‐ ‐ ‐ ‐ ‐ ‐ ‐ ‐

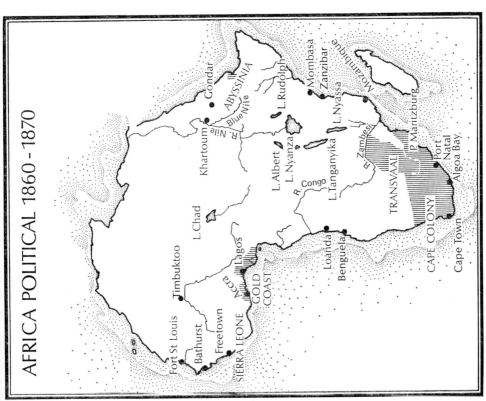

AFRICA POLITICAL 1860 - 1870

Gondar

ABYSSINIA

Blue Nile

R. Nile

Khartoum

L. Rudolph

Mombasa

Zanzibar

L. Nyassa

Mozambique

L. Albert

L. Nyanza

R. Congo

L. Tanganyika

Zambesi

P. Maritzburg

Port Natal

Algoa Bay.

TRANSVAAL

L. Chad

Timbuktoo

Fort St Louis

Bathurst

Freetown

SIERRA LEONE

GOLD COAST

Acca

Lagos

Loanda

Benguela

CAPE COLONY

Cape Town

BRIEF CHRONOLOGY

	NORTH OF THE ZAMBESI	SOUTH OF THE ZAMBESI
1787	Sierra Leone settled by freed black slaves.	
1791	Freetown founded.	
1795	Mungo Park's first exploration of West Africa and the Niger.	Cape of Good Hope occupied from Batavian Republic.
1805	Mungo Park's second exploration of West Africa and the Niger.	
1806		Cape annexed.
1820		British colonists arrive at Cape.
1822	Clapperton's expedition to Niger.	
1824	Sir C. MacCarthy defeated by Ashanti army.	
1833	Abolition of slavery in Empire, intensification of naval patrols.	Boers complain compensation for slaves inadequate.
1835		Great trek by Boers from British rule to Transvaal. British colony formed in Natal.
1841	Expedition up the Niger.	
1843	Gold Coast colony reconstituted.	War with Kaffirs entering British colony, extension of frontiers. Natal annexed.
1849		Byrne scheme settlers arrive in Natal.
1851	British navy captures Lagos.	
1862	Speke and Grant find Lake Victoria Nyanza as source of Nile.	
1868		Basutoland annexed.
1869	Dutch forts on West Coast purchased.	
1870		Diamonds found at Kimberley annexed from Orange Free State.
1871		Cape gets self-government.

	NORTH OF THE ZAMBESI	SOUTH OF THE ZAMBESI
1873	British expedition to Ashanti; treaty with Zanzibar; death of Livingstone.	
1879	Goldie forms Royal Niger Co.	British defeated at Isandhwana by Zulus.
1880		Zulus crushed at Ulundi.
1881		Transvaal Boers revolt, defeat British at Majuba, regain autonomy with 'Br suzereignty'
1883	African Lakes Co. formed to develop Nyasaland.	
1884	Somali coast forts occupied.	Bechuanaland annexed.
1885	Gordon killed by Mahdists at fall of Khartoum.	
1886		Gold rush to the Rand begins.
1889		De Beers monopoly formed by Rhodes.
1890	Zanzibar becomes British protectorate.	Rhodes becomes Cape Prime Minister. Swaziland under British and Boer rule.
1891		Rhodes sends pioneer column into Matabeleland.
1895	British expedition to Ashanti.	Jameson Raid to seize Transvaal for Britain failed.
1896	Kitchener advances against Mahdists.	Rhodesia created.
1897	Benin occupied and sacked.	Zululand annexed.
1898	Sierra Leone revolt crushed.	
1899	Kitchener occupies Sudan. Kenya–Uganda railway begun.	Anglo-Boer war begins.
1901	Ashanti annexed. Sokoto, Northern Nigeria, taken.	
1902		Boers sign peace.
1906		Last Zulu revolt crushed.
1910	Zanzibar annexed.	Union of South Africa formed.
1914	Britain seizes German Togoland and Kamerun with French; commences attack on Tanganyika.	Union seizes German S.W. Africa.
1923		Rhodesia votes not to join Union.
1924		Smuts defeated by Hertzog in elections.
1948		Dr Malan takes power in South Africa, speeds up apartheid.
1949	Coussey Commission recommends terms for Ghana independence.	
1956	Sudan independent.	
1957	Ghana independent.	

FOREWORD

When British adventurers began to explore the world during the sixteenth and seventeenth centuries, they discovered many ancient and well-founded civilizations, for example in the Middle East and Far East, that they recognized as not unlike their own. In India, Persia and China they encountered a social pattern that, although very different from anything they knew, was still largely comprehensible. But in Africa, to which they came last, they found little that they could understand, and less that they could wish to copy. At the best, their attitude towards native Africans was benevolent, if patronizing; at the worst, it was often crudely hostile.

'A savage *is* a savage,' declared R. M. Ballantyne as late as 1879, '. . . I have never met with what is styled "The Noble Savage" . . .' In 1874, the great English explorer, Sir Samuel White Baker, who, among his other disinterested achievements helped to crush the slave-trade, had expressed an even more contemptuous view: 'The treachery of the Negro is beyond belief; he has not a moral instinct and is below the brute. How is it possible to improve such abject animals?'

In the eyes of the nineteenth-century colonist, the African population was a dark, inert mass, on which he had undertaken to impose the benefits of technology and modern commerce. From India and the Middle East we borrowed much that was of lasting value; our conquest and occupation of Africa seems to have taught us almost nothing. No African words, for example, made their way into the English language. The relationship of British and Africans was particularly ill-balanced; and not until the opening of the twentieth century were intelligent Europeans first prepared to admit that the native peoples they governed and 'improved' might themselves conceivably possess a genuine artistic heritage.

The present volume depicts the rise and fall of a colonial system, that originated in the voyages of slavers and traders down Africa's long, unhealthy coastline; was built up over a period of a hundred and fifty years,

B   xvii

during which a succession of ramshackle trading-posts developed into prosperous settlements; and finally disappeared between 1956 and 1965. It is from the nineteenth century that Mr Roy Lewis and Mrs Yvonne Foy have drawn some of their most instructive data. Africa, in those days, was often the testing ground where British technologists tried out their new inventions. 'One of the first iron-hulled boats ever to be built . . . was constructed for Lander's expedition up the Niger in 1822'; and prefabricated ships and hutments were imported from England, and then assembled on African soil, very early in the century. Another useful import was corrugated iron, invented in the year 1832, with which perspicacious British settlers replaced the flimsy native thatched roofs.

Simultaneously, the British were introducing their peculiar social customs. As in India, they played their national games; and, in the eighteen-thirties, at Sierra Leone, a party of gentlemen, we are told, 'determined to brave the heat . . . by a game of cricket . . . They selected the scorching plain of the racecourse for the exertions of this exciting sport . . . Twelve or fourteen . . . blinded themselves to the folly. Abundant wines and liqueurs were at home for refreshment and hospitality . . . After a fortnight one only is said to have been living.'

Like every record of colonial enterprise, the story of the British in Africa is marked by strange and poignant contrasts. If midday cricket sometimes took its toll, so did the heroic struggle to build the African railroads. On the Beira–Umtali line, it was said that a white man died for every rail laid; and 1894 was considered a healthy year, as, out of every hundred Europeans employed, a mere forty-three had lost their lives. Lions, too, were a constant source of danger; during the building of the Kenya–Uganda railway, they carried off, besides many of the Indian labourers, two white employees and a chief of police. Later, a native tribe attacked the coolies, whom they accused of corrupting their women and boys. These hardy tribesmen put up a fierce resistance; but – a more sinister aspect of Anglo-African history – they were eventually reduced to order with the help of modern maxim guns.

PETER QUENNELL

I

THE LAST EMPIRE

The last British Empire was Africa. There were governors, judges, churches and clergy, schools and scholars, politicians and news-sheets, balls and banquets, marrying and giving in marriage among the British in the Americas for two hundred years before there were British homes in Africa. Sydney had been a colonial town for thirty years before the first British settlers struggled ashore at Algoa Bay. In the eighteenth century the British realized that their experience in the Caribbean and the American colonies was no guide to Africa's inhospitality. Freetown was colonized as a homeland for the domesticated African slaves of the English who had been liberated by Mansfield's judgement that all men who landed in Britain became free; a judgement which, however, did not provide them with employment or wages, so that, as was to be shown again and again, the liberated slave was often worse off materially and psychologically than he had been in servitude. Botany Bay was settled with white convicts, Freetown with African ex-slaves, and, there being a shortage of black women in London, a handful of English prostitutes for their comfort and the magistrates' convenience. From such beginnings two great adventures began, one leading to white Australia, the other to African nationalism.

DARK CONTINENT

The British experience of Africa was relatively short. It began with voyaging and slaving down a long, low, miasmic coastline whose real importance was that it was a backdrop and anchorage for the naval warfare that was dividing the new worlds between Britain and her European rivals. The coasts – Ivory Coast, Gold Coast, Guinea Coast, Slave Coast, Grain Coast – were charted, but only the outline of the continent was known when the Scots and English engineers were already experimenting with the locomotive steam engine, and the industrial revolution was in full swing in Britain.

What lay beyond the mangrove swamps, the breakers and the lagoons was largely conjecture – the reports of a few coastbound missionaries and traders, the myths of Prester John, a few travellers' tales of Barbary and Ethiopia, and the forest fires that could be seen glowing from the decks of inshore Indiamen making for Bombay and Calcutta. Occasionally an Indiaman was wrecked, but few if any of those who got ashore returned to tell of life among the African tribes. The hazard of English ladies becoming the bedmates of savages, and having to bear a line of half-caste children for them, seems to have stirred racial feelings in some who reflected upon the fate of the *Grosvenor* which in 1787 went ashore and broke up in the mouth of the Great Kei River in Pondoland. To ship off London's liberated black slaves with a few drabs to Freetown was apparently a natural expedient, but more than one effort was made to find out what happened to the white women passengers on the *Grosvenor*, and some relief felt at indications that they did not long survive their landfall.

Social life under the Union Jack in Africa began with the Gambia, bibulously, and ended ingloriously with Ian Smith. In 150 years the British built their Empire, most of it in the last two decades of the nineteenth century. It disappeared between 1956 and 1965. The British came in sailing ships, built forts and settlements on the coast, and in the 1840s began moving inland; in the 1950s they began to fly out in jets or stayed as B-class Afrikaners and Rhodesians. While they were *baas* and master there they told of their lives in books, diaries, articles and lectures, and letters home. From these records this impression of their life, the quality of their daily existence, the circumstance of the settlements they planted in the African environment, its impact on their minds and morals, has been put together. It is based on no new research. It seeks to pick out the changing form of outer living and inner feeling from the far more extensive expatiations on politics, on the African world, on the new flora and fauna. At home, there was a voracious market for accounts of Africa; anyone who could write, and especially who had a ready pencil – later a camera too – could find a publisher. 'It will be a great shame,' noted Alexander Stewart in his diary of Livingstone's expedition up the Zambesi, 'if I do not write a good book full of facts and graphic descriptions.' The public was eager for adventure, romance, travellers' tales, maps and routes and logistics of movement, amateur anthropology, descriptions of animals and recipes for killing them, and uplifting accounts of the progress of Christian evangelism. Social history touches all these things, but it is concerned essentially with daily life and its appurtenances.

The encounter with Africa was an encounter with Africans. There were no empty spaces for settlement; even when there seemed to be, Africans in hordes appeared as soon as the settlers had jobs to offer or cattle to steal. European life in Africa was as deeply pervaded by the personality of the black savage as in India it was by the Hindu and caste. Discovering, misunderstanding and rediscovering the African personality was a large theme in British historical experience in Africa. The process becomes inexorably the *leit-motiv* of studies in social history, even if it is essential in political history. British life in Africa was life with Africans – whether trading with them, fighting them or governing them. The black man was the module of all the natural marvels of the dark continent revealed to Victorian eyes by explorers. Yet the British kept aloof from him.

To Africa the British mentality brought all its previous experience, national or vicarious, of the exploration and subjugation of new continents. The British interlopers were ready, and indeed eager, to find something corresponding to the Inca Empire, and to destroy it. The hopes of early visitors like Jobson makes this clear. Rumours of such empires from Arab tales of Timbuctoo had reached Europe in the Middle Ages, but as the British progressed only from one barbaric authority to another, they ceased to expect marvels of that magnitude and often ceased to examine imaginatively what they did find. They came to expect mere savages, and the African kings who lived in some pomp, whether they were of Ashanti or Buganda or Barotse, were in the visitors' eyes only slightly more advanced savage chieftains. Africa became one of the several living Victorian museums of Darwinism. In the nineteenth century, the white man thought he saw in Africa clear confirmation that he stood on a pinnacle of evolution. The sensation of being *homo superior* seeped in irresistibly. The Hindus had their ancient cultures, religions, scriptures; so had the Chinese; elsewhere Islam had brought its science and literature; Africans were, it was felt, even less advanced than the Peruvian Indians. Such pleasure as there was in them was the return to the primordial past, a thing Victorian puritanism feared to indulge in too deeply. They found, specifically, that Africans smelt bad, without the least idea that African nostrils were offended reciprocally. 'A native's person has anything but a pleasant odour, which is natural to them, but does not agree with the taste of any white man.' This is a relatively perceptive reaction by an early visitor to the Cape. Eighteenth-century visitors rarely mentioned the 'sweaty multitude', but by the nineteenth century the British feared the smell carried contagion. Richard Lander worried when he saw Africans mashing his yams 'with hands that were far from clean'; a few years later Charles Livingstone complained that 'black humanity perspiring is not pleasant when one is eating'. So God, it emerged, had separated the African from *homo superior* not only by skin pigment but also by aroma. Victorian ladies sometimes tried to scrub it out. Failing, they required their 'boys' to wear white gloves when serving at table.

Some latter-day African savants have decided that white disrespect is a tragedy of chronology; how different it might have been if an Englishman from the illiterate court of Henry I had found himself in Songhai or Ghana, and had to bow as deeply as James I's envoys did to the Grand

Moghul! Instead they came to Africa puffed up with the virtue of emancipating black slaves – but with the conception of Africans only as slaves, porters, or eunuchs in harems.

British residence in Africa sprang dually from the philanthropic colony at Freetown, and from the take-over of Cape Town as a safeguard to the route of the Indiamen. And this imposes a difficulty in narrative, for the hinterland behind each toehold was for a century so different. Seaports have much in common, but West Africa and South Africa were for long quite separate white worlds, having in common only the African personality. The Central African plateau was a new environment again. Yet it is tedious to record their social development separately, because the motives as well as the equipment, mental and external, of the British were also common. So were the pipelines of experience and inspiration to the mother country. The same newspapers came off the mailboats, the same improved patterns of rifle were delivered, great as were the contrasts politically and climatically. It has therefore seemed best to make the distinctions broadly functional by the type of man and the type of vocation that went out, or grew up on the soil.

The communities were, after all, small. The British in West Africa never numbered more than a few thousands; for most of the nineteenth century the white population of Freetown averaged a bare hundred. The British settlers in South Africa grew to be a million strong and produced their fifth and sixth generations, but in 1875 there were only about 230,000, and in 1900 perhaps 450,000. The pioneer column which set off into Matabeleland in 1891 numbered 200 with 400 troops; today the Rhodesians number 240,000, the population – it was always said – of Bournemouth. (Some Bournemouth! was the retort.) The settlers of the Kenyan highlands never exceeded 30,000, apart from a contingent of businessmen and officials.

A man's life was as much determined by what he went out to do in Africa as by the part of Africa to which he went. We have therefore told in parallel, or perhaps in partial echelon, the story of the explorers and hunters, the traders, the officials, the settlers, the missionaries, the tourists, the soldiers. These professions, especially among the Victorians, frequently overlapped. Traders did duty as officials. Missionaries were among the greatest explorers. Almost everybody shot to destruction Africa's inconceivable wealth of wild life, probably the greatest such massacre in human history, unparalleled even on the United States' western frontier.

REDCOATS IN TANGIERS

The overture to British life in Africa was played in the seventeenth century. A settlement was attempted on James Island in the Gambia River, and another in Tangier, which was occupied by the British army from 1662 to 1684. In both places several of the leading themes of colonial life were introduced, notably drunkenness, maladministration, debt and a high mortality. Tangier came to Charles II as part of the dowry of Catherine de Braganza of Portugal and it was taken over and defended with two motives. The first was that it provided the king with an excuse to maintain Cromwell's standing army, which parliament was anxious to disband. The second was the vaguer hope that it might open the way to an empire that would give access to the fabled riches of Timbuctoo. This hope was also one motive for a colony on the Gambia River which it was supposed linked up with the Niger and provided a highway into the heart of Africa; when these hopes were disappointed, Fort James became simply the first of the British slave-forts. Fighting was almost continuous with the Moors at Tangier and with the French and Dutch over James Island, which was taken and rebuilt more than once. One important difference was that if you lost a battle on the Gambia River you lost your slaves to the French; if you were captured outside the walls of Tangier, you became a slave of the Arabs. The British withdrew from Tangier but hung on to Fort James.

The Tangier community was small – about 1,500 to 2,000 British, mostly troops, with Portuguese and Barbary merchants. Social distinctions were observed from the first. There was a *haut ton* of twenty top families headed by the Governor and his household; below them were the officials, the ministers, the doctor, the schoolmaster, the treasury agent and the junior officers. Below these were the common soldiers, merchants and shopkeepers, and sailors. At the bottom were the slaves.

Charles II paid erratically. The soldiers needed money for drink at the taverns that soldiers' widows kept. The shopkeepers battened on them and the Jews battened on the shopkeepers, besides making money on the side as double-agents. Pepys found, after twenty years of British culture, that there was 'in the whole place, nothing but vice of all sorts, swearing, drinking, cursing, etc: the women as bad as the men'. Pepys was exaggerating because it was his job to evacuate Tangier, and, like civil servants to follow him, he made the case for scuttle just as others earlier had made the case for colonization. In fact, drunkenness was as lightly regarded in Tangier as at Court, punishable only on duty. There were frequent brawls; robbery and murder were sporadic but punishments were severe even for coin-clipping, false weights, and selling drink without a liquor licence. A hangman was kept, but unhappily the hangman himself was under sentence of hanging for theft, so more resort was had to the pillory, houses of correction and the stocks. One form of punishment which was found useful in Tangier but was not, perhaps unfortunately, extended to the later British communities in Africa, was the ducking stool for female malice and gossip.

The climate was good, but the sanitation was contemporary, and mortality was high; yet Tangier was only two weeks out from Falmouth in favourable weather, and it was a place to visit. Entertainment imitated the Court at home. When the *Dreadnought* called in 1671, for instance, it landed 'Lady Midleton and several gentlemen of quality that come from Court . . .'. The Governor, Sir Hugh Cholmley and his wife entertained them 'at dinner and with dancing and at supper'; in 1669 the tone was set by Lord Henry Howard who 'streyned his fancy to find variety of divertisments', according to a letter from Colonel Norwood to Sir Joseph Williamson. 'It would challenge the notices in the Gazette . . . you get from France. Twice a week His Excellency has joyned men of his trayne to the woemen of this place to compose the rarest balls that have been knowne in Barbary. At back-sword, wrestling and bull-bayting we toyle as if the banke side of Thames were transplanted to Tangier.' Besides the balls and banquets there was a garden of pleasure 'where the ladies, the officers, and the better sort of people do refresh and divert themselves with wine, fruits and a very pretty bowling base'. There were amateur theatricals at Christmas with a theatre rigged in the storehouse, walks on the shore to watch the shipping passing through the straits, horticulture for the inevitable gardeners (Evelyn begged for cuttings), and church on Sunday. The schoolmaster was a Cambridge M.A., there was religious liberty, chaplains had an allowance of 6s. 8d. a day, the aldermen had scarlet robes and failed, as in England, to clear the mountains of offal in the streets. The Garrison hospital was a graveyard to which no patient went voluntarily. One Governor at least had the newspapers ('Newsbokes') sent in from home. The ladies had Spanish and Italian silks. But the best sport of the English upper classes – hunting and fowling – was usually attended by great risk from Moorish ambushes and snipers; even so, letters home extolled it, and when there was peace the local boars provided excellent pig-sticking for cavaliers.

The British also improved Tangier with walls, forts and a mole to make an all-weather harbour. When they left, however, they blew up their improvements, which was not a precedent for what has followed. They left because the upkeep was too great for Charles, and he wanted his redcoats home once parliament had got used to his having them – the Tangerines did good service at the battle of Sedgemoor. The Moors forced the British out by attrition. The fortifications were never strong enough to defy them as Gibraltar defied Spain from 1702 onwards. Seventeenth-century Britain was not capable of such a sustained effort of overseas administration.

COASTERS AND SLAVERS

These limitations were even more sharply revealed in the early history of the Gambia. The climate of Tangier was at least healthy; offshore one received from it 'a most odiferous smell like fume of cedar'. The fluxes to which the residents were prone had more to do with intemperance than with disease. In James Fort, malaria and the 'many sorts of distempers which are not known in Europe' took steady toll. They included cankers (yaws or frambesia), elephantiasis, worms, colic and the bloody flux (dysentry), which, noted Barbot in 1690, 'is not so common amongst the natives as the Europeans, many of whom are snatched away . . .'

The island was walled all round by the end of the seventeenth century, and was first defended with ninety small guns, later with thirty-eight great guns. Nevertheless it was five times taken by the French, and twice by pirates, apart from occasional mutinies arising from the intolerable conditions within. It lay in ruins for four or five years at a time, until the Royal Africa Company could get it rebuilt and reoccupied. Hence the British community there was an intermittent one. The high mortality soon gave the service of the Royal Africa Company a far worse reputation than Tangier had had, whither volunteers went in hopes of conquering all Barbary. The Gambia offered no such prospects. The attraction was less the service of the Company, for which its recruits were usually unsuitable, than the incidental rewards of peculation. When Corker was the Company's agent in 1699 the French Governor of the neighbouring and rival establishment at Albreda – which was frequently at war with the Fort – congratulated him on being recalled, on the grounds of his irregularities, to enjoy in a temperate climate the £50,000 he had made in a torrid one. The Factor Chidely operated his own mould for false coins in the Fort, cheated the troops of their pay and allowed a band of pirates to occupy the place in 1704.

The home government gave a subsidy to the Company to maintain a small garrison, and also allocated to it the proceeds of a ten per cent tax on the exports of non-Company traders when its monopoly was broken. This garrison, along with the local staff, formed the British community. As in Tangier, the soldiers at first brought out their wives, and attempts were made to create a residential community. When in 1721 the Company was once again occupying the island, they sent out a fleet of warships and transports under Colonel Whitney, which included about 170 factors, soldiers, artisans, women and children. The Fort lay in ruins after the last French attack and they encamped on the river bank. Within a year over seventy were dead, and the rest apparently did not last long. But Francis Moore in 1731 noted in his journal that 'In the evening the wife of our serjeant Mr Gilmore was brought to bed of a girl; they both did well, notwithstanding the opinion of a great many People in England who think it morally impossible for a White Woman to live in this countrey and bear children'.

The mortality of men was so great that their commander was at times a promoted private, and the garrison was reduced to two or three in number. The soldiers and company staff periodically deserted the fort to trade profitably on their own in the interior, and desertions to the pirates who periodically visited the river for dockyard repairs were not infrequent. A white woman is recorded as having committed suicide when her husband took this desperate course, for which another unfortunate factor, Rogers, was hanged in London in 1723.

Fort James was the first of a string of slave castles and forts which the British built or captured along the West African coast during the eighteenth century. It exported some 3,000 slaves a year, when in operation, and the other establishments did a larger trade. The hazards of war, tempests and disease – occasionally of African attacks – were tremendous, but the profits compared favourably with those obtained in trade at home, so that it was always possible to fill the places of the dead. The total number of whites involved was not in fact great, probably only a few thousand in the ships and shore establishments all told.

Not all the establishments were 'castles' in the full sense of garrisoned and defensible positions, like Cape Castle on the Gold Coast; there were lesser 'forts' and 'lodges' dotted between them, incapable of any real defence except against African marauders. These were subordinated to the 'castles' – for example, the British traders had two posts in Sierra Leone in the seventeenth century, a stone house in Sherbro surrounded by an earthwork and another at Bance Island long before Freetown was recognized as a natural site for a colony of emancipated slaves. Most were built of 'swish' – mud and wattle.

The Governor, or Chief Factor, of a castle normally had a council under him consisting of the 'commanders' of the neighbouring lesser stations, or country branches, up the rivers or along the coasts. These 'chief merchants' could live in some style, though the Dutch and French did themselves far better than the English. Under them were the factors, or merchants, the writers, or clerks, artificers in various skills from shipwrights to coppersmiths, surgeons, chaplains, officers and troops. At the bottom of the social scale were the castle slaves, who were, however, more like serfs in the later medieval period: they were paid wages, had considerable personal freedom and even conducted trade. They were capable of boxing a soldier's ears if they felt insulted and were only sold to the American plantations as a punishment for the worst offences.

The period of residence was about three years under the Royal African Company's service. The expectation of life was reckoned at five years. But while senior staff sometimes survived on the coast for twenty years, soldiers and juniors died like flies, partly because of their less healthy and more crowded quarters, and partly, no doubt, because of their diet – largely confined to smoked or salted meat, with preserved cheese, flour and butter. Scurvy was at first almost as great a hazard ashore as afloat. The growing of fruit and vegetables seems to have been beyond their abilities, and there was little market gardening among the Africans. Neither were clothes, except in so far as they became rags, nor buildings adapted to the tropics in the eighteenth century. Wigs and gloves astonished the Africans. The houses and lodges were built with verandahs after a time, and could catch the breezes. Cisterns were built to hold water, but it was frequently contaminated.

The steady loss of men by attrition and the difficulty of getting skilled workers led the British to commence the creation of a mulatto race which would be bound to their interest, but would resist the climate better. Concubinage with local African women was usual, notwithstanding the occasional presence of white wives. Francis Moore, the Royal African Company's factor in the Gambia, noted of the African women that 'If you will give them a little coral or a silk handkerchief you may take what Liberty you please with them', and even of the Christianized ones he added: 'If any white man has a fancy to any of them, and is to maintain them, they will make no scruple of living with him in the nature of a wife, without the ceremony of matrimony.'

According to William Smith in 1746, the provision of a concubine by the local friendly chief was 'a compliment always made to a European' and some early insights into the African personality were the result. Smith expatiated on the 'beautiful proportions and exact symmetry' of the girl with whom he was provided, and assured his readers that he was able to forget the complexion of his bedfellow 'and obey'd the dictates of all powerful nature. Greater pleasure I never found'. He reported that such vices as sodomy were wholly introduced by the Europeans, and 'the discerning Native account it their greatest Unhappiness that they were ever visited by Europeans. They say we Christians introduced the traffick of slaves, and that before our coming they had peace; but, say they, it is observable that whenever Christianity comes, there comes with it a sword, a gun, powder and ball.' However, the account of African society given by Mr Lamb, who 'was carried up country' from Ardah to the 'court of the king of Dahomey' was a good deal less favourable, and he anxiously wrote to the Royal African Society to ransom him 'with a cast-off white whore'.

As time went on skilled African labour became more available, but it was liable to all the usual hazards of coast life. Accordingly the castles were often in appalling disrepair. Though designed to ward off any enemy fleet, few were capable of it for long, if at all: an engineer who surveyed them said they were none of them equal to three or four ships of war. Part of the trouble was the lack of stone, or quarrymen to cut it, or transport to move it; much of it came out from Britain in ballast. Timber was also hard to cut and season, and such as there was soon rotted or was eaten by ants. One record notes that the kitchen roof fell in at Fort Commenda and nearly killed the cook.

Bricks were also sent out, but were used with mud and lime, not mortar, and the rains and rising damp soon made the walls bulge and crack. Roofs were thatched when tiles were not sent out. In the magazines, for example, the barrels would rot and split, spilling powder dangerously (the magazine blew up and destroyed Fort James in 1701), or had to be regularly spread on the battlements to dry off. Life was a round of desperate repairs, but one report noted that the head carpenter was 'an imposter' and the rest little better. In any event the castles were hardly built on the principles that would have deterred a strong landing party. They might have guns on their bastions capable of enfilading, but they were usually low on gunpowder and gunners, and the guns were frequently useless from rust and rotten carriages.

The main purpose of the castles in effect was to make a brave show, to keep the slaves in storage secure, and to deter African forces tempted by the stocks of trade goods they contained. Notwithstanding their seaward weakness, considerable African communities settled round them not merely to trade, but also for security, as in medieval England. Whether the insecurity of the interior was caused by the slave trade, or whether it made the slave trade possible, is a matter of controversy; the eighteenth-century traders in human muscle never asked such questions. Indeed, those on the coast had little idea, their writings show, of the cruelty of the trade as a whole. The middle passage, and conditions in the American plantations were largely unknown to them.

There are records of the daily routine. By day at Fort James there were three sentries, one at the gate, one at the door of the 'public room', and another patrolling and reporting the movement of boats to the Governor. At evening a lookout was set on the bastions to challenge all approaching canoes. A guard was set over the slaves to prevent a mutiny – necessary because on several occasions the slaves successfully rose and escaped. At intervals sentries called 'all's well' – or fired a musket to sound the alarm.

At daybreak the gates were opened, and the buying and bartering of slaves and trade goods took place. When ships arrived, the castle slaves and mulatto labour under a 'bumboy' unloaded them from canoes and lighters; the writers did the inventories, and the factors hastened operations, as ships' captains were in a hurry to leave before disease struck either them or the cargo. If the sailors spent long ashore they were soon the worse for palm wine, if not from the 'unwholesome mixture of limes, water, brandy and sugar which they call punch'.

Long periods of idleness, lethargy and illness supervened. There was little to do in one's leisure but drink, and bits of rum bottles are still to be found in profusion in the sands round the ruins of James Fort, the accumulations of 300 years' potations. Sailing for pleasure was unknown, and good hunting was on the whole too far inland to venture.

Exceptional men found plenty to interest them. Francis Moore was one of these. He survived twenty years of the coast to retire to Virginia, and both his intellectual curiosity and his temperate habits may have played their part. He studied and noted African habits, and made a major contribution to knowledge at that time through his book *Travels Into The Inland Parts of Africa*. His travels, however, were largely up the river and relied partly on the journal of Captain Stibbs, who disposed of the idea that the Gambia connected with the Niger, and reported that between its highest navigable point and the Niger was a distance of 250 miles – not to be traversed by a white man until Mungo Park's expedition.

Moore has provided an account of his routine in the Gambia in the eighteenth century; it is an epitome of the way Europeans could survive the West Coast climate for long thereafter; even at an early period his ingenuity was notable, and if all whites had been as careful they might have lived longer.

I got up at daybreak, in order to enjoy the Cool of the Mornings, and often-times took a ride of three or four Miles from Home, through Woods and Savannahs, the Air then being very pleasant: as soon as I came back I breakfasted on *Green* or *Bohea* Tea, or for want of it a sort of Tea which grows wild in the Woods, called *Simbong* . . . When I wanted sugar, which was seldom, I used Honey, reckon'd to be very wholesome; but if taken too much is apt to give a person the flux . . . for dinner I had frequently Beef, sometimes fresh, and sometimes powdered for it would keep in salt six or seven days without spoiling . . . Fowls are so cheap that you may buy them for three Charges of Gunpowder apiece.

The afternoon was the usual Time for Trade; but sometimes would last for three days together; which being my proper Business, I never neglected. If it ended soon, I would sometimes take a trip to the neighbouring Towns, and return'd home to supper; after which I amused myself with writing, reading or visiting my friends till bed-time, where I was commonly treated with Palm-wine, Honey-wine, or else a fruit called cola, which relishes water. I used frequently to go a-shooting, which was principally Doves and Partridges . . . Guests I used sometimes to have in plenty, some being Traders, and others messengers from the Great Men of the neighbouring kingdoms . . . The Negroe woman dressed my victuals for me in earthen ware, sweet and clean made by the Natives. I had a good large bedchamber and in the rainy weather I always kept a fire in it. My bed was raised from the ground about two feet upon Forks . . . I had a bed made of coarse cotton cloths, the produce of the country . . . six feet long and three wide . . . At the four corners of my bedstead I set up four poles to support a kind of pavillion made of thin cloth for keeping out the musquetoes.

WITH GUN AND CORRUGATED IRON

From the first the Europeans, and particularly the British, attacked Africa with their superior technology. If Africa resisted them for so long it was because her weapons were subtler and deadlier than those encountered in the East – and because the immediate rewards were meagre in terms of the casualties incurred. The Moors were too much for even a Cromwellian force in Tangier because, as was acknowledged, they had mastered the technique of European warfare. Gunpowder was effective against the Africans further south because they never learnt those techniques, and indeed the British could with equanimity sell them powder and firelocks made in Birmingham for sixteen shillings, because both deteriorated rapidly in the climate. But their wind-ships would bring the British to the coast of Africa: no further.

The rivers soon ended in sand-bars or cataracts, and on foot the be-wigged Briton was no better off than the negro. At the Cape, the Dutch were developing the ox-wagon and combining it with the musket; but they had penetrated only a short way inland when the British took over. Nonetheless in many ways the British astonished the Africans from the start: the way they conserved water and made it move in brick pipes, for example; their clocks and watches, their navigating instruments; their tools, down to the simplest (one of the greatest imports was nails); their capacity to build two-storey buildings and walk on each other's heads . . . and the simple savage's astonishment confirmed British conceit of its own prowess. The Africans were alternately impressed by British material appliances – a wizardry they compared with their own fetich – and contemptuous because of the fewness and sickliness of the men who deployed them. So alternately they submitted and rebelled in the belief that they were stronger.

Without the products of an industrial and scientific age, however, Africa could never have been subdued in the way America and Asia were. In Britain those implements were in the making. The slave trade itself was a stimulus to industrialization; the Africans, in return for slaves, wanted not just rum, but cloth and hardware. The demand for these from the Liverpool and Bristol merchants stimulated the Black Country, and it was among the mechanics of the Black Country that Boulton and Watt found the men who could make a reality of the steam-tight pistons and cylinders on which steam power was built.

Yet the taming by technology was a slow process. Life in the coastal towns could be based upon imports of the contemporary amenities of England, but the moment one tried to move inland the reversion to the primitive was quick indeed. Camp-life then became the norm of existence, a matter of rifles, tents, and portable living equipment. Waterproof cloth was going out to Africa in the 1820s and Mackintosh (rubberized cloth) from 1837. Steam and iron construction began to make an impression along the coasts from the 1830s. The tradition of prefabrication in English building was put to good use when iron began to be cast, rolled and wrought for largish structures. It was clearly valuable to meet the lack of African skills by using those at home, and a wide variety of prefabricated iron hutments, warehouses, churches and offices, were shipped out from early in the nineteenth century; Lambert and Holt were specialists in a popular type with semi-circular roofs. Wooden prefabs were mentioned by Anna Falconbridge in 1791–2: 'The last ship brought out a large house of 100 ft in length, which is to be erected in the vicinity of the Town as a hospital . . . the house is so constructed that it can be put up or taken down in a few hours, consequently may, at any time hereafter, be removed; and we understand several houses of the same kind are expected in two large ships, which are hourly looked for.'

The most conspicuous gap in materials available in Africa was roofing more permanent than thatch. Tiles and slates were imported, and among the first industries to be set up in South Africa were tile and brick factories, but the invention of corrugated iron sheeting in 1832 overcame the main difficulties. Iron girders, pipes, wire and tanks made European-style housing possible thereafter. Pumps, of course, were available in the eighteenth century to solve water and drainage problems.

Steam power was for almost the whole of the nineteenth century applied only to water transport in Africa, though a cornerstone of Cecil Rhodes' fortune was his possession of the only stationary steam engine in Kimberley in 1871. The rivers of West Africa, and a few in the east, above all the great African lakes, all offered obvious routes for steamboats, which could defy currents, and mount guns to deter war canoes. One of the earliest steamboats was in fact designed for Captain Tuckey's expedition up the Congo or 'Zaire' River. Sir Joseph Banks proposed an auxiliary twenty h.p. steam engine for a low draught sailing vessel to be specially built. It was to occupy only a third of the length, to consume daily about three tons of fuel (mango wood, it was thought, would burn well even when green), and to propel the ship at five or six knots. Boulton and Watt built the engine, which however proved quite incapable of the requirement; so it was left behind, though the engineers were keen to have another go at the design. One of the first iron-hulled boats ever to be built, the *Alburka*, was constructed by Harsley and Co. for Lander's expedition up the Niger in 1830. From the 1830s on, iron launches and small paddle and screw steamers began to appear in growing numbers on African rivers. Du Chaillu in 1862 records with satisfaction the stupefaction of the natives when a French steamer first puffed its way up the Gabon River. Steamers relieved the white man of the need either to row his own boats in the tropical heat, or trust himself to African canoes, but cataracts prevented them from getting far inland. The very design of iron hulls and girders, assembled from parts, suggested the portable boat, to be carried to inland lakes or above rapids in parts and reassembled, and they were being ordered by the missionary societies from the 1850s. Steamers were at times pushed above cataracts: the Mahdi captured the entire Anglo-Egyptian fleet of armed stern-wheelers after the fall of Khartoum, and operated them with captive Italian labour. The earliest African railway schemes were envisaged only as a link between steamer services on lakes and rivers.

Traction engines for road use did not appear in Africa until the 1870s when they were found useful in railway construction in Egypt and for goods traffic on the metalled sections of the Cape Colony roads. For railways Africa was at once too large and too sparsely inhabited until towards the end of the century, though Natal had the first short line in the 1860s. There were no roads, only bush paths and caravan routes where there were no rivers, and most of Africa was closed to pack animals by belts of tse-tse fly. Except on the veld, travel had to be on foot, or slung in a hammock between porters. The wheel was almost unusable over most of the territory. The bicycle was introduced as soon as the pedal and chain action was invented in the 1880s. The unicycle seems to have been an invention specifically for African conditions – a saddle or chair mounted on one wheel, sometimes between two wheels in tandem, and supported by African porters with poles, as a kind of improved hammock – bumpier but quicker.

Gas lighting was introduced into Cape Town in 1847. Other coastal cities gradually abandoned their oil lamps in its favour thereafter. It was laid on in hotels, theatres and public buildings, and in private homes by the end of the century. Electricity, both generated and in the form of hand torches was introduced about 1875. The African's day was, like that of the Englishman's remote ancestor, regulated by the sun: at first it could only be extended by candles and oil-lamps, but improved versions of the latter were introduced throughout the century – pressure and wicks in 1802, battery lamps in the 1870s. Hand tools were also improving – for example, by the introduction of the portable hand-drill in 1840.

It is fair to say that a large part of African social history is the social history of transport. This was Africa's basic theme, the abiding problem for explorer, hunter, merchant, missionary and soldier.

BY SAIL AND STEAM

Until the 1850s, and for many people long after, travel to Africa began with a lengthy sea voyage. The ships varied from 300 to 1,500 tons, and the journey from four weeks (to West Africa) to 60–90 days (to the Cape or Natal). The size of the ships likewise limited the tonnages that could be taken of both baggage and imported goods, such as machinery or building materials. The early passengers, whether steerage or cabin, brought their own food and drink for the voyage, bedding, clothing and utensils. Travelling receptacles were wooden boxes and chests, often horsehair covered, of traditional design and strength, leather handcases, and linen and canvas bags. The 'carpet-bag' began going out to Africa in the 1820s, and the 'Gladstone' followed. By an Act of 1842, ships had to allocate ten square feet per passenger, and to provide basic food. Even so, this meant 'close packing between decks'. The best ships were the Indiamen, which charged £50 for a cabin.

The steamers of the Union and Castle lines opened the way to Africa for settlers, tourists, visitors and officials. By 1857 mail steamers provided weekly sailings. By 1895 there were ships leaving almost daily and the

A NEW

VOYAGE

T O

G U I N E A:

DESCRIBING

The Cuftoms, Manners, Soil, Climate, Habits, Buildings, Education, Manual Arts, Agriculture, Trade, Employments, Languages, Ranks of Diftinction, Habitations, Diverfions, Marriages, and whatever elfe is memorable among the Inhabitants.

LIKEWISE,

An Account of their Animals, Minerals, &c. With great Variety of entertaining Incidents, worthy of Obfervation, that happen'd during the Author's Travels in that large Country.

Illuftrated with Cutts, engrav'd from Drawings taken from the Life.

With an Alphabetical INDEX.

By *W I L L I A M S M I T H,* Efq;

Appointed by the ROYAL AFRICAN COMPANY to furvey their Settlements, make Difcoveries, &c.

L O N D O N:

Printed for JOHN NOURSE, at the *Lamb* without *Temple-Bar.* MDDCXLIV.

Eighteenth-century Britain learned about Africa from travellers' reports. The title-page, incorporating publisher's blurb, of John Atkin's *New Voyage to Guinea*

The advertising wiles of promoters of emigration and land settlement schemes (such as that of James Byrne) exposed by George Cruikshank: the dream and the reality.

"All among the Hottentots Capering ashore !!! or the Blessings of Emigration to the Cape of Forlorn Hope (vie) To be half roasted by the Sun & Devoured by the Natives !!!

English and Scottish settlers coming ashore in 1820 at Algoa Bay: painting by Thomas Baines, founder of the nineteenth-century South African school of naturalist painters.

The reality of settlement was somewhat less terrifying than Cruikshank suggested. It began with the rough landing at Algoa Bay. Painting by C. Vandenberg.

time-tables were as much part of the mind of people dealing with Africa as was Bradshaw to those at home. Steamers introduced the Victorian shipboard routine on the Africa run, which became traditional and hardly changed between 1860 and 1920, though deck-space increased.

Early steamers took thirty-five days to Cape Town, which was gradually cut to twenty-one by 1900 as engines improved. Fares were fifty pounds to Cape Town, sixty pounds to Natal in 1860, but only ten to twenty pounds steerage, where the old rules about providing cooking utensils and bedding still applied.

Order and service gradually replaced the earlier cattle conditions. The voyages created friendships, and captains became well-known names on the Coast. They even insisted on rules for the chaperonage of wives, who began to be regular passengers by the 1890s. The ships were the lifelines to the metropolis – that 'great flagship of the race', as Conrad described Britain. Next in importance after settlers, the troops and the latest equip-ment, the ships brought newspapers, books and periodicals reporting that unconquerable advance of Progress which sustained morale in all dis-appointments in the African encounter. But before steamers plied, the gaps between ships could be wide, even at a major port like Freetown. It was not strange for a lady on shore to write a poem on 'A Light Barque from England', and a typical reference – in 1849 – runs:

On the 23rd [November] came in the 'Greenhow', the first vessel from England that has dropped anchor in the harbour since 19th August. Being so many months without hearing from home is one of the greatest privations we have. Everyone in the colony shared in the general anxiety for home news. M— tells me when he was here at a former period above *four* months sometimes elapsed without a vessel arriving from England.

Sir Charles Somerset organized the first England–Cape mail service in 1815, letters costing 3s. 6d. per ¼ oz. As in Britain, they were written on foolscap, folded and sealed with wax. When mails arrived from England at Durban a cannon was fired to advise people to call at the post office for letters. The colonies began to issue their own postage stamps in 1857 and Cape Town had pillar boxes from 1860. Internal postal services in South Africa began mid-century as postal carts to the towns could be organized along the routes. Post offices were set up, and by 1872 a regular daily post operated between Durban and Pietermaritzburg, and further inland one to three times a week. The letter rate was 1d. per oz. within Natal, 6d. to the interior or to Cape Colony, 1s. to Britain. Message carrying, however, in all parts of wild Africa was largely a matter of native messengers mounted or on foot.

The telegraph, introduced in Britain in 1850, did not begin to be laid in Africa until 1860–70, there being no railways to lay them alongside. The submarine cable was opened between London and the Cape in 1890, and the two English colonies were linked in 1878, so that Cape Town received the news of the Zulu victory at Isandhlwana within hours of its becoming known in Pietermaritzburg.

SAFARI OR TREK

In tropical Africa roads were few and local. In 1849 Mrs Melville, the wife of an official, noted that in Sierra Leone, occupied for fifty years or more,

There are no such things as carts, waggons, or even hand-barrows in the place ... everything that one person is able to carry is borne upon the head ... Unwieldy articles, such as casks, are slung upon poles of bamboo, which then are rested on the shoulders of several persons, while very large pieces of furniture are carried simply on the heads or shoulders of as many as are required to bear the weight.

In all Freetown there was but one sedan chair, and a few palanquins. Missionaries were to be seen dragged in rickshaws by liberated slaves.

The palanquin, for use in traversing bush paths, was described by Lady Hodgson, wife of the Gold Coast Governor in 1891.

There are two kinds: one is the ordinary hammock, in which the occupant travels lying down, and the other is known as a sitting hammock. The latter is by far the more comfortable, and it certainly is not so hot; it has also the advantage of allowing the occupant to see where he is going. The angle of the sitting hammock can be changed by means of a foot rest, and this is a great relief to your tired body on a long day's journey ... To every hammock are allowed 8 men, 4 carrying you when the road is wide enough for two to be abreast, and four ready to relieve their comrades on duty, or to assist them with the hammock over difficult ground. The hammock is made of stout canvas roped on to a bamboo pole, at each end of which is a flat cross-piece of wood which rests upon the bearers' heads, as two men walk in front and two behind.

For a century or more this was the method of transport for the sick, tired, women and children, though the last were occasionally moved in wheelbarrows, when horse or mule transport was impossible.

Crossing the many rivers of tropical Africa presented special problems. Where canoes or ferries were not available, this was a common method:

A rope would be stretched across, and a small packing case hung thereto, which was worked by pulleys. It is a very curious feeling to dangle 150 ft up in the air, with a roaring torrent beneath, and the knowledge that if the rope broke one would not be left to tell the tale. On one occasion, when soaring thus, the pulley would not work, and for a long time I remained suspended in mid-air. But, as it chanced, it was a broiling day, and the cool breeze up the river proved so delightful that I did not mind the delay. Once I saw an English lady who was so terrified at this mode of transit that she fainted and in this state had to be tied into the box.

In South Africa, the Dutch had made of the ox-wagon an instrument for turning almost the entire veld into a road, or land-sea; it could be disassembled for crossing mountains. The British at once adopted and praised it. The intermittency of the rivers hindered such transport in the wet season but never halted it for more than two or three weeks. Ox-wagons could cross the drifts like amphibious vehicles. But rinderpest, introduced from Asia in 1880, killed the oxen, and drought or locusts could stop them by destroying the pastures.

The resistance of tropical Africa to penetration is attested by the very slow introduction of railways, even light railways. Yet the light railway was the existing way to overcome the badness of roads and the want of mechanically propelled road vehicles. Four African obstacles stood in the way: desert, deep jungle, lack of water and fuel for locomotives, and hostile natives. The early lines in Natal and Cape Colony were local, indeed suburban, but they encouraged visions of what might be, as did the reports of the triumphs of British railway engineers in India and America. The first two locomotives arrived in Africa in 1859, one for the Natal line built by Robert Legg in London, and another by Hawthornes in Leith for the Cape Line; each came in pieces by sailing ship with its own engineer, who put it together and operated it thereafter. William Dabbs, the Cape engine driver, had a coloured man on the footplate to blow the whistle. By 1862 the link between Stellenbosch and the Cape was opened.

Major railway building hardly began until the 1880s. One railway at least failed under armed attack. When the Mahdists seized the Sudan it was decided to build a line westwards from the Red Sea coast at Suakin to the Nile at Berber, and run into them by train from the rear, so to speak, using railway know-how learnt in India. The line cost a million pounds, and ran only a few miles, and was chiefly notable for an armoured train; but Mahdist raiding parties prevented the railhead proceeding. Mountains of rails and equipment rotted at the port, and the project was abandoned in favour of Sir Garnet Wolseley's alternative of a rail link direct from Egypt. After the fall of Khartoum this had to wait until the 1890s.

The major railway sagas of the 1890s were four; Kitchener's line, which linked his Egyptian base with the Sudan; Rhodes's line to Bulawayo, Salisbury, Umtali and Beira; the link between Lourenco Marques and Natal; and finally the line from Mombasa to Lake Victoria, which created Kenya and Uganda – all built with the public money that became extractable from the Treasury when imperial policy at last dominated decisions. Railway supermen like Pauling and Lawson took charge, and systematic construction at the rate of a mile a day at predictable costs of between £4,000 and £9,000 a mile was introduced.

African labour could not build railways, so white men had to be brought in, or Indian coolies. Lines were built from ports at which materials could be landed, and advanced inwards, overcoming natural obstacles and other hazards, using working trains to bring up supplies of rails, food and water. The steaming 'working engine' drove like a drill slowly into the 'old' Africa and destroyed it, not without casualties. On the Laurenco Marques line, built first as a 2 ft light railway and later widened to 3 ft 6 ins, 500 Indian donkeys died in a few months, and 135 white men, from malaria and other African diseases. A white man died for every rail laid, it was said, and an African for every sleeper. Lawley, the contractor, fell from fifteen to ten stone in weight. When Pauling took over he kept samples of gravestones at his headquarters and all European staff had to choose their stone and pre- pare an epitaph. If a man was still alive at the end of his contract, he broke up the stone at a drinks party. Even so, his brothers and cousins died on the line; three successive book-keepers died in a month; five Scottish engineers died while building Fontesvilla bridge. 1894 was considered a healthy year as only forty-three per cent of the Europeans died. It was a repetition of early Freetown conditions in the heyday of the railway age.

The Kenya–Uganda railway was built by 'coolies' brought from India; their casualties were heavy as the result of malaria, blackwater, yaws and lions. The line was only one hundred miles towards Nairobi when it was almost halted by the attacks of man-eating lions at Tsavo, which preyed on the labour despite Indian army majors with guns and offers of rewards for pelts and cubs. The labour force nearly mutinied. Lions ate two white employees on the Beira line and nearly got Pauling himself on a trolley. At Tsavo they got, besides coolies, Ryall, the chief of police who had prevented the mutiny; he was scooped out of his bunk in his railway carriage. The completion of the railway was almost frustrated by the Nandi, who went to war with the 'iron snake' and the Asians who, it was alleged, debauched their women and little boys. By stealing the copper wire for the telegraph, they caused the first collision, which killed two more white men. The Nandi gave a good account of themselves until a hurriedly collected colonial force put them down with maxim guns.

From the new railheads, of course, traders and administrators had to take to the bush again by foot or in palanquins or on bicycles. The lines of rail were like tiny tubes or rhysomes boring into the continent; the 'bush' was vast. But the railway enabled the colonial authority to concentrate troops fast, and so to make administration ever more effective. By the 1920s the evolution of the internal combustion engine suggested freer locomotion in Africa, and road-making was put in hand – with the traditional inefficiency of the British. In South Africa roads came fast after the Boer War to meet the demand for the new motor transport. Steam cars are met in Africa from 1900; Governors wanted them. Elsewhere roads grew slowly. The first Cape to Cairo motor journey was not completed until the mid-1920s. Light planes were flying in Kenya by 1925 and demonstrating Africa's most obvious form of personal transport. Thereafter the need to 'adapt' to Africa to any degree progressively declined – and European standards, propped up by the consumer goods of Britain and America, and by cheap servants, rose spectacularly. . . .

This conquest of the bush was only possible because medical science complemented the progress in technology. From the first the Cape was found to be as healthy as Australia: the right destination for *poitrinaires*. Tropical Africa, from the experience of the Gambia River, was another world of deadly, hidden danger. Somehow only the most exceptional people supposed that the African had anything to teach the European about the best way to live in its heat, miasmas and exhalations. The first principle was to avoid the sun, which gave sunstroke 'with staggering and unconsciousness', and, as it was stated in *Coast and Bush Life in West Africa*: 'Never venture out in the deadly West African sun without wearing a helmet.' (It was specifically stated that a bowler would not do!) It was an illusion like so many others; for the West African sun is usually less powerful than the South African. From India were brought the spine pad, and helmet made of white rubber or cork, with a puggaree or light scarf bound round the base of the crown, both readily available from the Army and Navy Stores.

Sickness was inevitable. A medical treatise in the mid-nineteenth century warned the white resident that he must expect '. . . shivering, lassitude, headache and backache, cerebral excitement with raving delirium. Liver deranged – constant vomiting. Vomiting of blood. Chronic haemorrhage, Blackwater, shivering and rigors.' Other diseases of the coast were dysentery, jaundice, Asiatic cholera and typhoid. Malaria was, of course, the chief disease, for which a partial remedy was already known: quinine, used as a cure for all fevers in the eighteenth century. For one hundred and fifty years, white ears in Africa sang with the stuff, which was taken religiously, and without which indeed penetration of the continent would have been far slower.

Blackwater was scarcely known until Europeans went to Africa, and it was supposed at first to be an affliction peculiar to civilized living there, whereas leprosy was a malady of Africans, with whom it was supposed to have originated. Yellow fever, however, had been identified in Florida and was first seen in Senegal in 1778. Smallpox, which was a scourge to Africans, could be controlled by inoculation, which was made compulsory in Cape Colony in 1803.

It took time for medical science to find the antidotes; throughout the nineteenth century much of life in tropical Africa was lived in a condition of slight ill-health, and a sudden attack of 'intermittent' fever was always to be expected; it had to be fought or it compelled the abandonment of plans. The medicine chest was an essential component of travel in Africa: besides lint and bandages, it would contain Epsom salts, boracic powder, sulphur ointment, iodoform, and of course quinine and laudanum – which after the Crimean War came in the form of Dr J. Collis Brown's famous

'Chlorodyne' for bowel complaints. Other specifics were rhubarb pills, calomel and sulphate of zinc.

All these were needed at one time or another:

> It is astonishing how quickly that African fever prostrates a man, and with what equal rapidity he recovers – or dies – as the case may be. This is perhaps true only of its first attacks. Later on, when a man is saturated with malaria, he seems unable to shake off the fever. The recurrences are slight, but persistent, and it is then that complications arise and health is completely undermined,

wrote two nurses who joined the Rhodes column in Mashonaland in 1892. They also noted, however, that 'a great deal of illness which was attributed to fever and climate might with much truth be put down to the score of eccentric eating and drinking.'

UNDER THE HELMET

Merely shivering, or prostrate in a palanquin, the English staggered into the bush, building the African Empire which might, some fondly thought, rival their Indian one. They adapted themselves in dress only to the extent of the helmet. Otherwise in Africa they evolved slowly from knee-breeches, through trousers and frock-coats, to the Norfolk suit. But the growth of the cotton industry provided a growing selection of lightweight washable fabrics well suited to tropical life. They could not copy from the Africans – nobody 'went African' in clothing as elsewhere they 'went Oriental', beyond the decoration of hats and belts with animal trophies and skins.

But they did copy the Boers in the use of slouch hats and *veldschoen*, shoes made from animal pelts. In early Natal, for instance, the settlers soon found they had to make their own clothes. The first tailors in Pietermaritzburg were the Solomon brothers who opened a business in 1850, and six years later Miss Grant's millinery was set up in the same building.

For men, the Victorian outfitters produced the heavy woollen trousers and jackets used at home; the Norfolk suit became standard when it was introduced. Soldiers enjoyed wearing their regalia; Colonel Macdonald, for example, was bitterly upset when Lugard would not let him present himself in regimentals to the Kabaka in 1891 because the latter was suspicious of British warlike intentions.

The wearing of clothes, to the Victorians, was the primary expression of their civilization, and amid African barbarism its essential standard. It exalted them morally and technically: morally, because Christianity and Grundyism taught that nakedness, even partial, was wrong (indeed, African nakedness had to be described in roundabout expressions); technically, because European clothing was the primary product of a textile-manufacturing nation. Uncomfortable as the fabrics and cut of the garments now seem for tropical wear, it was a matter of national pride to be fittingly dressed for any occasion – as the explorers' journals indicate in particular; one wore full regimentals to be buried in if these were available. Watching the English leave their offices in Dar es Salaam at four, change into flannels for tennis, change again into stiff shirts and black ties for dinner, an American student of the colonial scene as late as 1920 declared that 'what will wilt an American, turn a Latin into a beachcomber, and make a Teuton look like a beefsteak wrapped in a wet rag, has no effect on the appearance of an Englishman. Neatness of appearance under all conditions is a shibboleth of the English, an interesting characteristic of their race.'

The first step in native enlightenment was the adoption of European garments. It was also a never-failing source of prim Victorian amusement at the black man's expense. The site for Freetown was bought from King Tom, the local potentate, for, *inter alia*, an embroidered waistcoat. To ingratiate himself with Mosilikatse, king of the Matabele, Cornwallis Harris the hunter brought him a many-mantled cape lined with silk, and a suit of tartan jacket and trews specially made for him by Mrs Moffat, the missionary. The top hat became the insignia of native authority, particularly in West Africa, and to a lesser extent in the south, where few white men wore it even in the towns. The convictions of the Victorians that their attire was itself a kind of armour against native hostility was perhaps strengthened by the many accounts of early explorers and the survivors of shipwrecks that the Africans or Arabs they encountered quickly stripped them naked and made off with their garments as items of the very greatest and rarest value and delight.

CHOP

The other great deficiency in Africa was a *cuisine*. There were game, vegetables and fruit, but they had to be cooked and served in European ways. Unlike China and India, Africa never enriched the British table with new dishes, or styles of cookery. The emptiness of Africa was enhanced by its gastronomic dreariness. The English despised the West African *fu-fu*, or yam-mash, but Coasters developed a modest taste for 'palm-oil chop' – meat or poultry, with vegetables stewed in palm-oil gravy. It never came to England, nor did that other great delicacy, ground-nut soup. In the bush, zebra could be cooked deliciously if you knew how, and elephant's heart was a delicacy, but the average fare was less interesting. From the first, what to eat in Africa was an obsession with visitors and travellers, who were, being Victorians, rather gross feeders. The appalling food at the hotels is a theme rivalled only by other discomforts. The Victorians from the first relied heavily on imported food, and benefited from the evolution of packaging. Preservation of food was developed by Durand in Britain from 1810, and preserving and pickling was an old tradition to meet the needs of the medieval 'hungry months' – though the Africans never attempted it themselves. The early visitors used ships' stores and imported such items as preserved hams and salted butter, as well as tea and coffee, which they soon tried to grow locally. Bottled perishables, like fish, fruit and vegetables, were largely imported from the 1840s, and tinned meat became a travelling standby from the 1860s onwards, after Pasteur's work had made it safer. Dehydrated vegetables were developed in the Boer War for the British troops. Frozen meat became available in the 1880s, but until the cities had refrigeration was little used in Africa. Shooting for the pot was the rule wherever game survived. Biltong – dried meat – was the traveller's preservative in South Africa, but humidity limited its use elsewhere.

The African drink, palm wine, though both nutritious and intoxicating when fermented, was never taken up except in severe droughts. The universal drinks at first were rum from the West Indies and brandy from France; the Cape vineyards began producing their own execrable brandy from the 1820s, and of course wine, which was otherwise imported. Soda water machines were brought into Africa in the 1830s. Ice machines came soon after, and the sundowner was then complete.

It was, however, necessary to eat some local meat, described by more than one housekeeper as 'fit to feed dogs with', and fowl which were always 'remarkably small'. 'One brings out loads of hams, tongues, cases of pre-served meat, fish, fruit, etc., and they are occasionally to be had tolerably good in the colony, but then one cannot live upon such things,' wrote Mrs Melville in 1849. 'I remember when small kegs containing half a dozen pickled tongues were sold here at £3 10s. . . . but people soon tire of such shipboard fare.' Imported staple foods for European consumption in fact fetched famine prices inland in Africa and whenever transport was difficult (as it usually was before railways, or during their construction). Few lived on 'native chop', and the long columns of porters that went with the white man inland were largely weighed down with his food as well as his tents, medicines, instruments and weapons. 'A large part of the cargo consisted of provisions,' wrote Mrs Hore in 1889 of her safari into Tanganyika. 'Such things as tea, coffee, sugar, and condiments have to be taken for the whole journey, and renewed year by year, and many other tinned goods, to help out the native foods, are taken, always remembering wheaten flour and ship's biscuits, which latter proved a great stand-by on all occasions.'

Eating properly was seen as a part of health. A recent article by a civil servant in West Africa recalls the advice given in the past:

A meal was enjoined half an hour after rising, that is at 5.30 a.m. if travelling, or 6 a.m. if in camp. This should be properly made up of coffee, tea or cocoa, preserved milk, a roll and butter or biscuits; a *caveat* was added that the last-named was neither so wholesome nor digestible as well-baked bread. 'One or two eggs, or a few sardines, may be advantageously added', for the experts on West African hygiene, nurtured on the merits of the *chota hazri* [early breakfast], con-sidered it highly improvident to start the day on an empty stomach. Next came breakfast, then still referred to as *déjeuner à la fourchette* and due at 11 o'clock. 'Begin with soup, then fish, game and meat of some kind, then vegetables, then a mere taste of some sweet, followed by a morsel of cheese. A little sound fruit for dessert, and *déjeuner* may be finished by a cup of *café noir*, drunk with a teaspoon of brandy' . . . For the nineteenth-century explorers of Africa, the proper time for dinner was considered to be 6.30 p.m. In its simplest [*sic*] form dinner was held to consist of the following courses, served in a carefully balanced sequence: a soup, a piece of fish, a *relevé* (the principal item), an *entrée*, an *entremet de légume*, a sweet, and a cheese savoury . . .

Nor did the Boers have much to offer the British in cuisine. A British governess in a Boer household noted the dull repetition of tasteless dishes: 'Always pumpkin, occasionally potatoes, usually rice, sometimes mealies. Meat always mutton. Beef rare and not good.' A book of South African recipes was not published until 1902, when Hildagonda Duckitt became known as the Mrs Beaton of South Africa, and her *Diary of a Cape House-keeper* became the prized possession of every South African housewife.

PALAVER

Nothing shows so strikingly the scant impact of African culture upon the British as the almost complete lack of any trace of African words or idioms in modern English. Social history is echoed in language. The English vocabulary was enriched by dozens of words from Hindi and military Urdu, as well as some Anglo-Indian colloquialisms. Though the colonial experience in Africa gave us many new and useful words, they come mainly from Afrikaans and Portuguese.

Historically the reason is that, as in other continents, the Portuguese adventurers first gave the natives the words for new European commodities, and named African or Asian novelties in Portuguese, lacking the native equivalent. These words the Africans politely handed back to the first English arrivals, and then took over more English words to create a new language, Pidgin English, and its more African variant, Krio, as a medium of commerce. Until the end of the eighteenth century no Englishman is known to have learned an African language, except Francis Moore, who may have had some syntax as well as a vocabulary of the Mande tongue. African languages were left to the missionaries, who began to understand their grammatical structure in the 1830s, but even their work had only a limited effect. The only two African languages widely studied by the earlier colonial administrators in the 1890s were Hausa and Swahili, since these were understood over considerable areas.

Words familiar to English newspaper readers, like *Veld*, meaning countryside, plain or plateau, of course came from Dutch. So did *Trek* (journey), *Drift* (ford), *Spoor* (trail), *Kopje* (low rocky hillock), *Laager* (encampment), and *In-* or *Outspan* (harnessing and unharnessing of oxen from a wagon). They evoke strongly the *Boer* (farmer) society which the British found and got to understand.

On the West Coast perhaps the most well-worn word the English annexed was *Palaver*, from the Portuguese *Palavra* (word), meaning anything from conversation and discussion to argument and trouble; one could talk of 'woman-palaver', for example, meaning trouble over a girl. *Pickin* (child) is also from the Portuguese, and so is the important word *Fetich*, meaning magic, or a God, from *Feitico* (idol). 'Chop', however, the universal word for food on the West Coast, is entirely Anglo-Saxon. It can be used as either a substantive or a verb. 'I go chop with you' means 'I will have a meal with you'. *Kraal*, which looks like an African word comes from the Spanish *Curral* (horse-pound), and *Assegai* is again Portuguese for a broad blade. *Sjambok* (whip) comes from the Malay, and 'Compound' is a corruption of the Malay *Kampong*.

Of African origin, all the Englishman picked up was *gorilla*, *tse-tse* (from the Bechuana word for a fly), *dash*, meaning a bribe or consideration, *ju-ju*, another word for magic, and *mumbo-jumbo*, meaning hocus-pocus, from a Mandingo word for God or bugbear. One African place-name, Mafeking, entered English permanently in 'mafficking' (rejoicing with hysterical boisterousness); *Zareba* (stockade) comes from Sudanese. *Askari* (soldier) and *Safari* (hunt) are both from Arabic. The basic East African word for a man, *Muntu*, plural *Bantu*, has barely entered English in the last few years, though it is used slangily in Rhodesia (and is now the accepted official word for African in South Africa – 'Native' having been abandoned because of its etymology). The word for African in the South was originally *Kaffir* ('Caffre'), the Arabic for unbeliever, and Negro in the West. The West Indians have left some traces on English usage, and have created a sub-culture of English patois, but the rich complexity of African oral tradition, none. In 1818 Captain Tracey was instructed to bring back examples of the written records of the Congo peoples. When the British discovered that there was no such literate culture in Africa they mostly assumed that there was no culture at all. A few individuals thought otherwise, but until ethnography became a systematic study, this view had little effect; it was assumed that the Africans had everything to learn from Europeans, but little beyond animal lore to teach.

Because the British were unready to study, even cursorily, African languages, African ceremonies and dances were likewise incomprehensible or uninteresting to them. They regarded the dancing and music as barbaric, the drums in various ways – menacing, tiresome, or amusing. They were, however, interested in the talking drums, the 'bush telegraph', and a few mastered its code. Even at recognized religious ceremonies the behaviour of the English could embarrass a more sensitive traveller. Lady Duff Gordon wrote, 'I went on the last evening of Ramadan to the Mosque, having heard there was a grand "function" . . . Priests, men, women and

English crowded in and out in the exterior division. The English behaved
à l'Anglaise – pushed each other, laughed, sneered and made a disgusting
display of themselves.' They turned from Africa to the re-creation in Africa
of a replica of British society. In the early stages it was simply insularity,
condemning Bantu and Boer alike. Bird, writing of 1820s society in Cape
Town, noted that 'An Englishman from the Orkneys to New South Wales,
is the same unbending creature. He accommodates himself with difficulty
to the manners of other countries; and nothing can ever be right or proper,
that is not English, and to which he is unaccustomed. The Scotch and Irish
mix more readily . . .' This English aloofness became superciliousness as
the century wore on, and finally under the influence of imperialism was
briefly transformed into a sense of mission in spreading British civilization,
constitutional and technological, to the benighted.

SOCIAL LIFE

The first problem was to establish the niceties of social life in small communities under the African sky. In the tropical colonies this was particularly
difficult. Mrs Melville, writing of Freetown in the 1840s, told her friends:

I cannot tell exactly how many Europeans there are in the colony, but I am
pretty sure they do not altogether amount to a hundred. They are made up of
civil and military officers, merchants and missionaries; while occasionally the
presence of a man-of-war in the harbour gives a pleasant addition to the colonial
society. There are no public amusements, except annual races. Dancing parties
cannot well be got up, where there is seldom even *one* unmarried lady in the
whole place; but there are dinner parties as at home; and a solitary friend quietly
drops in, now and then, to breakfast, or to spend the evening.

The lunch or dinner party was the staple social event, to which British
conventions were nailed like the flag. They were as stuffy and boring as
their counterparts at home, but with tropical variations. 'The dinner parties
are far from lively,' wrote Rankin, an authority of the 1830s.

Profusion of viands, fruits and wine, and a hospitable reception, strive to
counter-balance the uniformity of suffocating air and a reunion of the same
individuals perpetually repeated. The variegated locust, painted in purple, red,
and green, leaping into the soup-plate; the large black cricket plunging into the
wine-glass; the fat-bodied mantis plumping into the hot-spiced pepper-pot,
which needs no such addition, are novelties; but any charm the novelty may
possess soon subsides. Every contrivance to create a cool sensation fails: in vain
the refreshing orange and lime flower float in the finger-glass; in vain the water
in its porous red-ware jar evaporates, and sprinkles the globular surface with
dew; in vain the claret, Madeira and Sauterne have been for hours exposed to the
sea-breeze, the bottles encased in wet cotton and standing in a cooler; heat reigns
triumphant, favoured by the cloth clothing ceremoniously worn at such times.
Matters of local interest there are none to excite conversation; and, during a great

part of the year, arrivals from England are too few to afford new foreign topics. Coffee follows dinner, the horses are ordered, and the guests separate.

One such description can stand for the many on record.

PLAYING THE GAME

National festivals were the great occasions for communal relaxation, the renewal of traditions. The Boers met regularly at '*Nachtmaal*' to renew family ties and arrange marriages; the British ceremonially observed Christmas and, after 1837, the Queen's birthday. Poor George Mason and his friend, struggling to establish themselves in the early days of Natal colonization, found themselves with a shilling left on Christmas Day: 'and how could we employ our last shilling better than in procuring a Christmas dinner? Fortunately beef was cheap, so that 6d. bought about 3 lbs of prime meat, the other 6d. for 2 lbs of Cape raisins, which, with flour, sugar and eggs, etc. (that we possessed previously) furnished us with material for a good Christmas dinner.' The Mellys, travelling in the Sudan about the same time, did themselves better on the banks of the Nile: '*une dinde parfaite, des poulets farci à la turque, du mouton sauce aux câpres, du riz au currie, des gateaux de pommes de terre, plum pudding, et custard pudding, le tout arrosé d'ale, de champagne, et de St George en négus.*' In Mashonaland the first Christmas had to be done in such style as was possible: the day 'dawned on an already excited community,' wrote one of the pioneers; 'I do not think it exaggerating to say that by noon everyone, with the exception of three or four men, was very tipsy indeed . . . till the end of the year, says my diary, camp and township remained "on the burst".'

Organized games were taken early to Africa, even, some feared, to dangerous lengths. Rankin records that in the 1830s a party of gentlemen:

determined to brave the heat, and insult its power, by a game of cricket, with the thermometer probably at 98° in the shade; they selected the scorching plain of the racecourse for the exertions of this exciting sport, and in full exposure to the meridian sun . . . They left the cricket ground, burning with fever voluntarily sought; and after a fortnight only one is said to have been living.

Croquet required less exertion than cricket, and was introduced wherever grass could be grown (as at Government House). Where horses could be kept, polo was introduced from India – as Indian maharajahs played, emirs in Nigeria were expected to do the same in the Imperial heyday. Indeed, sport became almost compulsory as the public school spirit spread through the colonial empire in the 1890s. It was seen as another of the props to morale, like dressing for dinner. Training Africans in 'teamwork' became the great imperial duty. The diaries of district commissioners are full of it.

Practical joking was one of the greatest of home-made entertainments, sport, theatre and discipline in one. It has a long history in British social organization: cruelty and mirth, spontaneity and invention, closely inter-twined. It was the great relief of pent-up spirits before conformity became too powerful. In Africa the natives provided a stimulating audience for the pranks of the white man. It sometimes rose out of the sheer boredom of colonial life, as when a trader in Beaufort West wrote:

Here we are awfully wild coves, shy stones through windows and such like, the only amusement we can get just now. The people here never invite anyone to their houses at night; in fact a fellow may be here a long time before he passes the threshold of any of its worthy citizens ... everyone turns up his nose at his neighbour. I assure you I don't like to run any place down but for society I don't think there's a more beastly place on the globe.

It was common to plant insects in other people's beds, pretend to be wild animals, shoot out lamp posts, impersonate bishops; the stories, curiously boring so long after, stud nearly all African travelogues. Even Cecil Rhodes had his leg pulled, and taking such a setting down in good part was essential to popularity.

In South Africa, on the other hand, social gaieties were introduced earlier than on the West Coast. Within a few years of the arrival of the British settlers, Bird tells us that:

the private entertainments, whether given by the Dutch or the English, are in good style, and abound in all the delicacies of the season ... Musical parties occasionally take place at the Cape; and there are not wanting private performers of taste and execution; but the professors are few and not eminent. Dancing is the favourite amusement of the Cape ladies; for all prefer to do that in which they most excel ... The ladies of the colony, whether English or Cape-Dutch, appear to be little, if at all, inferior in grace and activity to the usual standard of London dancing, and superior to most of the provincial assemblies; but they cannot be expected to keep pace with the exquisite movements of the elegantes of a court. The waltz or quadrille are now the high Cape tone ... to these dancing assemblies a lady may go with her brother, or a friend, or alone, without fear of impertinent remark or intrusion. And she may return on foot at night, unattended, except by her slave with a lantern, without the slightest apprehension of alarm or insult ...

A theatre was built in Cape Town as early as 1807 and amateur companies were easily made up. Actors sometimes came to the Cape and Natal for their health. They could make money at performances at the Masonic and Trafalgar Halls in Durban, and the Dramatic Hall in Pietermaritzburg, which actually had dressing rooms and a portable gallery by the 1860s. Recitation, nigger minstrels, variety turns, the repertoire of the Victorian hall in London, were replicated.

Gradually, indeed, an African type emerged, though it varied a little from one colony to another. Whether it was the creation of writers at home, such as Kipling, Rider Haggard and lady novelists setting their romances in

Kenya or Rhodesia, or whether they took their portraits from life, is hard to say, but a self-reliant, humorous, compassionate, brave and versatile character emerges by the end of the century. Whether he runs a farm, or is revered by the tribe he rules alone, he is 'good with the natives' in a sense that people at home recognize as a very special art, only to be learned on the veld or in the bush. Once an ideal like Sanders of the River has been invented, people model themselves on it.

THE RETURN OF THE NATIVE

Somewhere between 1900 and 1930, the African knocked at the door and announced that he had taken the treatment, and had become civilized, if not an Englishman. There was nothing surprising to Coasters when Sir Samuel Lewis, who had become as rich and respectable as any white merchant, was presented to the Queen; but somehow he was felt to be egregious, not a portent. The British had become used to living among, doing good to, and being served by, smiling, obedient, tamed savages; some day perhaps they would become civilized, but the time got further off the more Africa became amenable. It became important to remember that they were, after all, savages, and no rash concessions should be made too soon. In 1879 R. M. Ballantyne wrote:

I use the term advisedly, because I wish to call things by their right names. A savage *is* a savage, and in my experience among the natives of different parts of the earth I have never met with what is styled the 'Noble savage', nor even heard of a genuine specimen, except in cases when individuals have embraced the civilising Gospel. Let me not be misunderstood. I have no sympathy whatever with those who regard 'niggers' as an inferior race of ignoble men, who are only fit to be killed or turned into beasts of burden for the benefit of the highly exalted and much self-praised white man ... But, on the other hand, I have little sympathy, and no agreement, with those who, forgetting, apparently, that this red-Kafir is in truth a savage, would treat him as if he were already a Christian and civilised man. To treat him kindly, justly, considerately, lovingly; to try to do him every possible good, and chiefly, to bring his soul in contact with the Saviour, is our simple duty, but to *trust* him is no part of our duty. It is worse than folly because it defeats our philanthropic views and prolongs his debasement. Who would trust a thief, or a liar, or a murderer? The whole Kafir nation, root and branch, is a huge thief, an inveterate liar, and a wholesale murderer.'

It was a statement made in the fear of a Zulu invasion and a more charitable expression of the view was usual. Mary Kingsley a few years later began to urge that the African be judged more seriously, insisting on the value of his traditions, and the need to understand his behaviour as intelligent, not childish. Her views were enlisted by those who advocated indirect rule as a means of keeping African village society intact. Meanwhile, the missionaries were educating Africans to the third and fourth generation to understand Europe and Europeans; but when they did it proved disconcerting. By 1900 complaints about the mission-educated boy was a cliché on every settler's lips. The odium for missionaries by every other branch of British society in Africa sharpened. Why did they have to teach Africans to read? Why not just carpentry? And cleanliness?

By the end of the century the problem of how to employ educated Africans, except as clergy, was becoming bothersome, particularly of course in West Africa where it was often felt that a suitable educated black man might well be appointed to the legislative council of some *other* colony, but it could not happen *here*. Nevertheless, Mathers voiced the general opinion in writing in 1907 that the 'destiny of the British people to open up Africa from South to North may safely be left to the hereditary capacities of the race.' Ewart Grogan, reviewing history, was not put out by the size of the African population, or its demonstrated capacity to survive the worst that nature and conquest could do to it, declared that the white man would take all in Africa as he had in North America. 'It is pathetic, but it is history,' Grogan remarked with relish as the new century opened and the 'old Africa' passed away.

2

EXPLORERS, HUNTERS AND TRAVELLERS

In 1795 Joseph Banks, on behalf of the African Association, engaged Mungo Park to find and trace the course of the Niger. With Park's travels, the systematic exploration of Africa by white men began. Banks had accompanied Captain Cook on his first voyage in the capacity of the expedition's botanist. He shared the fame of the team which opened the Pacific suddenly to western eyes, discovered New Zealand and charted the vastness of Australia. Cook's expedition was organized by the Royal Navy at the instance of the Royal Society: only public money and the Navy's resources could have won such a harvest so quickly. To Banks it seemed clear that Africa would not yield its secrets until land expeditions into its interior were similarly organized, equipped, financed and sent out with the backing of governments and the advice of scientific bodies at home. A critical French geographer, d'Anville, had shown how little was known of that immense interior once the legends of the mountains of the moon were set aside, along with Prester John and Monomotapa, and if the assumption that the Senegal River 'must be' the mouth of the Niger, and like assumptions, were treated as unproven. If the map were to be filled in, Europeans would have to go, see and survey in person.

FILLING IN THE EMPTY MAP

To promote that object, Banks formed the association in 1788, a year after Sierra Leone was colonized about a hundred subscribers, including some ladies in society, came in at two guineas each. The sum raised sufficed to project Park into a series of adventures which, when written up and published, rivalled Cook's travels in popularity. The association thereby made its point. Under pressure of public interest, the government, in its niggardly way, had to find the money, or part of it, for further exploration. Cook's feats, it was safe to surmise, could be repeated elsewhere in the

Transport

The main means of river transport were African canoes propelled by African muscles for the British explorers, traders – or tourists, here seen viewing the Victoria Falls.

The Victorians were, however, quick to use their steam power on the African waterways. David Livingstone's *Ma Robert* made slow progress against the Zambesi current in 1865.

The rickshaw was widely used for town transport in West and southern Africa.
The once-feared Zulu warriors were glad to find work pulling 'missie'.

The 'machila' for carrying white men along bush paths was a Portuguese innovation, readily adopted by the British. The reclining missionary used the slung-hammock type, but in 1907 the Army & Navy Stores catalogue offered an improved version.

The "Bellamy" West African Carrier.
(Registered design.)

Consists of a Roorkhee chair, suspended from a bar with cords and springs, leg rest and awning. Head pieces are provided for either 2 or 4 bearers. Invaluable for travelling in the bush. Each £5 15 0

The I. S. Carrier.
Long Wooden Pole, arranged with head boards and springs, for 4 bearers 20/6

Almost the entire veld, or South African plateau, was navigable by the ox-wagon. It could move before there were roads, could be dismantled, provided a mobile home, and, locked in a laager, these wagons formed forts.

The gold rush to the Rand in the 'eighties stripped the colonies of men, draught animals and vehicles, whose value soared. A string of carts for the Transvaal, about 1886.

Hotels were primitive until the gold boom opened up South Africa with roads and railways. The 'goldfields coach' at the Royal Hotel, Potchefstroom in 1888.

On trek in South Africa, surrounded by all worldly possessions.

Railways came to Africa in the 'sixties. The Royal Engineers played a leading part in pioneering their use – a short line from the Red Sea base of Napier's Abyssinian expedition in 1868, provided important lessons.

When the crisis between Britain and the Transvaal under Kruger became acute, the 'Outlanders' put their families on the train to Cape Town. The Jameson Raid in 1895 produced a crush at Park Station Johannesburg: in 1899 men fought for seats in the carriages.

Railways first played an important part in war in Africa in the Boer War. The British used armoured trains effectively against the Boers – the first operating under Baden-Powell on the outskirts of Mafeking.

Traction engines were tried in African conditions by Wolseley in Ashanti in 1873, but failed. They proved effective later in Rhodes' column in Matabeleland to generate electricity for searchlights and to power machinery.

Motor cars stimulated the building of roads. *Above* As early as the 1890s motorised vehicles were being built. This vehicle, amalgamating a cart-type body and a military chassis, was built in the Sudan for desert conditions in about 1895. *Below* A car with trailer at Dodowah, Gold Coast, in 1922.

world, but as the charting of coastlines neared completion after three centuries of navigation of the oceans, the next stage was to strike deeply inland. Park's expeditions were invaluable pioneering efforts – a sort of 'feasibility study' – which revealed what the problems and dangers of tropical African travel were. On Mungo Park's experiences ever more elaborate techniques and instrumentation of African travel, from the one-man mission to the military expedition, were developed in Britain during the following hundred years.

Popular interest in Africa was sustained by the century-long British fight against the slave trade. This was partly a government responsibility, partly the concern of the missionary societies. For both, exploration was necessary if the facts about slavery, which did not begin and end at the coastal forts, were to be obtained.

The growing profession of science also demanded facts. Africa's flora and fauna must be collected and classified. Beyond scientific knowledge lay the possibility of economic measures; Africa's mythical reputation had always been of wealth, and governments dared not ignore the possibility that it was deserved.

For the explorers themselves there was the pure excitement of discovery, which many of them described in full-bodied prose when they wrote up their journals for publication. More important, profitable careers and world-wide fame were to be built on travels into the unknown. Africa, populous and varied, was bound to produce more excitements than travels in Australia or even the American West.

After Waterloo the whole world was open to British explorers and travellers. Peace reigned in Europe. The seas were policed by the British Navy, whose ubiquitous sloops and gunboats constituted a launching-pad for British travellers, explorers and missions everywhere.

The Foreign Office maintained a corps of remarkable consuls dotted among the seaports of Africa and the world, one of whose tasks was to compile political and economic information about the interior. The English, secure in sea power and technical prowess, felt a profound self-confidence as they undertook all travels, major or minor, easy or dangerous. English-women shared that national self-confidence and took to travel likewise. The market for travel books began to grow; John Murray was the first publisher to make big profits for himself and for African explorers. A social forum for travellers was needed in London; the Raleigh Club was formed to provide it. A more expert base for explorers and the promotion of exploration was needed too; in 1830 the Royal Geographical Society was founded, to disseminate facts, prepare maps, collect books, issue instructions and test instruments and equipment. Lord Goderich, the Colonial Secretary, became first president of this 'point of union to travellers and scientific men, and depository of geographical information'. The Society became immensely influential, second only to the missionary societies, in the century of inland exploration. It financed some expeditions itself, but its real importance lay in the access of its officers, like Sir Roderick Murchison, to the government, and its ability to extract financial grants and other assistance such as naval passages and such useful appointments as temporary consul for explorers. Its medals were almost as coveted as the titles and orders that the government conferred on successful explorers. Its 'African nights' became a focal point of literary and scientific life in the capital, drawing the largest audiences for the reports of Grant, Speke, Livingstone and Burton.

It was obvious what had to be done. The great African river systems, which presumably were commercial routes, had to be found and surveyed; above all, the sources of the Nile, the courses of the Niger and Congo, and the upper reaches of the many other rivers whose mouths were already charted. The peoples and states of the interior had to be encountered and studied; and their co-operation and respect had to be gained. They must have cities and marts, but only Timbuctoo was known of. Was there a Monomotapa? Baird reached the heart of Abyssinia in 1770 and described its small cities and primitive customs, disposing of Prester John. The problems of getting in emerged. To the north there were the appalling perils of the desert crossing in camel caravans, and Arab hostility. Benjamin Rose, an American sailor, the first westerner to get to Timbuctoo, went as a slave after his ship was wrecked off Rio de Oro in 1811. (The African Association had his claims published.) The Arabs also held the east coast. The Egyptians or 'Turks' were on the Nile and their permission was needed to ascend it. After the treaty of Vienna, exploration northwards from the Cape became possible for the British, and the use of ox-wagons provided a method – until the fly-belt was reached. Tropical Africa was a terrain for walking and river navigation. Mungo Park was the first to test what this involved.

Park's preparations included a servant, a horse, provisions for two days, a change of linen, an umbrella and a 'small assortment of beads, amber and tobacco' as trade goods for barter. His instruments consisted of a pocket sextant, a compass and a thermometer. His armament was two fowling pieces and two pairs of pistols. One of his qualifications for the assignment was that he spoke Mandingo. His plan was to purchase food and shelter with his trade goods as he advanced. He quickly found that the price of his *laissez passers* from successive chiefs was very high, and that virtually everything a white man had was plunder to the impoverished natives. At Jong half his stores were taken, at Koonitang half of what remained was taken, by the chiefs of the territories through which he went; finally he himself became the prisoner of the 'moors' or Fulani who robbed him of his horse and compass. Here was the first lesson of African travel over any distance: how did one retain enough of one's stores to get any distance, for the exactions laid on travellers were so heavy from the outset that one soon became a pauper. Park was reduced to selling the buttons off his rags to buy food.

The white traveller proved to be not only a walking store of wealth to be stripped, but a store of technical knowledge to be exploited. Park was only the first explorer in Africa to be ordered to mend the broken guns and other imported European gadgets for his hosts who lacked the skills to do so. Park also learned to live off little but his curiosity value for four years. He brought back the information that the Niger flowed eastwards, and the more dubious impression that the native city of Sego provided 'a prospect of civilization and magnificence which I had little expected to find in the bosom of Africa'.

The logistics of the southward route from Tripoli, and the northward route from the Cape, were tested by a series of expeditions which followed Park's description of his journey to the Niger from the Gambia. Joseph Ritchie's attempt to cross the Sahara from Tripoli in 1816 only got as far as Murzah, where Ritchie and one of his companions died, while the third, Lyon, managed to return with a slave caravan, and with the unreliable surmise that the Niger was a tributary of the Nile. Clapperton, Denham and Hillman crossed the desert from Tripoli to Sokoto, but Timbuctoo remained unattainable till Laing reached the city in 1826, only to be murdered, however, on the way back. Grey's and Peddie's expeditions from the west both failed.

From the Cape, the first scientific journey northwards was made by William John Burchell, a Fellow of the Linneaen Society, in 1811; he was finally stopped by the waterless stretch of the Kalahari, and got no further than Bechuanaland. He returned after four years with 63,000 specimens of the flora and fauna of southern Africa. He was financed by the British Governor of the Cape, Lord Somerset. Alexander's large expedition overland to Delagoa Bay in 1830 was financed by the Royal Geographical Society to the tune of £750, from which he paid £40 for his wagon and £90 for ten pack animals.

The requirements of travel by both these routes was thus clarified; so were their hazards. Park's misfortunes revealed the need to take enough trade goods on porters' heads, with a sufficient guard, to get any distance from one native ruler's petty kingdom to the next. The Admiralty undertook a well-found expedition up river accompanied by Lander in 1830 with steamboats; but while these could move with success against warlike canoes, and carry adequate trade goods and armament, the expedition only got a limited distance before its members were prostrated with malaria. Lander himself was killed in an attack by African war canoes. The horrors of the Saharan route were fully revealed by Laing and his predecessors. While camels could carry 400 lbs compared with 30 lbs to 40 lbs for a man, and go for weeks without water – whereas a man needed five gallons every three days – their range was stretched to the extreme by the distances between oases. The caravans had to be both large and well-armed to hold off the Tuaregs and other marauders who operated from their own watered bases, rather like medieval robber barons who preferred plunder to trade. Though the British consul was foolish enough to suggest in 1822 that the route from Tripoli to Chad was as open as that from London to Edinburgh, the pioneers learnt that even for an Arab four or five crossings was considered an achievement of a lifetime. The desert routes were found to be marked mile by mile by the bones of human beings and camels; as a Golgotha for slaves it rivalled the middle passage, and the first of the British to return brought harrowing tales of their sufferings.

In a military sense the Arabs remained masters of the desert routes until the French began their gradual occupation after 1830. The southward route had to rely on the Nile in the 1860s, after Laing had found that Timbuctoo, so far from being a centre of manufacture, arts and learning, housed in buildings roofed with gold, was a sordid slave mart of mud houses, four mosques and crumbling walls, frequently at the mercy of the Tuareg.

PAYING THEIR WAY

To cross the desert Laing provided himself with four camels at £15 each, £10 for subsistence for himself and his three servants, and presents worth £40 2s. 0d. to obtain permission to proceed. When he exceeded the estimated all-in cost of the expedition, £640, Lord Bathurst became frantic. It was at the time when noblemen in England could 'rub along' on £40,000 per year.

The superiority of the wagon as transport for an explorer was clearly shown by the inventory of goods which Burchell took with him first in one and subsequently in two. His trade goods included, besides beads, which were light and easy to carry, such heavier items as bales of cotton, brass wire and copper sheeting. He took a great deal of provisions – rice, bread, biscuit, wines and brandy – besides casks for water. He had a complete tool chest as well as wagon and harness spares, a large armament including four barrels of gunpowder; nor did he forget medicines, instruments and artists' materials. His inventory, in every detail, as given in his book of travels, provided a checklist for any traveller in the south until the 1870s. But the moment the wagon disintegrated, or the oxen died of thirst, sickness or lack of food, any such expedition found itself in trouble.

Explorers faced the same problems of rapacious native chiefs in the south; and, if they did not encounter the formidable military power of the Arabs, powerful tribes organized for war, of which the fiercest were the Zulu, stood in their path. The Africans were as interested in the oxen, on which the travellers utterly depended, as in their trade goods. Two or three hundred miles from the coast the risks by this route were almost as great as on the other.

The routes from the East Coast, which began to be used by Burton, Livingstone, Speke and their successors in the 1850s, exhibited the disadvantages of the others combined. The Arabs looked with the greatest suspicion on the British who, they knew quite well, would end their profitable slaving industry as soon as they were strong enough. The Arabs knew it, and the British knew they knew it. The native chiefs in East Africa were more primitive than in the west, their culture sometimes neolithic, and therefore they were eager to possess the white travellers' valuables and magic appurtenances. The system of extorting *hongo* or gifts from visitors amounted to an onerous and arbitrary travel tax. The Arab readily fed African suspicions of the white man's intentions. Pack animals by the eastern route were unusable (though sometimes attempted) because of tse-tse, while fever was often as dangerous to health as on the West Coast.

THE EXPLORERS

But the difficulties were also the opportunities. They made the adventure a path to glory and sometimes riches. The dangers of Africa were irresistible to two types of men: the ambitious who wanted fame, and the scientific mind which sought new knowledge and the recognition its discovery ensured. To both Africa was a quarry, even if it was a graveyard. It helped some (Burchell, for example, and Lugard) forget a woman; for others it would prove one's manhood to a woman (Laing, for example, and Grogan).

When the Napoleonic Wars ended, the mass of half-pay and retired officers yielded a number of born explorers. They had endured the rigours of eighteenth-century campaigning, they were no strangers to danger and could assess a situation and the character of any other race they met in a conflict of wills. The big prizes – Timbuctoo, the source of the Nile – were there to be won.

Mungo Park was prepared to be obsequious and inconspicuous to gain his ends, even darkening his face on his canoe trip to Sego, on the way to Timbuctoo. Even Burton made his trip to Harar in disguise as an Arab merchant. After 1815 the tone of explorers became more imperious. Park did not take a Union Jack with him, but even Burchell did in 1811 and thereafter it became standard equipment. Clapperton, after his death in Sokoto, was wrapped in the flag by his servant Richard Lander. Explorers felt that in raising it they gave themselves its protection, though they were in the midst of African states two thousand miles from the nearest gunboat. In 1864, Samuel Baker proved the flag's mystic powers when the grasping but cowardly potentate, Kamrasi of Bunyoro, became terrified of an approaching army of Mbaras, strengthened by a Turkish (i.e. Arab) contingent, and called to the English visitors to fly with him. Instead the flag was raised, and to Kamrasi's amazement, the hostile forces retreated when informed that all beneath it were under the Great Queen's protection.

35

When Swann, a naval officer, and his three companions launched their steel lifeboat on Lake Tanganyika in 1882, for the London Missionary Society, they flew the Jack at its mast, and that evening 'we had not the heart to haul down the grand old British flag, emblem of liberty and justice, but left it at the masthead all that night. As I rose to retire to rest I raised my cap in respectful salute to the dear old flag, for it was the first time I saw it fluttering over a British craft in darkest Africa.'

Nor did explorers hesitate to tell African potentates that they were King George's or Queen Victoria's envoy, and that they were great princes or noblemen in their own country, instead of impecunious Scots, or the shifty agents of a joint-stock company. With the flag and nobility went, of course, the manner. It was obvious that one should not sit on the floor in front of an African kingling, as his subjects by custom did, let alone grovel there. The folding chair became an essential item of equipment. When Speke brought out his iron folding chair, opened it and sat on it as an iron throne before Ruwanika, he evoked the despairing refrain, 'Oh, these Wazungi, they know and do everything.' Speke stormed out of Mutesa's palace when the king was unpunctual. White men felt they were lost if they were not treated with respect.

In the eighteenth century, perhaps naturally, Africans could mock European clothes, or even declare them indecent, as the Fulani did poor Park's shrunken nankeen breeches. But European garments soon proclaimed the superiority of both the white race and its representatives in Africa, as well as the power of gun-backed Christianity. When Dixon Denham joined the Oudney-Clapperton expedition from Tripoli in 1822 he noted that 'we were the first English travellers who had determined to travel in our real characters as Britons and Christians and to wear our English dress; the buttons on our waistcoats, and our watches, caused the greatest astonishment.' Laing only put on European dress when he reached Timbuctoo. The prevalence of acacia thornbush made it hard to keep up appearances at times, so it was advisable to have a change of clothes in reserve for great occasions. Ladies took needles, thread and safety pins. Soldiers would carry their regimentals in a tin trunk. Clapperton presented himself in his naval uniform to the Emir of Kano. Kamrasi of Bunyoro was contemptuous of Baker's rags, until the explorer changed and strode in dressed in the kilt, sporran and glengarry, which he had kept in reserve. Gordon Cumming, the hunter, also impressed King Mosilikatse with the full glory of Highland attire.

The flag, moreover, was backed by superior weapons. The Africans, except in the remotest spots, had muskets; but even when the British had only flintlocks, they were usually of superior construction; more important, their owners knew more about their use. James Bruce astonished the King of Ethiopia in Gondar in 1770 by firing a candle end from his musket through three shields, and shamed the King's general. He knew the force of powder whatever the missile. Already the rifle was coming into use; and as soon as breech-loaders and percussion caps replaced muskets, revolvers replaced pistols, the explorer's superiority was even more easily demonstrated against man or beast. At Salah, the Arabs were amazed that Laing could fire a gun without a flint. African chiefs were eager to enlist expeditions in any forays they were making, knowing the effect of even a few accurate shots from rifles by Purdey or Bissett.

In some strange but not easily traceable way white prestige was rising through Africa. Perhaps less in West Africa than elsewhere. Richard Lander noted ruefully that in 1822 he was often 'coldly received', and that the curiosity of the natives was 'glutted with satiety', and that a 'European is shamefully considered no more than a man'. But this was on the Niger. Further from the coast they found that the words 'I am a white man' promoted awe, that they were considered 'a superior order of beings' because the Africans 'had heard marvellous stories of Europeans'. The renown of superior instruments and fetiches (watches were thought to be alive by Africans who had never seen them before) in some way preceded explorers by tales; consequently African chiefs felt complimented to have them as guests as well as allies. To have a British visitor raised a chief's prestige, even as he robbed him and sometimes even plotted his murder. The British insisted on talking as equals to chiefs, though up to the 1890s they were careful to accord them their ceremonial titles, such as 'Your Majesty'. In their journals these honorifics were narrated with humorous contempt as 'His Sable Majesty', 'the Royal Couple' and the like.

His prestige ensured the white man his safety from the Africans, if not from the Arabs; the Arabs, however, were conscious of the gunboats on their sea life-lines from the coast. Henry Drummond in 1888 opined that the reason why a white man could walk alone and unprotected among savage people was still 'a mystery at home', and supplied the answer: 'It is his moral power, his education, his civilization. His commonest acts are miracles; his clothes, his guns, his cooking utensils are supernatural.' Drummond asked the Nyasa peoples among whom he moved, and where a white man was then still a rarity, 'Why do you not kill me?', to which the reply came, 'Oh, we would never kill a spirit.'

This sense of moral power was strong in all the explorers. It enabled them to fight down tropical sickness, or march despite it. 'It is the mind that will bear Laing through,' wrote Laing. 'Should it fail me, what doctor could strengthen it?' To his father-in-law he wrote, 'You must always consider me safe, for it is my destiny to be so.' Alexander said he did not expect to survive his expedition but was content to serve his country, and Speke was determined to complete his discoveries or die in the attempt. Livingstone carried this sense of destiny to its highest point. Not all explorers were as certain that God was with them as of their indomitable British destinies; but the missionaries were.

Fame being the spur, and the very greatest prizes relatively few – there could only be one Nile, one Niger – ambition was a strong component of the African explorers, but so was egocentricity and even jealousy. Laing was consumed with anxiety lest Clapperton should get to Timbuctoo by the southern route before he did. There was friction between Denham and Clapperton about the discovery of the Niger, and Denham went so far as to blacken Clapperton in the eyes of Lord Bathurst with allegations that he was having homosexual relations with an Arab. Burton could not bear Speke to have discovered the Victoria Nyanza when he prospected for it alone, quarrelled with him and unwisely denied Speke's claims. Baker was chagrined when Speke and Grant turned up at Gondoroko on the Nile in 1864, having found the outlet at Ripon Falls – but was indebted to them by their kindly assurances that much was yet to be done in tracing the river's course to Lake Albert (where he found the Murchison Falls as a recompense for his and his wife's sufferings). Livingstone broke with the London Missionary Society for a single phrase of caution, and belittled or denied other explorers' work. During expeditions, quarrels between explorers were not infrequent; James Stewart joined the 1865 Zambesi expedition of David and Charles Livingstone with a profound veneration for the former; they parted coolly. So did Stanley and Emin Pasha.

LOGISTICS

As the century advanced, the logistics of an expedition into Africa were raised to an art; distance was almost directly proportionate to size, because of the amount of trade goods that had to be carried. The first consideration was the type of goods that the Africans would want en route to provide victuals, shelter and possibly protection for the expedition. Too little, and one ran out and became almost reduced to Mungo Park's or Clapperton's condition. As the century advanced, however, this became less of a disaster because relief expeditions, of which Stanley's for Livingstone was the most sensational, would be mounted, while the mere fact of being an Englishman kept the natives within limits of respect. Too much, and the cost of porterage became excessive, quite apart from the cost of feeding the men. 'Every day I must *give* – to the Turks, *give* to the natives, *give* . . . for twelve months I have had to talk, to explain, to manage, and to lead the brutes in this direction, like a coachman driving jibbing horses,' Baker said, and Stanley noted how fast *hongo* dues rose as caravans and expeditions multiplied between 1875 and 1889.

Richard Lander in 1825 attempted to travel with modest bartering powers. To penetrate the Niger, he and his brother took only fifty yards of 'sergeant cloth', 110 mirrors, 50 razors, 100 combs, 50,000 needles (but he found that the bottom had fallen out of the market), 100 pipes and 2 medals, in all worth £260 and weighing nearly 10 cwt. Beads soon became a drug on the West African market, but up to the 1880s the East and Central African natives wanted them. Cloth was important in East Africa where the natives were found to be wearing tree bark cloth, admittedly beautifully worked, the art of weaving not having reached them either from Egypt or West Africa. It was estimated that an African porter required about a yard of cloth a week to buy his subsistence, which meant a weight that could be calculated by the length of the journey. Though cloth was readily exchangeable, wire and sheet metal were equally important – indeed, what was needed was a variety of wares, so that the explorer could set out a small shop-window wherever he halted. Baker and others found, as the traders did, that the more you showed Africans, the lower the value of your goods became and the greater the cupidity of the buyers.

Chiefs expected a present consonant with the standing that the visitors gave themselves. The dilemma was that the more important you gave yourself out to be, the more princely the presents you were expected to give, and the sooner your capital was exhausted, or the longer and more expensive your train. This cupidity among the African princes annoyed the Victorians, hoist as they were on their own petard in this matter. African princes wanted more than trumpery; they wanted instruments and guns, down to the last items on which the successful return of the expedition depended. It infuriated Speke to be asked for a watch by a savage who would destroy it in two hours, and indeed Kamrasi complained to Baker that Speke's chronometer had 'gone dead'.

Above all the chiefs wanted the explorers' superior guns and ammunition. Baker saw Speke's rifle in Kamrasi's hands. When Baker wanted the girl Bacheeta as an interpreter, his obvious need put up her price to three double-barrelled guns, and on her side, since she disliked the change, she had to be appeased with his wife's petticoat and beads. Powder, bullets and caps were just as important, so improvident was native use of them; in West Africa chiefs were even known to demand cannon to defend their stockades and mount on their war canoes.

THE BLACK MAN'S BURDEN

The difficulties that the explorers had with porters is a major theme of their books. It was easy enough to hire men for the early stages, but Africans had less stomach for venturing into foreign parts than Europeans, fearing, with reason, for life and liberty. They often deserted, taking what was on their own heads with them and especially their rifles. One way and another the explorers' capital shrank rapidly. It was then necessary to hire, at fresh expense, new sets of porters as each tribal frontier was passed, or persuade a chief to lend slaves. Baker in vain gave half the wages in advance, hoping that the lure of the other half would keep his porters loyal; but a man might carry more than his entire wage on his head. Explorers swapped comparisons of tribes and types of loyalty and stamina. Gibbons in Barotseland, for example, recommended 'Matoka' boys. The management of carriers was an important assignment in any large expedition. Desertion by porters could be a matter of life and death. The power to inspire loyalty reached a unique level in Livingstone, who was never deserted.

Rapacity reached its ultimate when Kamrasi, having wheedled almost everything out of Baker in 1864, finally demanded Mrs Baker before he would help the explorer proceed to Lake Albert.

'I will send you to the lake and Shooa, as I have promised, but you must leave your wife behind with me,' said the King. Baker levelled his revolver at him telling him 'in undisguised contempt' that if the trigger were pulled not all his guards could save him, 'and that if he dared to repeat the insult I would shoot him on the spot. At the same time I told him that in my country such insolence would entail bloodshed, and that I looked on him as an ignorant ox who knew no better, and that this excuse could alone save him. My wife, naturally indignant, had risen from her seat, and made him a little speech in Arabic (not a word of which he understood) with a countenance almost as amiable as the head of Medusa'.

Kamrasi's reply, as reported by Baker, would seem reasonable to any modern anthropologist. 'Don't be angry. I had no intention of offending you by asking for your wife. I will give you a wife if you want one, and I thought you might have no objection to give me yours; it is my custom to give my visitors pretty wives, and I thought you might exchange. Don't make a fuss about it.' It all reads splendidly and titivatingly as a triumph of British female independence in Baker's best-selling book. When the Livingstones were trying to ascend the Zambesi in 1865 they asked what a local chief thought about Mrs Livingstone's female companion; he longed for her, he said wistfully, but could not raise the number of cows required to buy such a wife. Macdonald Duff, who recorded the first Universities Mission expedition to Central Africa noted that the chiefs, when refused rum, demanded white wives from the missionaries.

The explorers' own equipment – 'survival kit' in today's parlance – became a matter of commercial interest. The earlier travellers often wore a mixture of Western and Turkish dress – Lander wore a straw hat, a muslin *tobe*, boots and baggy Turkish trousers. In 1860 the explorer was recommended to take flannel underclothing, whatever the climate, and to allow for shrinkage in shirts, which should have pockets. Heather-coloured tweeds were best for outerwear; jackets to be tailored as shooting jackets for the moors, and trousers to be strapped up outside and fitted with cavalry-type leather buttons, supported by serviceable braces made by a saddler, not bought from an outfitter. Oxford cord hunting breeches could be worn with long boots, vital in grass and thorn bush, which tore so many Victorian rig-outs to tatters; on his expedition to Lake Tanganyika in 1882,

Swann soon regretted leaving his gaiters behind to save weight. Waistcoats were to be cut long, with four flapped pockets, the front lined with leather. Buckskin gloves were considered essential for bush whacking. Butcher boots with laces greased with mutton fat would last on the march (in fact explorers complained of the collapse of footwear, though Speke walked from ´Zanzibar to Gondoroko without mentioning the problem), and woollen socks. A soft felt hat, Boer-style, was acceptable for southern Africa, and sou'westers for the rainy season; as the century wore on, the helmet and puggaree became general in the tropics, but Livingstone was famous for his peaked cap.

For those trekking in Cape wagons, or in river steamboats, solid leather bullock-hide trunks carried the stores, but for head porterage sheet copper lined boxes measuring 16 ins × 12 ins × 12 ins with ring handles were recommended, loaded to only 20 lbs. (Porters had also to carry their food, arms and ammunition.) There were a variety of instructions about tents, but tent technology barely advanced in the nineteenth century until Stanley extolled proofing with sulphate of copper. The eighteenth-century explorers did without them.

The important developments were in firearms and instrumentation. To the middle of the century nobody was quite sure if breech-loading shot-guns, rifles or revolvers would stand up to African travel. Once the hinges were wrenched the guns were useless, and up to 1860 explorers still swore by muzzle-loading flintlocks, at least for reserve, and certainly always for one's black attendants. But the appearance of hingeless breech-loaders from Wilson of Birmingham, with cartridges that could be made in the jungle from wads and tissue changed this. Only with the arrival of the Irish Webley in 1876 did explorers have a revolver light enough to carry on foot (Burton carried them under his Arab robes to Harar), the Colt being essentially a cavalry weapon. Until then they preferred a double-barrelled pistol. 'It is no good having small bore popguns', wrote one expert. Until cartridges became general every expedition carried a mould and lead to cast bullets and buckshot.

Compasses improved, so did sextants; the Casella rain gauge eased the surveyors' task; ruled and squared paper accompanied every expedition. Most explorers, with an eye to illustration, made sketches which the wood-engraver could copy. A good water-colour painter was a godsend to naturalists at home. Cameras were taken to Africa from about 1860 – Livingstone was furious at failing to photograph Lake Nyasa. Explorers astounded natives by making fire with their watch-glasses; by 1875 reliable lucifer matches provided both a quick fire or light, and proved white magic. Explorers were advised to be carpenters, blacksmiths, tinsmiths, gunsmiths and veterinary surgeons, in addition to being artists and map-makers; many who survived were not.

Until the last years of the century the only real increase in health aids for explorers and travellers in Africa was the introduction, first of chloroform, which could be carried, then a knowledge of asepsis, which books of instruction began to promulgate. Mosquito nets improved in lightness, but their use was to prevent mosquitoes keeping one awake with their bites. Quinine was the specific against fever, but if one got it, or ran out of quinine, an alternative was to induce perspiration. Against dysentery there was no real defence although everybody had their nostrums: the Rev. Dennis Kemp in 1898 advised a flannel belt to ward it off. Lander noted in 1827 as he sat by Clapperton's deathbed that it was 'a disorder that causes hope to die within the patient'. Water filters were early recommended as part of a large expedition's equipment, but regulations on boiling water were rarely advocated before the turn of the century. Exploration was largely carried through by desperately sick men – and women. When the first missions were being founded in Nyasaland, McDonald Duff recorded 'a large part of each man's time was spent in bed'.

Samuel Baker describes how, crossing a river with his wife behind him, he chanced to look back and see her transfixed and sinking into a bank of weeds, 'her face distorted and perfectly purple'. He dragged her ashore and found her in rigor and coma. 'It was *coup de soleil*.' Then followed a heart-rending description of Baker marching on beside his unconscious wife's litter 'carried mournfully forward as a corpse. A painful rattling in her throat betokened suffocation.' Finally he forced a wad between her teeth. Slowly they staggered on, spending the night in miserable huts, while Baker feared she would die any moment.

I was ill and broken-hearted as I followed by her side through the long day's march over wide park lands and streams with thick forests and deep marshy bottoms, and through valleys of tall papyrus rushes, which, as we brushed through them on our melancholy way, waved over the litter like the black plumes of a hearse. We halted at a village and again the night was passed in watching. I was wet and coated with mud, and shivering with ague; but then cold was greater than them all . . . in the drawn and distorted features I could hardly trace the same face that for years had been my comfort through all the difficulties and dangers in my path. Was she to die? Was so terrible a sacrifice to be the result of my selfish exile?

She did not die; in fact as Lady Baker she went on his next expedition up the Nile, but that does not make the story any less impressive. Sometimes man and wife were too ill to leave their litters but lay side by side under leaking thatch, for a month together, speaking of England and singing patriotic songs.

HOSTS AND GUESTS

These trials strengthened the impression that Africans were utterly heartless. 'They have no compassion for the sufferings of the white man,' complained Richard Lander, 'and if they can mortify him by any means, they think it a praiseworthy deed.' Baker spoke of the 'unfeeling brutes that composed the native escort' who were 'yelling and dancing as though all were well', when Mrs Baker seemed to be dying, and recorded Kamrasi's malicious pleasure at their thin appearance after he had left them marooned in a malarial marsh without porters. It took Swann's perspicacity to realize, by 1882, that African servants were afraid that if their sick masters died, they might be accused of poisoning or otherwise killing them, and therefore kept away from their beds.

The explorers' accounts of Africans were almost consistently unfavourable. Baker sometimes admitted that his trials made him a little irritable, and granted that the Arabs were even worse than the Africans – 'scoundrels among scoundrels'.

The key to African behaviour was seen as double-dealing. 'The treachery of the Negro,' wrote Baker disgustedly in 1874,

> is beyond belief, he has not a moral human instinct and is below the brute. How is it possible to improve such abject animals? They are not worth the trouble, and they are only fit to be slaves, to which condition their race appears to be condemned. I believe I have wasted my time and energy . . . by my attempt to suppress the slave-trade and thus improve the condition of the native.

Speke was just as sweeping. The African, he reported in 1860, 'works his wife, sells his children, enslaves all he can lay his hands on, and, unless when fighting for the property of others, contents himself with drinking and singing like a baboon, to drive dull care away.' He admitted young Africans had a marked proficiency in learning but specifically 'in telling lies most appropriately in preference to telling the truth'.

Many explorers' accounts were evidently aimed at disabusing the home public of the idea that the African was a simple noble savage, merely waiting redemption, a line that pulled in the subscriptions at Exeter Hall. Their choicest epithets were reserved for the chiefs they met and whom they found to be bloodthirsty despots whose subjects were too spineless to dethrone. Most British explorers quite consciously felt themselves forerunners of the blessings of white rule in some form. 'I was under the roof,' remarked Burton in Harar, 'of a bigoted prince whose least word was death, among a people who detest foreigners, the only European who had passed over that inhospitable threshold, and the fated instrument of their future downfall'; Lander spoke of chiefs 'with villain, murderer and cannibal stamped across their baboon-like faces'.

Of the Zambesi people he met, James Stewart concluded that 'the greatest kindness that can be done to them is to tax them whenever and wherever it can be effected to pay for good government.' 'The obtuseness of the savages was such,' runs a refrain in Baker, 'that I could never make them understand the existence of good principle: their one idea was "power", force that could obtain all – the strong hand that could wrest from the weak', but he added wryly: 'This miserable, grasping, lying coward is nevertheless a king, and the success of the expedition depends on him.' He and others painted an unrelieved picture of rapine and anarchy, petty principalities endemically at war with each other from Zanzibar to the Sahara, made worse by the Arab slave-trade. Baker spoke well of Mutesa of Uganda because he forwarded messages and thus inaugurated the Central African post. Speke, who stayed with him, drew an unflattering picture of brutality, greed and cruelty. He often adopted a tone of jocular contempt, as when he described a Bunyoro chief 'who covers his children with bead ornaments and throws them into the Nyanza to prove their identity as his own true offspring, for should they sink it stands to reason that some other person must be their father.'

Inevitably the explorers got caught up in the politics of the palace which would occasionally be put to good account, as when Speke played off Mutesa and his royal mother against each other. The great explorers prudently refused to be drawn into marauding forays though Stanley fought a dozen battles with tribes who tried to stop him. As white men evidently had to deal with native potentates, advice was given on the subject, as with the management of natives in general. Francis Galton, who was for a time secretary of the Royal Geographical Society, advocated 'a frank, joking but determined manner, joined with the air of showing more confidence in the good faith of the natives than you really feel ... if a savage does mischief look on him as you would a kicking mule.' He pointed out that an explorer was beyond the law and had to make his own, fix a scale of punishments for his native entourage, but warned young men, fresh no doubt from public schools, to discriminate 'in the licence he allows his stick'. Mansfield Parkyns, who travelled extensively in Ethiopia in the 1860s, and decried its reported risks, was contemptuous of 'treaties with nigger "majesties" who find unutterable amusement letting off a box of lucifers', and concluded that 'a savage might be treated like a child. He must either be persuaded in a manner he can understand or be whipped.' Speke gave his absconding porters three dozen lashes, and Stanley excused 'the application of a few cuts to confirmed stragglers' to hasten the process of reaching camp and to deter would-be deserters. Explorers reported expertly on the thickness of African skins.

The fear was that the African dread of the white visitor's guns and the awe of his power would wear off, but Galton noted that 'they require time to discover he is not very different from themselves and easy to be made away with'. The apparent remedy was to take adequate military protection on an expedition. The early attempts to use redcoats for the purpose were disastrous; all but three British soldiers sent with Mungo Park in 1805 died quickly, the remaining three were killed with him in a canoe on the Niger as they attempted to reach the coast downstream.

Other explorers enlisted African troops or armed and trained their porters. Baker's huge expedition up the Nile in 1880, on the Khedive's firman (or order), was defended by Egyptian troops, inefficient and un-disciplined as Baker often found them. By that time, an unarmed, unaccompanied traveller could hardly have retraced Speke's track: Baker was frequently in action. His expedition was perhaps the ultimate effort in the elaboration of its equipment. He built a riverhead base at Gondoroko with corrugated iron magazines for stores, including immense supplies of Manchester goods and every gadget he could think of to excite or amaze the Africans in the areas he hoped to explore and annexe for the Khedive: they ranged from musical boxes to galvanic batteries for demonstrating electric shock. He set up machine shops and sawmills, and even brought agri-cultural implements. 'Thank God I had forgotten nothing in the pre-paratory arrangements,' he wrote. 'Without the spades, hoes, etc., we could never have succeeded on this journey.' Stanley, for his fourth expedition, which crossed the continent from the Congo to Zanzibar, took fewer native troops, but used steamers and portable boats, and demonstrated the fire-power of the maxim donated to the expedition by its inventor.

The difficulties of porterage early turned explorers' minds to the carriage of boats and steamers to the inland waterways. Once steamers were estab-lished, stores in bulk could be carried, dependence on porters and canoes reduced, and a base established on which white men would be safe – and comfortable. The early boats were often defective, or broke down; Livingstone was disappointed in the *Ma Robert*, supplied in parts by Lairds for £6,000; it proved unequal to the current of the Zambesi, and could not be carried inland. Many boats, small and large, were. Between 1830 and 1890, scores of them were either sailed up the estuaries, dis-mantled and carried round cataracts and barriers, or carried in as many as a thousand separate packages, on porters' heads, for hundreds of miles. Again, Baker's expedition was the most lavish: he brought no less than three portable steamers up to Gondoroko, one paddle-wheeled and two with screws, quite apart from his stern wheelers which were brought up from Cairo or Khartoum. One boat was brought in sections from Suakin to Berber slung on Trieste fir-tree poles between pairs of camels. He per-formed the astonishing feat of working a paddle steamer through the Sudd papyrus marshes to the river above Lake Albert. But his advance was achieved with a dwindling force, and finally he was in danger of being exterminated by the blacks as he retreated by forced marches, short of ammunition, deserted by his porters, his pack animals dead. To get so far, he had started with six steamers and fifteen *diabeeahs* in Cairo, and added nine steamers and other vessels at Khartoum to move 1,650 troops and two batteries of artillery. Stanley in 1887 had a far smaller force to rescue Emin who took over from Baker in Equatoria, but his force also dwindled steadily, his rearguard was almost wiped out, and hardly a hundred of his original company of nearly eight hundred arrived with him and Emin in Zanzibar.

It is difficult to resist the conclusion from these and other expeditions that if the Africans had been as determined to keep the white men out of their territory as had been the Moors in the north, few explorers would have got very far; but the Africans had no such unanimity of feeling. Despite the explorers' disparagement, the record shows that the Africans often rescued them *in extremis*. Mungo Park was once rescued by an African woman on whose mercy he, ill and destitute, threw himself. She kept him for months and certainly saved his life. Other African women helped Clapperton and Lander; the widow Zuma, for example, rather pathetically hoped to marry one of them. All the explorers, while denouncing African treachery, record other occasions when they received assistance which was not merely bought with trade goods, indeed after these had been exhausted.

Yet it was obvious to the Africans that the white visitations were preludes to conquest. Bello, the Sultan of Sokoto, declared to Clapperton that he realized that he must take India as precedent; and later in the century the travellers and missionaries did not conceal their belief that they and their flag were the precursors of British rule. Speke and others were minutely questioned on their motives for travelling, which deepened their contempt for African intelligence, as well as their view of the prevailing anarchy which prevented Africans from travelling; but the Landers were openly accused of deceit, and of coming to the Niger with 'no good intentions'. After the partition of Africa, travellers warned Africans that the British were coming. Gibbons obtained Lewanika's grudging permission to map the country, and proceeded not only to survey the best areas for white settlement, but warned his servants that they would have to behave themselves when they became servants to the settlers.

THE HUNTERS

One of the advantages that European explorers and travellers had in African eyes, and which secured them porters, servants and hospitality, was their capacity to kill game. They could feed their entourage well, simply because of their better weapons, with or without the help of African tracking skill. On long journeys, hunting was a necessary activity; in moments of the greatest anxiety, the explorers took days off to kill for food, sometimes for sport; on rare occasions in self-defence. Their requirements were, however, by most accounts modest. Alexander complained that 'this thirst for blood is discreditable', when he saw four hippos killed in a day, while Gibbons wrote, 'I confess to occasions when I have been compelled to shoot animals for no other object than to feed my gluttonous carriers.'

White hunters, on the other hand, explored only to find the game, not the

Explorers and Hunters

British notions of African society in the eighteenth century were vague, even libellous. The tradition that the explorer was offered a black wife is the first tribute to African hospitality – which the cartoonists made fun of.

On Safari – a mid-Victorian picture of an explorer and his porters moving into the East African interior.

Between rivers there were only bush paths. The Victorians early constructed portable and sectional boats, often with engines, to be carried from river to river, as Stanley's steel boat *Advance* here demonstrates.

Dr Livingstone's adventure with a hippopotamus from a coloured engraving; no doubt the artist had to draw from a highly exaggerated account, before the advent of the camera (though the great explorer's brother used one in Africa).

The early missionaries thought it perfectly right to take their children on expeditions, and many were buried in Africa. They had a safe entry to heaven in that way. Livingstone's expedition of 1850 reaches Lake Ngami, by Alfred Rider.

At the Inkisi Falls, Stanley wrote 'inviting my friendly natives to my aid, we buckled on to the two largest canoes, while the weaker Wanguera cut through the forest'.

Africa had become a venue for newspaper scoops by mid-century. The *New York Herald* sent out H. M. Stanley to find the missing Dr Livingstone, and the scene at Ujiji was duly recorded in writing and by a sketch by the indefatigable Stanley.

Victorian explorers had to know when to run – and when to run up the Union Jack. John Hanning Speke escapes from a group of angry Somali.

The Victorian explorer was advised to have the rudiments of civil engineering, as well as of medicine, at his disposal. Lt V. L. Cameron building a bridge to cross the Lovoi for the Central African expedition in 1875.

White strangers were valuable as hostages, curiosities and repositories of new skills to many African tribes, whose chiefs occasionally made them prisoners, even slaves. The missionary families of Ramseyer and Kuhne had a longer spell than most – four years in Kumassi, partly in irons.

Mary Kingsley was not the first, or last, white woman to become an explorer as well as traveller, but her dry and amusing style, and her accurate observation made her a best seller, and a legend on the Coast.

Elephant hunting and the ivory trade dominated much early African travel and exploration. A sepia study by A. A. Anderson, 'Death of a young elephant'.

Hunting the lion in Africa became the great sport, a source of immense profit to publishers, gunsmiths and travel agents. Before the camera, the hairbreadth escapes of the hunters were transcribed by artists from the heroes' own accounts.

The camera sometimes caught the sense of butchery of wild life that changed the aspect and ecology of Africa in the nineteenth and early twentieth centuries. *Above*, the vast spoils of bushbuck hunting from the album of Robert Harris, 1888. *Below*, a hunter with his native bearers in 1906.

TROPHIES.

The following approximate prices are published for Members' guidance. It will be well, however, to avoid any misunderstanding, that Members should have an official estimate given before any trophy is proceeded with, as variation in sizes, &c., of hoofs are liable to cause difference in cost. Members will oblige, when giving orders for hoofs to be mounted as inkstands, by stating whether they require them with or without pen-rack. Mounted specimens can be seen in the Department. **HOOFS AS TROPHIES.**

	Electro.		Nickel.		Brass.
No. 1. About	42/6	...	37/6	...	35/0
„ 2. „	50/0	...	40/0	...	40/0

No. 7. As Match stand in electro-plate and chased 50/0

No. 8. As Candlesticks, in iron and copper .... each 35/0

	Electro.		Nickel.		Brass.
No. 3. About	55/0	...	45/0	...	45/0
„ 4. „	42/0	...	40/0	...	35/0

No. 9. As a Trinket Box, electro-plated and chased 50/0

Engraving inscriptions on Hoofs, &c., 1/6 per dozen letters extra.

NOTE.—In addition to the prices given for mounting Hoofs, Pads, Slots, &c., there is a preliminary and extra charge for curing, viz.:—
Hoofs and Slots, 2/6 each; Pads, 1/6 each.

No definite time can be given for completion of mounting hoofs, as they **must** be thoroughly dry before mounts can be fixed, and this takes from 2 to 3 months.

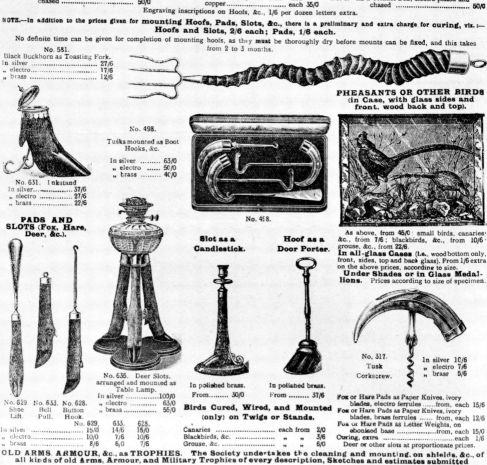

No. 581.
Black Buckhorn as Toasting Fork.
In silver 27/6
„ electro 17/6
„ brass 12/6

No. 498.
Tusks mounted as Boot Hooks, &c.
In silver 63/0
„ electro 50/0
„ brass 40/0

No. 498.

PHEASANTS OR OTHER BIRDS
(in Case, with glass sides and front, wood back and top).

No. 631. Inkstand
In silver 37/6
„ electro 27/6
„ brass 22/6

PADS AND SLOTS (Fox, Hare, Deer, &c.).

As above, from 45/0 ; small birds, canaries &c., from 7/6 ; blackbirds, &c., from 10/6 ; grouse, &c., from 22/6.
In all-glass Cases (i.e., wood bottom only, front, sides, top and back glass). From 1/6 extra on the above prices, according to size.
Under Shades or in Glass Medallions. Prices according to size of specimen.

No. 635. Deer Slots, arranged and mounted as Table Lamp.
In silver 100/0
„ electro 63/0
„ brass 55/0

Slot as a Candlestick.
In polished brass. From 30/0

Hoof as a Door Porter.
In polished brass. From 37/6

No. 317.
Tusk Corkscrew.
In silver 10/6
„ electro 7/6
„ brass 5/6

	No. 629.	No. 633.	No. 628.
	Shoe Lift.	Bell Pull.	Button Hook.

	No. 629.	633.	628.
In silver	15/0	14/6	15/0
„ electro	10/0	7/6	10/6
„ brass	8/6	6/0	7/6

Birds Cured, Wired, and Mounted (only) on Twigs or Stands.

Canaries .... each from	2/0
Blackbirds, &c. .... „ „	3/6
Grouse, &c. .... „ „	6/0

Fox or Hare Pads as Paper Knives, ivory blades, electro ferrules ......from, each 15/6
Fox or Hare Pads as Paper Knives, ivory blades, brass ferrules ...... from, each 12/6
Fox or Hare Pads as Letter Weights, on ebonised base ....from, each 15/0
Curing, extra ....each 1/6
Deer or other slots at proportionate prices.

OLD ARMS, ARMOUR, &c., as TROPHIES. The Society undertakes the cleaning and mounting, on shields, &c., of all kinds of old Arms, Armour, and Military Trophies of every description, Sketches and estimates submitted

Big game hunting in Africa contributed enormously to the Victorian interior decoration industry. Nothing of the slain was wasted except their screams – the natives ate the flesh, and the hunters had hoofs and horns made into objects of ghastly good taste.

other way about. For these men there were three motives: to kill in order to obtain trophies, trade and sport. From the British occupation of the Cape in 1815, men of this type began to arrive to hunt, and for no other reason.

It would be untrue to suggest that the British big-game hunter in Africa was solely or mainly responsible for the colossal destruction of its wild life which has transformed and impoverished the continent. It is clear that, quite apart from climatic changes, the Africans had made substantial inroads before the white man arrived. When the British traders and slavers began to sojourn on the West Coast, they found but little game on their short trips inland other than wildfowl. The fowling-piece was a better provider for the pot than the rifle. The Africans, with snare, spear and musket, had already killed much of the game in the search for protein. There was plenty of evidence of malnutrition and hunger, and this may have added to the urge of the black man to sell slaves to the white.

In other parts of Africa, where the black man often lived in a fairly stable symbiotic relationship with wild life, game was abundant, as the explorers reported. But the destruction was gathering pace. The Arabs killed animals and trees as prodigally as they killed men, extending the Sahara Desert and making a waste of the jungle. Their big objective was ivory, their main quarry the elephant. In the south, the Boers had been living off the vast herds of antelope with no care for the future for a century before the British sportsman arrived. He was late in the day, but he set to with a will.

A library of books, often mere amplification of their game-books, testifies to the keen interest and admiration of those at home. They narrate almost every conceivable way of being attacked by lions, hippos, elephants, rhinos and the like, and getting away with it; and every part of every animal pierced by a bullet is itemized. For the scores who got their repetitious accounts published, hundreds more merely decorated their English villas with mounted heads and skin rugs. It was largely, but not wholly, a sport for military men, who might stop off at the Cape on their way to their regiments in India, as well as for the officers of the regiments in Africa itself – some went on regular lion hunts on the Somali coast and nearly exterminated the game there. Only rich men could come out from England specially to hunt, and none until comfortable steamships could transport them. The hunt was taken up, of course, by the settlers who found game a pest, and then by District Officers. As Africa became safer, the Great began to arrive and kill in the perfect security they expected.

The abundance of game astonished the first British hunters and explorers. Much of tropical Africa seemed only just out of the Pleistocene Age. The drying savannahs were over-populated with ungulates and supported a substantial cadre of predators. It has been estimated that in the early nineteenth century there were 500,000,000 springbok alone between the Karoo and Kalahari Deserts. Close to the little colony at the Cape, only a short ride was necessary to find rhinoceros, giraffe, elephant, zebra, kudu and hartebeest. Sometimes herds swept down from the desiccated pastures to the sea in such quantities that the shore stank with corpses for thirty miles. To cull such vast migrations was like beating off a swarm of locusts with a fly swat. Olive Schreiner's husband, S. C. Cronwright, as late as 1895 made a calculation that he himself had seen a herd of antelope 500,000 strong from horizon to horizon, so that it might have been ten million in all. Valleys were filled, rivers were choked with bodies over which the survivors pressed on. Men shot till they could no longer hold their rifles; *biltong* (dried flesh) became unsaleable, hides fetched 6d. each. Reports of such occurrences assured hunters that Africa's wealth, animal as well as human and mineral, was inexhaustible. By 1870 the land was almost shot out to the Limpopo. Hard times then faced the trek-Boers who had been virtually self-contained for years together, living almost entirely on the slaughter of antelope, and even living in hartebeest hide huts.

The prototype of the big-game hunter was Captain William Cornwallis Harris, Royal Engineers, who took two years' leave from his regiment in India in 1836, went north to the Vaal from the Cape with a Parsee servant, a white brother officer, Richardson, and an entourage of Hottentots. He took 18,000 musket bullets and seems to have used most of them, charging the herds, firing from the saddle and not bothering with the wounded. He found elephant and hippo on the Vaal, giraffe on the Limpopo and sable antelope on the Eland River. He explored far into Matabeleland long before other white men, and was sustained by the game without difficulty, returning with stuffed heads for an exhibition in London which electrified the county gentry, who also pored enviously over the book he published soon afterwards.

His feats were more than emulated by Gordon Cumming, who represented the killer *par excellence*. In 1846 he mounted an expedition similar to Harris's, taking 3 cwt of lead, 400 lbs of gunpowder and 50,000 percussion caps. He shot anything that moved and exulted in the trail of wounded and dying animals he left behind. He founded the cult of the elephant as the animal most worthy of a Briton's steel, and recounted many hairbreadth escapes, as well as devoting pages of his book to loving, almost pornographic, descriptions of the dying screams and squeals of the huge animals into which he pumped round after round of heavy shot, expatiating on the astonishing absorptive quality of their thick hides.

I followed, loading and firing as fast as could be [runs one of his descriptions] sometimes at the head, sometimes behind the shoulder, until the elephant's forequarters were severely punished; notwithstanding which he continued to hold stoutly on, leaving the grass and branches of trees scarlet in his wake, until I began to think he was bullet-proof ... Having fired 35 rounds with my two-grooved rifle, I opened up on him with the Dutch six-pounder; and when forty bullets had perforated his hide, he began to show symptoms of exhaustion. Poor old fellow ... !

48

Such prowess overwhelmed the Africans, who made him welcome wherever he went. Ranging ahead of his wagons with a train of saddle horses, he learned everything the Boers and native hunters could teach him. He bore a charmed life; one of his dinner-table stories was of surviving an attack by wild dogs, but he was also charged by buffalo, elephant and lion. They all failed against Cumming's dexterity with the rifle. He returned from the trip having killed 105 elephants, 80 lions, 60 hippo and 800 antelope, having preserved his specimens in hermetically sealed tins, and having sold dozens of muskets to the natives to continue the slaughter. The trip showed a profit of 3,000 per cent on an outlay of £800, and his book *Lion Hunters of South Africa* made more. Lionized in London, he died of drink at forty-seven – whereas Harris's exploits won him the leadership of a mission to Menelik of Ethiopia and a knighthood.

Such exploits inspired the greatest hunter of them all, F. C. Selous, a man *sans peur et sans reproche*, who dedicated himself from boyhood to big-game hunting, possibly to compensate for a weedy physique. His career in South Africa began in 1872, and after learning the rudiments from a Boer professional, Jan Viljoen, he went to Lobengula of the Matabele to get permission to hunt in his domains. Lobengula gave him permission in the assurance that the elephants would deal with him, and indeed one did sit on him. But he survived to kill them by the hundred. In Barotseland his retinue was attacked and wiped out, but he escaped and walked, starving, to the sanctuary of a mission. Within a single lifetime, Selous had to explore ever further afield to find game.

By the 1880s most of the game was extinct in South Africa, and it had become scarce throughout central Africa. A single hunter with the small-bore high velocity rifle firing the nickel-covered bullet introduced in 1895 was far deadlier than the earlier hunters with their gas-pipe flintlocks; he had the power to pick off what game they left. Smokeless powder, and magazine action, increased his deadliness to animals.

British visitors to Kenya found the country teeming with game in 1890, and soon restarted the process. Lord Cranworth remarked that the 'timid but fierce looking rhino' was a nuisance, and noted that seven hundred were destroyed in the years 1910 and 1911 alone; the zebra was 'an unmitigated pest' which broke down fences, and should be shot as food for natives and pigs; the hippo was ruinous to cultivation, the baboon should be destroyed without mercy as it had no respect for men or dogs, while the bush pig carried deadly swine fever. 'If the presence of game at all, or in excessive quantities, is deleterious to the wellbeing of the population, then the game must be banished,' he declared. But he, like other transplanted English farmers, wanted a close season for ducks, and control over fishing streams. Reluctantly Cranworth admitted that there was a case for game reserves, as even he could not accept the total extinction of many 'splendid and beautiful' species.

The British conscience began to move from close seasons, and the preservation of particular species, to reserves as the century wore on. Lord Grey was the first at the Cape to adopt the practice of declaring some animals 'protected', and this practice developed in other British colonies. In 1884 Kruger introduced a game regulation law into the Transvaal *Volkraad*, as ruin impended for the trek-Boers. This proposal was taken up by the Wild Life Protection Society after the Anglo-Boer War, and the Kruger National Park could probably only have been established as the first of the great reservations because of the determination of Stevenson-Hamilton, the first game warden, who began his career in Africa exploring the Zambesi in a portable steamboat. Harris himself had shown the other side of the British attitude to animals by making superb water-colours of the game he encountered. Burchell, early in the nineteenth century, had amazed the Boers by sketching animals and refusing to kill them himself, even when they were needed for food. 'This poor creature,' he wrote of the rare kudu, 'to whom I was indebted for so favourable an opportunity of obtaining, without hurry, a careful and correct drawing of the species, appeared so mild and harmless, and had so much speaking solicitude in its beautiful clear black eyes, that I could not witness its fall, but turned away.'

Licensing was brought in widely in British possessions at the turn of the century for the hunting of large animals, and visitors to Uganda, for example, grumbled at paying £80 for the right to kill two elephants. This revenue pleased local finance officers, but it did not preserve the game which began the century by being extremely tame, and ended being extremely fearful of man. The stalking of animals with cameras was increasingly extolled as a manly sport, with plenty of opportunity for risking one's life, if that was what was wanted.

British sportsmen generally felt that stalking without killing was like playing Bridge for matchsticks. Only blood gave the authentic thrill to the hunter. The problem was therefore to provide the maximum thrill for the minimum damage, and the trade of the 'white hunter' arose after the First World War, particularly in East Africa. His function was to conduct licensed sportsmen through the bush, organize and run camps for them, make sure they got satisfactory trophies, and see that the killing was clean. The 'white hunter' who helped to reduce big-game hunting from near-warfare to a chivalrous duel became a folk hero, combining in himself the love of animals which became a British obsession in the nineteenth century (the RSPCA was founded in 1824 to deal with cart-horses), and the role of victor of dozens of fights with lions and other beasts which had to be culled to maintain the 'balance of nature'.

The hunter in many ways completed what the explorers began: not just the opening of paths through the bush to admire Africa, but its preparation for colonial rule, the antithesis of tribal anarchy and the wilderness in which wild animals had precluded domestic herds. Their efforts were complemented by mission stations which formed bases from which Christianity could be preached, and hunting and exploratory expeditions could be assembled. They were indispensable to the surveyors of railway routes, protecting them from animals, running their camps and finding the best gradients. The change in atmosphere in Central Africa was lamented by F. C. Selous in 1900:

Ah, but the old days were best, after all – or at any rate I think so. The traveller by rail will journey at his ease it is true, in a saloon carriage, through seemingly endless wastes of low forest and scrubby bush, and will probably think it a terribly uninteresting country; but no man will ever again sit by a camp fire by one of the little rivers that the railways will cross, eating prime pieces of fat elephant's heart roasted on a forked stick, nor watch the great white rhinoceroses coming to drink just before dark ... the abundance of big game – elephants, black and white rhinoceroses, giraffes, buffaloes, zebras, and many varieties of antelopes – made it always interesting alike to the hunter and the lover of nature ...

THE TRAVELLERS

In the wake of the explorers and hunters came the travellers – the men and women who wished to see the country opened up and settled; to observe the natives, and to conquer the remaining natural mysteries. In 1883 Joseph Thomson, for example, established that the snows of Mount Kenya and Kilimanjaro were permanent, and in 1899 Halford Mackinder, using Alpine experience, climbed Mount Kenya, and was photographed as the first man on its summit. The tradition of picturesque travelogue was deep in the English character, and for one hundred years or more an African itinerary had been on most professional travellers' list. Thousands of books, of which a few are still worth reading, were written.

Early travellers stuck to the West Coast, and only went inland when the way had been opened up. In the south, the excellence of the climate and the Cape wagon or cart made travel easier. In central Africa, however, travel hardly became possible until colonial government had been imposed after the 1890s. To the Victorians, the Nile and the Cape – the Egyptians and the Zulus or the Boers – were the main attraction. Thomas Cook began his tours to Egypt in 1869, and indeed helped to organize Sir Samuel Baker's expedition in 1874. Travellers could not normally mount expeditions with carriers. Their way into Africa was by camel from Suakin to Berber, or by Nile steamer from Alexandria to Khartoum, where travel was for the wealthy, the eccentric, and the intrepid.

In 1850 André Melly, a Liverpool cotton merchant born in Geneva, with an English wife and his two sons and a daughter, decided to visit the land from which his raw material came, took steamer to Egypt; and in Cairo fitted themselves up cheaply. They hired twenty camels and a number of servants – a dragoman, a valet, and a cook as well as camel drivers and two sailors. On travelling days the dragoman rose at 4 a.m. and woke the other servants who prepared breakfast for the English party, which set off at 8 a.m., reading Shakespeare aloud to enliven the desert travel. At midday they halted for lemonade and bottled beer; in mid-afternoon they set off again, and in camp in the evenings wrote up their journals, dried flowers, stuffed captured birds, and talked. Mr and Mrs Melly dressed as they did in Liverpool, though the latter protected herself from the sun with shawls, and her husband wore a pith helmet. Son George wore a fez and turban against the sun, his brother Charles a wideawake, and their sister Louisa a large straw hat; both ladies had sunshades. At Khartoum they found plenty of European society, and were visited by the Egyptian Governors who wanted to look the ladies over; they, in their turn, visited the Pasha's harem. They went upstream in a *diabeeah* laden with gifts of vegetables and fruit from the Governor and the local Catholic fathers. Their dragoman purchased for them a small black slave for £5 8s. od., which they thought too much when the lad proved to be stupid. They reached Berber on 7 January; on the 13th Mr Melly fell ill, and died on the 19th. On the morning of 24 January, two Italians riding south from Assuan sighted a caravan which they first supposed was led by Turks wearing white turbans. At last they realized that the approaching figures were ladies. They had no doubt to which nation these ladies belonged; who but an Englishwoman would dare to attempt the desert crossing in straw hat and green umbrella? The Melly ladies were continuing their journey alone.

The most celebrated of late nineteenth-century travellers in Africa was Mary Kingsley. A 'frail spinster' from Cambridge, niece to the writer Charles Kingsley, and daughter of a traveller, she decided to travel herself when the death of her father gave her liberty from domestic duties. On a visit to the Canary Islands in 1892 she met a number of Coasters, whose conversation decided her to tackle the dangers of the West Coast. She made two trips, in 1893 and 1894–5; her account of what she saw, heard, did and had to undergo provided material for another Victorian best-selling travelogue. Her style is discursive, gently humorous, at times arch, but saved by the spice of irony from becoming tiresome even to the modern reader: from it emerges almost the quality of a Jane Austen character. Among the ingredients of her success was the novelty of a woman travelling alone (though for a short time as companion to Lady MacDonald, wife of the Governor of the Gold Coast) in the years when white mortality from malaria was still appalling; the chanciness of Coast life runs through her narrative. She was no mere sightseer, though her verbal descriptions of town- and landscape were evocative, because she undertook quasi-scientific investigations to give her trips a purpose. She studied beetles, fish, and above all fetiches and made drawings or collected specimens. She was factual and thorough as well as anecdotal and picaresque; finally she arrived at completely new interpretations of a region that few English readers knew, and generally regarded as totally inhospitable, dangerous and given over to shady characters. Mary Kingsley returned with the warmest admiration for the Coasters, defended the traders' morals and profits, presented almost for the first time 'the African point of view' in rational terms. She put West Africa in a new light, demolished its reputation for evil, and turned it into an exotically dressed stage for vital and human characters. She captured the mysterious charm of Coast life whose power to summon back those who felt it was inexplicable in England.

Her travels and books were models of the genre. Mary Kingsley used the facilities available; she did not strike into unexplored country. She took passages on mailboats and river steamers, and engaged canoes and African servants for her fishing expeditions and visits to backwaters not touched by steamboats. She relied on traders and missionaries, occasionally officials – English, French and German – for hospitality and help; she became famous for her remark 'it's only me' as she returned to them from visits to bush communities in search of entertaining characters and fetiches. Her itineraries took in most of the coastal towns from Freetown to Luanda, though she spent most of her time in Calabar and Gabon. After Mary Kingsley and Sir Ronald Ross* the Coast was wide open to the inquisitive traveller, but few have surpassed her descriptions of selling off her clothes when she ran out of trade goods, falling into rivers or game pits, and spending nights in native huts or getting soaked in mangrove swamps.

Complementary to Mary Kingsley's travels in West Africa was the journey from Cape to Cairo made by E. S. Grogan and A. H. Sharp in 1898. The colonial powers were technically in full possession by then, and Grogan planned the trip to show that a railway route was feasible as well as to obtain the favour of his future father-in-law. At the time war was looming in South Africa, the Belgian *Force Publique* had mutinied for the first time in Leopold's Free State, and Kitchener was still dealing with the Khalifa. Grogan's journey was from the Cape through Rhodesia, Nyasaland and Tanganyika, and thence along Speke's trail through Toro to Gondoroko on the Nile. His bitter aspersions on British colonial laxity, commercial torpor, African laziness and savagery, missionary futility, and his descriptions of his narrow escapes from big game and careless gun-bearers, made a book to warm the heart of hard-nosed settler and adventurer. 'Shabby! Shabby! is the only word for our methods in Africa,' he cried, denouncing 'The poor-dear-black-man-down-with-the-maxim-Africa-for-the-African Creed.' He blithely provided a map with a route for the railway and telegraph marked in through natural obstacles greater than those which were being overcome by Whitehead for the Uganda Railway. The travellers saw the depredations of slaving, mutiny and cannibalism round Lake Kivu, and were about to provide descriptions almost as macabre as those of the great explorers, when they were attacked by the Dinka and other tribes in the southern

* Who identified the mosquito as the malaria vector.

Sudan. Grogan became convinced that in one of the African tribes he had glimpsed the Darwinian 'missing link', so much discussed in controversies on evolution, in which he believed.

While exploring with a small number of followers, I observed some ape-like creatures leering at me from behind banana palms, and with considerable difficulty my Ruanda guide induced one of them to come and be inspected. He was a tall man with the long arms, pendant paunch and short legs of the ape, pronouncedly microcephalous and prognathous . . . The stamp of the brute was so strong on them that I should place them lower on the human scale than any other natives I have seen in Africa . . . Their face, body and limbs are covered with wiry hair, and the hang of long powerful arms, the slight stoop of the trunk, and the hunted vacant expression of the face, made up a *tout ensemble* that was a terrible pictorial proof of Darwinism.

Twelve years later Melland and Cholmondley, two British officials, made a similar journey in totally transformed conditions. By now travel was largely a matter of proper camp equipment bought from the big stores in London, quinine in regular doses, mosquito nets, and the hiring of porters and servants; if these deserted or behaved badly, they could be reported to the nearest D.C. who often applied the stick. Chiefs though still expectant of modest gifts or dashes no longer levied *hongo*, and had become obsequiously co-operative. The problem of overcoming natural obstacles had been reduced to routine, the dangers from animals and tribes were small; the telegraph was operating almost all along the route, except for breaks in Tanganyika and between Toro and Gondoroko.

Melland and Cholmondley decided to test the use of bicycles on bush paths in tse-tse areas, and covered most of Grogan's route in three months, though the bicycles broke down because of the relative fragility of two-speed gears. They relied for safety and comfort on their carriers to whom they paid 4s. 8d. per month each. It was estimated that for a three-week journey thirty carriers were necessary, and for six months sixty. Their equipment included cameras, carbide and five loads of spirit tanks and specimen equipment, besides tents and camping equipment; they noted that travellers should not skimp on porters and have to omit books and tables, essential to morale on long bush journeys.

They moved without serious problems from one government *boma* (government station) to the next, in comfortable steamers on the lakes, and in Entebbe found stretches of motorable road, and a government lorry of which they made use. The *machila*, they noted, was fast being superseded. Marching through Bunyoro and the Sudd they encountered none of the hostility or sullen suspicion which met the Bakers forty years previously, the natives, if prone to noisiness and excitement proving 'a happy sophisticated crowd. They are really very friendly and well-disposed, and their outbreaks are really due to their exuberance of spirits, which is liable to get out of hand in the beer season.' They got through the Sudd easily, thanks to the earlier mapping expedition of Dr Milne and Captain Gage. From Gondoroko it was a simple if slow matter of Nile steamer and Sudan Railways.

By 1900, the British tropical outfit had been fully worked out: Turkish trousers and the fez had been discarded in favour of pith helmets or terai hats, drill shirts and shorts to below the knee (for officials), with puttees to protect legs from the long grass, though spine pads of solero cloth were still recommended. Dark glasses did not become general until the 1920s. Missionaries were advised, when on safari, that pyjamas were essential for Christians. Bowels could now be moved by Carter's Little Liver Pills, and Beechams' Powders were helpful. Travellers could take the new patent thermos flasks to provide cold water or hot tea at the end of a tiring day, and ladies on safari could take portable irons heated by blocks of solid fuel. Victorian ladies preserved their modesty by means of their voluminous garments and any convenient foliage. On the small steamers it was a mystery to males 'how they performed their morning toilet', for which the men found the paddle boxes most convenient. Mrs Lippert, on trek in Mashonaland soon after the Rhodes column had cleared the route, was presented with a small cabin convenience in camp and described it as 'an extraordinary but acceptable luxury . . . for in a camp with a lot of gentlemen it was awkward to say the least of it . . .'

By 1905, not only were there electric fans for the D.C. (though these were rarely installed), but battery operated fans for the traveller, as well as auto-rotary hand fans which the Army and Navy Stores claimed were 'useful against the annoyance of flies, gnats and mosquitoes' – but by then it was impossible to buy a small boy at £5 8s. to crank it. Anti-mosquito head guards were the alternative, fitted in hat or helmet. Insect and moth powder was now available, based on the natural insecticide being produced by the white settlers in Kenya, pyrethrum.

The contents of medicine chests, however, though more lavish, were hardly more efficacious than they had been twenty years earlier. One advertised brand contained the usual selection of cascara, salicylate of soda, ipecacuanha, Easton syrup, essence of ginger, chlorodyne and quinine. Washing vegetables in potash permanganate was a new precaution, and boiling drinking water was a routine that naturally followed the discovery of dysentery bacilli after 1900. The 'Congo' chest (as supplied to Sir H.M. Stanley) was sold by The Army and Navy stores at fifteen guineas, and weighed forty pounds.

Much of the material in travel books consisted in description of the conditions of travel and the behaviour of the African servants en route. One constant of African travel for the Briton was his boys; and the picture hardly changed since Alfred Swann set the scene in 1882.

We became attached to our black attendants, to the boy who anticipates our every want, who serves us cheerfully at all hours. Strong men who would scorn the idea of being helpless absolutely lean on these children of the forest so far as their personal comfort is concerned. Does the long march end in rain? The boy is there. Wet firewood? No matter, dinner is cooked. Hot bath ready. Pipe, tobacco, dry clothes all at hand in the tent. It is 'Boy!' all the time; without him bush-life would be unbearable.

The more adventurous travellers not only took unusual routes, but also visited and lived with remote tribes; if their observations fell short of the canons of anthropological science they made vivid journalism. Two attitudes prevail in this vast literature; the arch and half-defensive description of African ways and the imperially condemnatory. A typical traveller of the second type compared the 'boy' with whom nothing useful could be done, who was 'lazy, inordinately vain, deceitful and dirty', with the boy who 'takes kindly to the white man, and to whom the white man is an everlasting surprise and mystery'. Training them was an endless subject for argument, born and reared as they were 'on the wholesale plan, mothered by a refuse heap, christened after an empty bottle or an undergarment . . . the minds of children and the habits of pigs'. For fifty years African customs, their pidgin, their magic and superstitions, their comical misunderstandings of the white man's new world being brought to them, formed an almost inexhaustible theme, now totally ignored. The heroism of missionary narratives sharply declined in the same period.

After 1910 the automobile began to enter seriously the African travel scene. Africa was a natural challenge to the motor pioneers. In South Africa the problem was one of building roads; elsewhere the problem was to see how far cars could be taken into the wilds. The day of the 'first' by car in Africa had arrived. The Court Treatts made the first Cape to Cairo motor journey about 1925. In 1928, Frank Grey decided to test the suitability of British cars for African conditions, and mounted an expedition from Lagos to Khartoum in two Jowetts; cars were already being railed to areas where they could be used, but long through connections were missing, so that their cars were the first ever to reach Kano on their own wheels. The excitement of car trips in Africa soon seized the imagination of a motoring age, and the virtual inability of the British to build trunk roads in Britain found a perfect parallel in Africa.

In 1920 the first plane flew from the Cape to Cairo and opened Africa's air age. In 1927 Air Commodore Charles Samson led a 'routine' R.A.F. flight of four aircraft from Cairo to Durban and back, refuelling at Heliopolis, Wadi Halfa, Khartoum, Kisuma, Nairobi, Tabora, Abercorn, Bulawayo, Bloemfontein and Grahamstown. Africa henceforth could be surveyed, mapped and fought over from the air.

3

THE MISSIONARIES

The missionary life has probably been a more marked component in British social life in Africa than in any other part of the British Empire, with the possible exception of the Pacific. The great missionaries were not only explorers of the unknown African map; they stayed and explored the African mind. For nearly a hundred years missionaries played a dominant role in the politics of Africa's subsequent subjugation and settlement. The greatest of them, such as Livingstone, were among the high heroes of Victorian adventure. Their exploits, depicted imaginatively in the *Illustrated London News* and other papers, were as much a source of national pride as military victories. For Africa was to be, for Church and Chapel, but especially for the evangelicals, the field of atonement for the slave trade. It was to be the modern field for the expansion of the gospels, a place where the early Church could be relived, where the Oxford ordinand could walk in the metaphorical footsteps of the apostles, complete with martyrdoms and miracles. Africa offered a field for holy work wherein to test God's power which would be far from the uncouth, corrupted, unbelieving savages of the new industrial slums – a continent where virgin (if darkened) minds awaited the message of salvation and redemption.

THE ATONEMENT

In many missionaries' imagination there floated a vision which, had it been realized, would have given Africa, or most of it, a period of Christian theocratic government like that of the Jesuits in South America in the sixteenth century. This vision embraced a great chain of mission stations which would link east and west Africa with a road between them for Christianity and gospel-guided commerce to move along. In the innocence of African conditions that prevailed in the 1840s this was not thought to be unduly arduous to organize fairly rapidly, given the men and the funds. It was solemnly estimated that, to cover the nine hundred leagues between Mombasa and Gaboon, and with the stations spaced at intervals of four to the hundred leagues, each costing £5,000 a year to run, the work could be completed in five years. In some undefined way branches would link up with Abyssinia and with South Africa, where stations were pushing up what was becoming the Great North Road.

Joseph Krapf, who was working for the Church Missionary Society in Zanzibar in 1851, declared: 'Africa must be conquered by missions, though a thousand warriors should fall to left and right.' On the West Coast David Hinderer in Yorubaland declared that 'Two good links were already made towards it – Babagry and Abbeocuta; and I am sure God will hear our prayers and give us Ibadan about two days' journey northeast as a third. Next to that Ilorin may, by the providence of God, in time constitute a fourth; and the same number, if not less, in Tchad, where we shall soon shake hands with our brethren in the East.'

The guilt of slavery was at once an abiding memory and a scandalous reality in Africa. Until late in the 1860s there was still slaving off parts of the West Coast until Brazil, the last country to fall in line, prohibited the traffic. Before it was finally put down in the west, the missionaries were grappling with it in the east. Arab slaving was not stamped out till the end of the century. The missionaries found that what they had come to atone for was looked back on with simple nostalgia by the Africans, at least in the west. As late as 1895 a chief complained to a missionary: 'Since your arrival we have had to give up this kidnapping and selling of people; I made £20 a week out of it.'

The first great missionary effort was the settlement of Sierra Leone as a homeland for freed slaves. At that time, the end of the eighteenth century, the only other British settlement, the Cape, was the scene of missionary efforts to end slavery there. The origin of mission interest in Africa was the religious revival of Wesley and Whitfield; until then, the clergy had generally defended the slave trade in negroes. Thomas Thompson, sent to America to convert the Red Indians, wrote a book defending the trade as consistent with revealed religions and engaged in it himself. Perhaps the need to defend it indicated that Christian consciences were beginning to prick. The governors of Cape Coast Castle evidently scented the danger, openly ridiculed religion and limited baptisms to fifty a year.

The agitation, writing and preaching of the 'Clapham Sect' in the last quarter of the eighteenth century developed Christian conscience with remarkable speed. The efforts of Wilberforce, John Venn, Granville Sharp and Zachary Macaulay led to the founding of Sierra Leone in 1787 as a private venture; it was to be the forward base in Africa of the missionary invasion. From the turn of the century Methodist and evangelical clergy everywhere were reading pamphlets on the scandal of the trade and the sins of the Bristol merchant élite. With the battle for its extinction, grew the

58

desire to convert the benighted heathen in his own lands. Young men felt the call to sacrifice themselves. The missionary societies came into being to organize their self-dedication, to provide them with passages, Bibles and translations. Thus William Carey's *Enquiry into the Obligation of Christians to use means for the conversion of the Heathen* led to the founding of the Baptist Missionary Society in 1792, to be followed by the London Missionary Society in 1795 and the Church Missionary Society (after the Archbishop of Canterbury gave it his cautious and unenthusiastic blessing) in 1799. Similar societies were set up in Scotland (not in Wales or Ireland, of course), and in 1804 the British and Foreign Bible Society was founded to provide the essential ammunition, copies of the Gospels. To give Africa these priceless spiritual things was seen as complete 'reparation for Africa's wrongs'.

Feeling the call and going out to convert the heathen was one thing; doing it was another. Between 1795 and 1820 martyrs' crowns were won by many of those who went to West Africa; by 1812 some dozens had died and all there was to show for it was a few churches and a school with one hundred and twenty pupils. Even so, it had not been the English clergy but Lutherans who got the first stations organized, building the villages and roads, baking the bricks and bringing in artificers. The English clergy at first were set on more spiritual things – to reproduce in the African soul the same sentiments that they had felt in their own drawing rooms or studies when called to the Lord's work. Governor McCarthy wanted mass baptism as a political necessity and complained that the Sierra Leone Society was 'a set of fanatics' when the Rev. Johnson refused, because he insisted on the authenticity of conversion according to the New Testament, rather than the bulk conversion of later Church history.

By 1840 the C.M.S. had some fifty schools going, with 6,000 pupils, the Wesleyans 1,500. The first assault of the Church on the Gambia failed, due to a combination of fever and Islamic imperviousness to Christianity. The S.P.G. reported back in 1838 the natives' 'decided preference for Muhammed'. Every missionary sent to the Gold Coast in these years died, and continuity was only established by the arrival of Thomas Birch Freeman, son of an African father and an English mother, at Cape Coast Castle. 'I stand,' he said, aptly enough, 'in the deadly breach with humble confidence that God will spare my life.' He lasted fifty-two years. The Societies had to learn that they had to man their missions with their own African converts, capable of withstanding the climate, and these converts were the clergy that began to create the chain of missions up the coast to Calabar and beyond, and northwards to Kumassi.

Bishop Crowther was perhaps the most eminent of these African converts, and when he joined Buxton's Niger expedition, he returned in full health when 130 of the 145 members went down with fever and 40 died in the steamers. Only in the last quarter of the century did white missionaries find means to survive. As late as 1859 yellow fever carried off half of them. But by 1860 the missions were moving inland in advance of the flag.

As the missionaries spread inwards from Sierra Leone, they spread outwards and northwards from the Cape. In 1800 William Anderson forsook Mammon in Aberdeen for the London Missionary Society, went to the Cape, and set up a mission among the Bastaards, or Griquas, escaped slaves of the Boers, who had set up their own little 'republic' north of the colony. They trekked as far as the Vaal, knew the bushmen, and the game, and finally settled down with Anderson on the Orange River. Visitors, like Burchell the naturalist, and Lichtenstein the scientist, carried back reports of his work, other missionaries joined, and finally the Cape Government claimed them, with the ultimate result that they were demoralized, and subsequently attacked by the migrating Bantu. But the reports of the missionaries showed the effects of Dutch slavery and the L.M.S. sent Dr Philip to the Cape in 1819 conscious that 'in so weighty a matter we dare not look to a man of ordinary make'. He proceeded to battle for simple access to souls, first of the Hottentot slaves of the Boers – who denied they had any – then for the bushmen, and finally for the Kaffirs themselves. Philip wanted an Indian land policy. Had he got it – as in West Africa – the colony might never have become a white settlement. It was the missionaries who, seeking to maintain African rights in the land that the settlers needed, were also responsible for preserving some African kingdoms, such as the Basutoland of the great Moshesh. The missionary leaders were deep in politics from the first, and were unpopular with the settlers. Their influence accordingly declined sharply once the colony got self-government in 1871.

To the Boers the missionaries were intolerable hypocrites and mischief-makers, and their intentions were magnified. As one Boer said when the slaves were emancipated in 1834, 'Dr Philip spoiled the Hottentots, he had got a law passed that obliged him to marry his daughter to a Hottentot, that he would rather shoot her than see her so degraded, and that Dr Philip had taken all his slaves from him and he wondered at the mercy of God in suffering such a man to live.' This remained the folk belief of the Boers.

Despite the succession of Kaffir Wars that alarmed the outward expanding frontier the missions spread northwards until the Boer republics barred their way and threatened the 'missionary road' to central Africa. But the missionaries got through to Matabeleland, linking up with the Church of Scotland in Nyasaland. There was an Anglican church in Pretoria as early as 1861.

By 1840 in the southern African area there were twenty-six stations of the L.M.S., thirty-two Wesleyan, five Scottish and thirty-three non-British missions. By the outbreak of the Boer War in 1899 the number had doubled. Livingstone's journeys had drawn the Scottish missionaries

into Nyasaland in 1872, and the L.M.S. sent its advance guard into
Uganda in 1875.

THE CALL

In Jane Austen's England, as in the Victorian age, the poor clergy provided
a stratum of impoverishment and blighted prospects from which, inevitably, the missionary societies could expect to draw their rank and file
to the army of Christ. Scores of young men in holy orders, and many
dissenters too, took up missionary work because there were no other
outlets or preferment at home. Of the nobility and gentry it might be
true that the eldest son inherited the estate, the second went into the army
and the third into the Church; but the third son at least got a living in the
pleasant countryside – at worst in London. The lower-middle-class or
working-class boy who wanted a clergyman's life found the going harder.
If he baulked at the industrial slums, the colonies offered him a career of
a sort and a field of labour, not necessarily converting the heathen.

Clergy were an urgent need in the Cape the moment the British took
over, and more so when the settlers began to arrive. Salaries were small.
Many abandoned the cloth for trade. Some combined both. Yet, even
before Victorian respectability spread, the demand for the same church
rituals, ministrations and consolations were wanted by the settlers as were
available at home. Church buildings seemed a natural priority to the early
settlers – they knew that churches were being built all over England in the
new towns and suburbs at that period. Often the church was the first form
of public works after the pioneers' huts were up and their seed planted in
alien soil. (At the end of the century it was to be hotels.) The clergy, often
sent out at some expense, were tempted to exaggerate the progress they
were making with white souls as well as black ones. White souls needed
saving – as witness the joy recorded in the Cape when an English farmer
asked to be married to his black concubine after fifteen years of sin.

A serious call to convert the heathen, whether these were in the Cape,
amid the terrors of Kaffraria, or in 'Darkest Africa's' fever-ridden swamps
was a different matter. The missionary societies at least in the early stages
were fairly discriminating as to whom they sent out. Sound theology was
the basis of training and the diploma of fitness for the work. Calloway, for
example, felt that 'my ulterior labours as a missionary would be of a much
more efficient character if before going I could spend a few months with
some learned divine to give consistency to my theological knowledge.'
Often theology was the only equipment a man sailed with. But many
missionaries had other skills to offer, and as the century wore on, and
reports on the failures came back, this was seen to be essential.

However, the call to Africa was usually an individual decision, and it
was sometimes hard to convince the societies of its validity. It was a

practical period. Faith was little use without works; faith had to be expressed in works. Faith abounded in a country overweeningly conscious that it was technically ahead of the world, and the achievements of the engineers were a challenge to the Church. This challenge had scant effect on the bishops or the universities. It did affect the attitudes of the young and ardent, impressed by the stream of writings on the slave trade, and increasingly the first-hand tales of missionaries on leave, who lectured up and down the country, raising funds and inspiring recruits as they did so. They were a different type from the Trollopian incumbents of vicarages and palaces, and to the young in an age of exploration their lives were cast on a wider screen than the earnest but dilletante Kilverts of the parsonages.

First came the conversion, then later the call to the work. Robert Moffat, grounded as he was in the Bible, heard the message of the Methodists, and had to ask himself if he really believed; 'then followed the struggle between hope and despair. I tried to reform – not by avoiding grossly immoral conduct, for I had never been guilty of that, but by foresaking foolish and worldly company, vain thoughts and wicked imaginations.' For weeks he hung between hope and despair, gazed into the pit of wickedness he could embrace if he failed to believe, and suddenly in a little garden while reading the Epistles to the Romans, knew he was redeemed. The supreme moment had happened. It pained his friends that he should turn Methodist, but this was his lightest cross. Strong in faith he was now able to plunge into good works. Then, on a calm summer's evening, walking to Warrington to buy something he needed, and dreaming of promotion and future comfort, his eye was caught by a missionary placard.

It announced that a missionary meeting was to be held, and the Rev. William Robey of Manchester would take the chair. I stood for some time reading it over and over again, though I found the time for the meeting to be held was past. Passers-by must have wondered at my fixedness . . . the stories of the Moravian missionaries in Greenland and Labrador which I heard my mother read when I was a boy, which had been entirely lost to memory, came into vivid remembrance as if fresh from her lips. It is impossible to describe the tumult which took hold of my mind.

He could not rest until he had seen Mr Robey, though he trembled at his fateful door, and was even refused entry; but at last he was set to work in the nursery garden where he pursued his long courtship simultaneously of the nurseryman's daughter, Mary Smith, and the London Missionary Society. Both gave in finally, and with the briefest of preparations the young man set off, with momentous results for Bechuanaland, which he was fated not only to Christianize but to preserve from becoming another Boer republic.

J.W.Colenso lamented at Cambridge in the 1830s that so few would

Missions, Medicine and Education

The missionary as the missionary societies saw him – converting savages to the faith. *Above*, an idealized figure preaching in West Africa. *Below*, Robert Moffat preaching to the Tswanas, from a picture by Charles Davidson Bell.

The missionary in his natural surroundings – the Rev. A. N. Wood mending his boots at a station in East Africa.

Nursing was one of the earliest women's professions to transform war, missionary life, and even native life in Africa, after Florence Nightingale laid down its principles and training. Nurses at the base camp of the Pioneer column moving to Matabeleland.

The teacher as the African saw him, complete with sun helmet, bible and benevolence. A carving (said to represent Mr Kenneth Robertson) from Yorubaland, Nigeria, about 1930.

British women were generally shocked by the low estimation in which Africans appeared to hold their women, and from early on laboured to transmit to them the Englishwomen's attainments of the day. Lagos 'Female Institution', c. 1875.

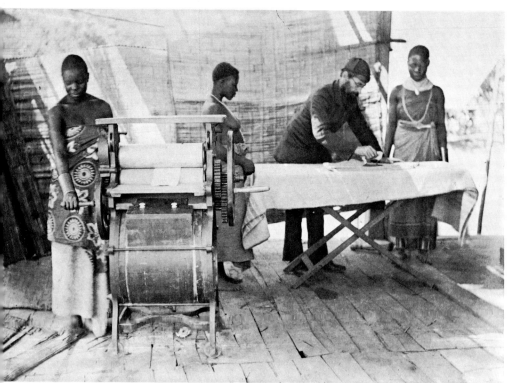

It was a matter of concern to Englishwomen in Africa that so few African women could be employed as reliable domestics, but every effort was made to train them. *Above* a sewing class in East Africa and *below* the laundry at H. M. Consulate in Nyasaland Protectorate, 1886.

feel the call to the heathen and declared that 'Parents must learn to train children as missionaries from the womb.' The example was however all about the Victorian child, as missionary lives provided the safest of improving books for Sunday and week-day reading. A perhaps fairly typical case was that of Rivett, who in the 1850s went regularly to missionary meetings in Yarmouth, and heard from the bishops of Bombay, Cape Town and Natal of the work to be done. Mackay of Uganda heard of the missions to Madagascar while studying engineering in Berlin. He was one who admitted that there was work to be done at home – 'in fact, missionaries can be nowhere more necessary than here, but I cannot, once having been led to set my face to Madagascar, turn to other work instead.' He was diverted to East Africa by reading an advertisement by the C.M.S., asking for a lay superintendent for a settlement for liberated slaves in Mombasa. This led to his twelve years in Uganda, beginning at Mutesa's court at Mengo.

For the Anglicans the path sometimes led through Church careers. Robert Gray at Oxford was converted by the Tractarians, became a friend of Pusey, and in 1840 was appointed secretary of the Society for Promoting Christian Knowledge. He had been a conventional pious clergyman, the son of the bishop who organized the ragged schools in Durham. The bishopric of Cape Town was offered him as a preferment with more pomp than position, but during his consecration he heard the blast of the trumpets of St John the Divine in Revelations and felt assured that he was destined for great work; it led to his quarrels with Colenso, scandal and schism.

David Livingstone began to sense the need for personal atonement when he was twenty. He felt unworthy until he read Dick's *Philosophy of a Future State*, whereupon he decided immediately to accept salvation and devote his life to his Redeemer's service. Its form was revealed to him in an appeal by Gutslaff to the churches of Britain and America on behalf of China; but as that country was cut off by the war to assert British rights to run opium there, the L.M.S. diverted him to Africa when the time came for his departure. Livingstone, when he applied to the L.M.S. in 1838, was clear what was involved: 'to make known the Gospel by preaching, exhortation, conversation, training of the young; improving ... the temporal condition of those among whom he labours by introducing the arts and sciences of civilisation, and doing everything to commend Christianity to their hearts and consciences.' He foresaw that the heathen (then the Chinese, rather than the Africans) might scorn the teaching and contaminate the teacher's faith. He assumed that the life would be full of hardships, but said 'I have no hesitation in saying that I would willingly submit to them, considering my constitution capable of enduring any ordinary share of hardship and fatigue.' He proved it could.

In this state of certitude the missionaries went to Africa, where, except in the north, they did not meet any ancient civilization deeply rooted in its own scriptures and religious culture, but complex societies in a state of turmoil which they found hard to understand but felt sure were evil. The missionary in Africa might die, with or without making discoveries, but at least he could never doubt the rightness of his call. As in the Pacific, he was among savages, and was able to reveal to them not only the superior truths of Christianity, but its incontestably superior material fruits in the form of Victorian gadgets. Danger there might be, but there was, blessedly, no intellectual opposition, except in Islamic areas (and not even much there). The missionary was, until the twentieth century was advanced, buoyed up by a comfortable sense of superiority. He had the truth; no one else had.

Theology, it was soon seen, needed the reinforcement of technology. By the 1830s it was clear that a medical degree was a valuable adjunct to the Bible, while the experience of Sierra Leone showed that missionaries should be all-round handymen if intending to go beyond the towns. The missionaries, like the settlers, came from an agricultural country and largely from farming stock or from an environment of simple craftmanship, so they automatically brought to Africa a working knowledge of subsistence economics. A few, like Livingstone, began in a factory. Fewer still came from the superior classes that depended on servants for everything, or from the mercantile orders that never used their hands. The employment of servants was of course natural to them. When the universities' missions began to send men into East Africa in the 1870s and 1880s the situation changed. 'Marples carried the English Oxford days with him everywhere.' wrote the venerable Percival Johnston of one of the men who answered Dr Bradley's invitation to undergraduates to meet Livingstone's call, and found life in a room in Africa much the same as one in College. 'There was Randolph who rowed for Cambridge', and the university men proved to be tough enough to build houses, plough the land and live on pumpkin soup. 'Bishop Steer looked as if he could live for a month on the smell of a sardine tin.' By the time Britain had become largely urbanized and divorced from rural verities at the end of the century, Africa had been conquered. The mission stations were established, and Africans did the work and were fully instructed, so that the pioneer spirit was less necessary to missionary work. The professionals had arrived.

THE LIFE

The first task of the arriving missionary was to establish his base, and to travel to it with the necessary gear. It was usually tough going. The first party of Methodists reached the interior of Gambia by canoe, set to work to cut down trees for a clearing with English axes, and build houses, with the idea that a church was to follow. Eight of the eleven were dead in three months, while the agriculturalist who had been prudently added to the party to sow the crops that were to sustain them when initial rations ran short, died in forty-five days.

They had to build their huts of mud and wattle like the Africans, while living in tents. They immediately surprised the Africans when they adopted rectangular shapes that could be enlarged instead of the beehive huts, which Africans duplicated when they wanted more living or storage space. Many, however, accepted native huts to live in at the start, as did settlers and prospectors. 'The little round huts, the company of uncouth and all but naked Kaffirs, and in their midst the two patient Christian men . . . singing the song of Zion, while the dim light lit up the dark faces' went one report from an S.P.G. circuit. Another described 'some sorry hovels where our brethren reside. A packing case, or wooden bench from school, or an old chair, was all we had in more than one house.'

In 1844 Livingstone went through the same experience and told another missionary:

I am just finishing my house. It is something like your own I suppose, only rather more primitive. 52 feet in length and 20 broad, walls 18 inches thick and 11 feet high. Verandah 6 feet broad, containing a study, bedroom and parlour – pantry, kitchen apart from house. Is it stone do you think? Nay, but a much easier material to mould, very plastic mud. We dash it on about a foot thick and cut it straight with a spade . . . one hour's exposure makes it difficult to cut. We run up walls in no time after the foundation is laid . . .

Bishop Calloway's first house consisted of four rooms in all, measuring 42 × 10 × 7 feet.

According to Mary Moffat, the typical mission house in southern Africa was a single unit, consisting of 'fore-house', bedroom and sitting room with a separate kitchen usually full of gossiping natives who frequently stole strange utensils that appealed to them; there were store houses apart. The siting of the whole complex, as it might be called today, or *kraal*, as the natives called it, was often made with a view to the availability of building materials, as well as water and communications. Clay was naturally important on a site, for the missionaries soon learned to make bricks when they established themselves in timberless regions, and used them everywhere for solidity in church structures. They first adopted cow dung in the native fashion for flooring.

In the towns, of course, living was more like home. By the 1840s in Cape Colony the clergy were very comfortable. 'Bishop's Court' had a drive into a shady quadrangle by the house, the school and the well-inhabited servants' wing. 'Entering the house, and passing through the large hall to the verandah beyond, one found oneself in another world. Flanked by two wings, the drawing room on the one hand, the study on the other, a succession of terraces ran down to the grassy lawn below . . . to a superb view of Table Mountain.' Thus Victorian clerical class distinctions were preserved from an early age.

The inland missions had early to become self-sufficient in food, as they were set up deeper into the interior. Mission life resembled that of the farmers in many respects. In Sierra Leone and later in other parts of West Africa (later still in East Africa) this meant discovering what crops would grow and the missionaries made the usual mistakes of people coming to the tropics from temperate climes. In time they learned how to grow the local food, and gradually to grow it better than the local people, as well as to introduce plants such as cocoa, that would acclimatize. But on the West Coast they were long dependent on local markets, buying their necessities with money sent out by the societies at home.

Where the missionaries were inefficient or easily discouraged, the stations soon collapsed, and they went home – or died of disease aggravated by despair. Gradually, missionary penetration began to be planned with more forethought. 'When I am in bed swallowing camomile and my bones aching,' wrote one, 'my head burning and loathing all kinds of nourishment, I feel I must leave. But no sooner do I feel strong than Sierra Leone seems too pleasant a place to leave just yet.'

In southern Africa the stations were in theory fixed, but the peoples to be converted were nomadic. This was disconcerting, and soon the missionaries had to adopt native cattle-keeping and pastoral methods, often moving with the tribes in their wagons. Gladwin, forced out of his mission to the Shona by the Matabele in 1850 described such migrations:

Imagine 5,000 people of all ages, 30,000 cattle, together with troops and wagons moving like a black cloud; men, women and children drinking up every puddle of water they met with; kaffirs attacking – thus we moved on amid the lowing of cattle, musketry and crying of children, enveloped in a cloud of dust, which rendered every object invisible at ten yards, the whole of the scene heated with the hottest of African suns.

The domestic scene about 1820 is set by Mary Moffat:

With regard to animal food, all missionaries, however small the family, kill a sheep (but the sheep are small in this land) every week in the moderate weather ... The chief part of the sheep's fat is in the tail, which is an enormous size, a burthen for it to carry ... this we melt, it assists cookery ... and (of it) we make candles and some people soap; but that is an immense and troublesome business ... As much of the mutton as we can we salt for the summer ... sometimes an ox or cow is killed and the chief part of it salted ... we smoke the meat to keep the moth out of it ... Most missionaries have a brick oven for their bread ... we have the wheat all ground down together, and I like it better than sifted for household bread.

The wheat, of course, was brought up from the Cape by wagon and at that era mostly imported by sea from Europe.

The advance guards, penetrating ever further, had to rely on African hospitality, and they bartered teaching for food. The exploring missionaries like Livingstone had to take with them trade goods, including guns in some cases, as well as the Bible, but supplies were limited and usually gave out early in the journey, as African rapacity was excited. The missionaries found that they were, for all their poverty, far richer than those they had come to serve, and who, lacking the things the white man had, hated to let a stranger carry further for others' use what they coveted. Consequently when the trade goods were all gone, and even personal possessions, the missionaries shared the hardship and starvation of all explorers; and their plight was usually worse because they had to remain; nor could they fight or bluster to retain property as secular explorers did. God had to be trusted to provide. Burgess, on tour, wrote: 'Sometimes I have only one meal a day, [maize] porridge without sugar or milk. I get wet through three or four times a day.' Mackay in Uganda reported that he lived on plantains for days at a time.

Livingstone was uplifted by following the diet of John the Baptist: 'Locusts and wild honey,' he wrote home, 'abound. Perhaps I may be excused if I mention the physiological effects of the Baptist's food. The former is excessively constipating and the latter has just the opposite tendency. The locusts, pounded and mixed with honey, are just as good if not better than shrimps at home.' He was one who took great pains to find out from the natives how much the arid Karoo had to offer: they showed him no less than forty edible roots and thirty fruits. It seems he was too skilful in life support ever to go really short. On the other hand, some were less well equipped. At the Primitive Methodist missionary station that had been established at Sesheke in Barotseland, when rinderpest broke out, as late as the 1890s, absolute famine supervened, and Mathilde Goy, a mission helper, narrated how she walked two hundred miles with her baby and fifteen Africans to get food, losing her way and nearly dying on the march.

THE FALLEN STATE

The missionaries were theoretically prepared to find their subjects plunged in heathen darkness, but their books and reports back indicate that they were frequently taken aback by African primitiveness. Few ever had doubts that the reform of African society was urgent, and that they knew how to apply it. Admiration for African achievements was not entirely lacking, but it was rare; however, friendships and understanding developed between the early missionaries and notable African chiefs – like Coillard and Lewanika, Owen and Dingane, Moffat and Mzilikazi. The chief was so powerful, or so it seemed to the Englishmen, that his conversion was the great goal – he was the Constantine of the savage empires. So missionaries laboured at the top. Livingstone is the special example of the Christian who achieved close and natural association with Africans as men and women, colour and culture apart; his attitude generated the devotion of the servants who went with him on his journeys, often without pay, enduring all hardships – and in the end carried his body back to his own tribesfolk. But his example was not to be followed in black and white relations. It could not be.

For the most part, missionary impressions of Africans were highly unfavourable. It was assumed, in keeping with Victorian precepts on environment and self-help, that Africans were individually capable of attaining any heights. Bishop Crowther's career was the example of this. One simply had to start at the bottom. But he was exceptional; besides, black clergy attacked African savagery roundly. In the eighteenth century William Carey declared that 'they are without the gospel, without government, without laws'. Of the Kaffirs the missionary view was thus summed up: 'Prior to his conversion his life is purely animal; its features were sensuality, greed and craftiness.' African dancing particularly horrified the missionaries, who could see only lewdness in it, whatever the occasion. African art was mere making of idols. One report found that 'the religious sense is so thoroughly dead in the Kaffir, their conquest or their civilization must precede their conversion in numbers. Their abominable rites and their nationality are so intermingled; . . . to abolish the one we must break up the other by arms or by arts.' This view reflected a growing militancy as the early struggles to achieve moral improvement by persuasion proved slow work.

Particularly in the south the presumed degradation of African society from a higher condition was a constant theme: the missionaries recognized in it a parable of the Fall in which they believed and which they taught. (This was a doctrine familiar to many Africans, if not in the Edenic form.) Bishop Henry Calloway's first conclusion was that 'there is not a single thing the kaffirs do not require to be taught, from the washing of their bodies to the building of their homes', though he modified it later.

The missionaries soon found that slavery was not just a matter of reparation for white wickedness in the past, but an endemic condition of African society to be combated. The brutality of African life seems to have astonished the English clergy. In Ashanti Freeman reported that the towns of the chiefs were 'charnel houses' from which the reek of blood was never absent, and Dahomey was worse; Mackay from Buganda reported that the native armies went out to pillage and enslave even before the Arab slavers arrived. Painful indeed was it to this worthy man when, after long intellectual conversations with the Kabaka Mutesa, from which he hoped much, he finally discovered that the King was totally indifferent to human life and, for example, acquiesced in ritual killings designed to relieve him of a slight illness. Mackay reported that the swamps round Mengo were filled with 'countless skeletons', just as F. S. Arnot reported that the Matabele grain-pits were full of human skulls about the same period (the 1870s). The Matabele merely smiled at missionary calls to repentance and continued to wash their young men's spears in Mashona blood as the Zulu system prescribed. In Benin the altars were found stinking with blood and decomposition, 'the smell no white man's internal economy can stand'.

Such scenes, which shocked men whose concept of European civilization was derived from nineteenth-century optimism, set the missionaries the problem of the African personality – dismissed by traders with a shrug. (Trader Horn extolled the morality of cannibals.) Unequipped with scientific anthropological techniques, they puzzled helplessly over the contrasts of kindness and cruelty. In the years of Florence Nightingale and the Crimean War, Livingstone called for deeper study of it. So reckless were the chiefs of human life, Livingstone reported, that a man could be put to death for a single distasteful word; yet sometimes he saw 'exhibitions of very tender feeling'. Some Africans were kind to him, others indifferent. He consciously turned his mind to the grandeur of nature in his travels lest he become depressed by man's depravity.

The missionary problem, in short, was where to begin. The initial contacts were often rebuffed on the grounds that Christianity was bad for African society. After the Ashanti War a chief even refused a school, saying that they would accept the presence of a mission, but would not select children for education as 'Ashanti children have better work to do than to sit down idly all day to learn hoy! hoy! hoy! . . . God gave the fetich to us – we know God already ourselves and we cannot do without human sacrifices. It is your religion that has ruined the Fanti country and brought high men down to the level of low men.'

The Dahomey chiefs feared that Christianity would make their people cowards, Freeman found. In Buganda, on the other hand, Mackay's early converts became martyrs to the church, dying bravely – as did Bishop Hannington, toiling up towards Mengo and slaughtered in his camp, with the words on his lips, 'Tell the king I have bought this road with my life.' It was one thing to entertain the chiefs with biblical stories, another to get permission to proselytize. And Lewanika referred to 'that rubbish heap of fables you call the Bible', after he had heard the stories, which was the missionary way of introducing religion. Paterson, more shrewdly, noted that the natives 'imagine that the gospel is the white man's word, good for him but not good for them', arguing that they would only accept it when black men preached it.

The problem was to get permission to settle among the Africans, yet steadily to work against their beliefs and customs, particularly fetichism, which included all forms of witchcraft and rainmaking by ceremony (rather than proper prayers), polygamy, going about naked, and misconceptions about God and goodness. Missionaries who believed in the efficacy of the

Book of Genesis in grounding the Africans in a better understanding of man's place in the universe were much upset when the reverberations of the Darwinian controversy were felt in the 1860s. The new learning was deeply unsettling, and mission work could actually make a man unsound on doctrine. For years the Cape was scandalized and riven by a bitter battle between Bishop Gray and Bishop Colenso over a book the latter wrote during his missionary work, which seemed to throw doubt on Moses's authorship of the Pentateuch.

Witchcraft was an early difficulty, for the Africans assumed that the missionaries practised their own brand, since they moved fearlessly among warrior tribes, came from over the oca, and possessed many odd devices. Counter-accusation was useful too. Coillard tells how, after a misunderstanding over a gun, some Primitive Methodists had their storehouse burned down as a punishment for witchcraft. Other missionaries were nearly killed for drawing up a design for their houses in the sand with sticks. But in general the Africans were impressed that the missionaries rarely succumbed to their local magician's spells; some may have done, not from mesmerism, but from poison. The strictly limited power of the gospel to cast out devils has been something of a disappointment to the African missions down the years.

Those who could see the objective knowledge that lay behind much African sympathetic magic were few – but Livingstone was naturally one of them. He reported that he observed strict medical etiquette with the witch doctors, treating them as colleagues in the same arts and only employing his own when called in for a second opinion, if even then. He undoubtedly believed in the efficacy of the herbal, and even surgical, methods of the 'witch-doctors' long before this became a respectable study in Africa. Maugham, a Foreign Office administrator in Nyasaland, was one of the practical men who in the 1890s advocated putting these powerful figures on government payrolls, but missionaries bristled at any such idea. Witchcraft and Christianity were irreconcilable. So was polygamy.

The denunciation of polygamy annoyed the tribesfolk who knew it was an essential part of their chiefly system and their authoritarian society, and noticed there was plenty about it in the white man's own Bible. An immediate difficulty arose over polygamous converts; in the main the missionaries followed St Paul strictly, insisting that the concubines be put away before a man was accepted for Communion. The missionaries, even Bishop Calloway, could hardly credit that Africans had any family life, reporting that 'there does not exist any strong bond between the man and his family, the marriage bond easily broken; child obedience slight – these people are to be regenerated by God and the Gospel alone.'

In missionary eyes, the position of African women was deplorable. They sent home sad stories of African men who replied to their protests: 'Who ever heard of a woman feeling anything? The woman is man's property.'

The ill-treatment of African women is a continual theme in missionary life; but it was a little naively assumed at first that Christian marriage would put an end to it – or at least raise married women to the level of married women in civilized England, where they owned no property, as they could in most parts of West Africa.

PREACHING AND PRESTIGE

The direct attack with the Gospel proved at first discouraging. Calloway found that he talked 'but very few come'. On the coast, in the eighteenth century, the natives had to be bribed with liquor to listen to sermons – perhaps not unreasonable with sermons of that era.

Preaching was apt to be somewhat haphazard in its effect until the preacher could speak the African language, and even afterwards. On the West Coast it was surprisingly long before the study of West African languages began with Koelle, but almost from the first men like Paterson and Calloway realized that they must learn Zulu, Sotho, Sechwana, and other Bantu tongues to put the Bible stories over without making theological or other bloomers. Macdonald Duff noted the difficulties of translating 'Judas kissed him', because, as the Yao and Angoni never kissed, the translation always came out 'Judas bit him' or 'Judas smelled him'. Worse still, the word 'guilty' proved untranslatable. Colenso got into difficulties with Zulu descriptions of God, which also fitted the caddis-worm. Indeed, the Zulu word for God appeared to him to be 'a dangerous approximation to Arianism'. With that realization came the exciting challenge of translating the scriptures into these languages, using appropriate orthographies. It led to the regular installation of printing presses in missions from about 1830 onwards. The Moffats carried a parlour press in their ox-wagon.

The leading missionaries accordingly spent much of their time between 1830 and 1860 in learning vernacular languages, and in translation. Moffat, for example, translated the Bible into Sechwana. Bryant and Grout produced a Zulu grammar and Zulu hymns. The Bible did not get into Xhosa until 1865, translated by Appleyard, and it was much criticized at the time.

There was a perceptible difference between the attitude of missionaries beyond the frontiers of British authority, and those within it. In Tongaland the missionaries were at first refused permission to reside because 'the idea of a white man coming to see them, seeking nothing for himself but only to do them good, was too impossible to be received.' Nevertheless the idea that missionaries 'wanted nothing for themselves', unlike the concessionaires or the Boers, did spread in southern Africa.

The first missionaries had to live, humbly and cautiously, in the kraals, and to give to the African Caesar what was Caesar's. In colonies it was different. Colenso, the champion of the Zulu in defeat, even when called upon by a chief dressed in European clothes, his biographer reports, 'did not yield to an impulse to shake him by the hand. Natives, for all their honesty and other admirable traits, had to be kept at an arm's length, or risk making them pert and presuming.' Missionaries were firm that Christian brotherhood did not imply undue familiarity, that the relationship was largely between wise parent and obedient child, and that it was necessary to teach Africans that in the process of bringing them the Gospel and civilization, the privilege was theirs. Helping them otherwise simply made them feel that the missionary was a servant, 'and this was the very thing to make them show off their airs for they are so disobliging,' wrote McVicar of the Bakwenas. 'I am trying a different plan with them. I make my presence with them a favour, and when they show any impudence I threaten to leave them, and if they don't amend I put my threat into execution.'

As time went on, and the missions grew powerful in some areas, the clergy began to introduce punishments of a much more severe sort for their converts and servants. When the Livingstonia mission had administrative powers, it introduced flogging, first for theft in 1881; and in lesser missions, particularly for the young, the precepts of Victorian Britain about sparing the rod were applied ruthlessly, and justified on the ground that Africans beat each other without compunction. 'I am not to be imposed on,' said McVicar. 'When they want to be paid to do things in their advantage [I insist] that they ought to pay me rather than be paid.'

COMPETITION

In adversity, at the beginning, the missionaries of all denominations were united amongst themselves. Whatever their differences of communion, the field was enough for all. In South Africa, indeed, new stations were set up away from rivals. Lutherans, Moravians, Anglicans, dissenters of all types, shared the work. But it was 'painful' when lack of the right pastors led to laymen going over to other communions. There was soon outright strife between Roman Catholics and Protestants, particularly as the devotion necessary to go to Africa at all proceeded generally from the intense type of mind that was intolerant of all other ideas. The biggest crisis came over MacKay and the Catholic priests at the Kabaka's court in Uganda, which would have been a ludicrous tale had it not ended in a short re-enactment of the Christian wars of religion, in which Anglican blacks killed Catholic blacks with European rifles. Mackay was determined that Africans should live by the word of the Scriptures, which he was determined to import, translate and finally print, as were all the early Protestant evangelists. He found himself called in by Mutesa to argue doctrine with the first Catholic fathers, who of course refused to kneel in prayer with the Protestants, and proclaimed the C.M.S. a bunch of liars to the king, which put MacKay to the necessity of explaining the great schism and the Reformation to the monarch, who, when in difficulties, could always turn to the Moslems – though he feared their political designs on Buganda – who were warning him that the Christians would end by annexing the land. 'Look and see in the book if Christ appointed a line of popes,' the engineer implored the king, who, however, had to be refused baptism when he asked for it, no doubt thinking it useful enough, since he insisted on polygamy, and indeed asked MacKay to obtain for him an Englishwoman to add to his seraglio.

Painful as all this was, the cheerful native comment was more painful still: 'Four kinds of Christian is like a man with four cows; he can always get milk.' The African could not, or would not, worry about the doctrinal differences which had killed so many millions in Europe. It continued to worry the Churches at home, and one missionary, according to Macdonald, got a hint from headquarters about 'distinctive principles', but replied that he could not find a native word to express these differences. Yet it was, and remained, a missionary problem that it had to teach Africans that the proper way to worship God was in dispute; this led to the argument that if white men could secede from the Church, and form something more truthful, why should not African Christians select their own truths?

SIGNS AND MARVELS

The real force behind the missionaries of all varieties was not so much the Holy Spirit as Victorian technology and the protection they could give Africans against exploitation by Boers, settlers or traders. The Tswana called in the missionaries, after they had seen Moffat, for help against Boer raids, traders, game hunters, and would-be concessionaires. The great string of missions might almost have been established on that basis alone, quite apart from the preaching. The very clothes that the missionaries and their wives wore produced an impact on Africans that induced them to listen to the new message. The nudity of African women in many areas was, of course, very painful to the incoming Christians, prepared for it as they were (occasionally they found the women clothed, the men naked). Livingstone noted that the women, going about almost totally naked, seemed to know no shame. The first step to grace, as the converts came in, and as the children were taught, was the wearing of European clothes; even though some thoughtful missionaries had occasional doubts about the effects later. Many spoke of the beneficent exchange of the 'dirt and indecency of native clothing for European dress'. McVicar thought that the garments sent out by the societies sometimes made the wearers get a bit above their station in life; but Calloway approved native hygiene more than 'our half-civilized people who dress but do not wash as they should'. A missionary lady in Barotseland enforced discipline by turning away those who called at the house for food with nothing on – even when one of them claimed that nudity *was* his 'national dress'.

After the Africans had got used to the heavy apparel of the 'Ambassadors of Christ', as Coillard called missionaries, they could be made to wonder at the gadgets they brought. Livingstone's own equipment for crossing an unknown continent was calculated down to the last ounce; yet he took a magic lantern with him which showed biblical scenes, but made the startled Africans believe that he was raising the spirits of his ancestors on the spot. The firearms that the missionaries brought were only to secure game, not for self-protection, but were naturally prestige-giving. Trade goods – cloth, beads, wire and so forth – they also brought, though these were of more use in southern Africa than in the west, where African traders had been appraising western exports for two hundred and fifty years. More impressive, as the century went on, was missionary mastery of steam and iron; then they were increasingly able to demonstrate a far-off but potent civilization of notably superior power and indicate that these achievements flowed ultimately from belief in the right God. The wheel's importance could not be demonstrated in tropical Africa far in advance of roads; but by by 1880s the missionary bicycle was astonishing pedestrians along the bush paths. In 1896, for example, John White and Stanlake reconnoitred on bicycles the Mashona preparations to revolt against the Chartered Company. Portable iron buildings enabled the missionaries to put up small churches quickly by the 1860s, but much more important were, of course, the portable steam launches which were expected to give the intrepid missionaries mastery of Africa's lakes and rivers. They were perhaps effective only in giving Nyasaland access to the sea; but they naturally impressed natives everywhere. From the first impact native kings believed that it was the missionaries' duty to teach their own people the new magic skills, even though in Africa, as elsewhere, tribes tried to keep their technological knowledge secret.

MacKay in Uganda was perhaps the greatest missionary engineer, though only the first of a long line that has followed. He learned engineering in Leith and then in a Berlin locomotive works. He designed, before leaving for East Africa, a steam-raising boiler in welded ring-sections each portable by one man; the rest of the marine engine being similarly broken down into seventy-pound portable loads. Such was the organization that nothing was lost on the seven hundred mile journey and he was able to report from his portable workshop on Lake Victoria: 'The engines for our steamer stand complete to the last screw; the boiler is ready to be rivetted.' In addition he had brought the inevitable printing press and founts of type, as well as a forge, tools and instruments. When the natives marvelled he firmly denied that it provided any proof that white men came from heaven: 'I told them they can easily know all that white men know; I tell them we were once naked savages – but God began to teach us, and we became civilized.'

MacKay noted that no Muganda knew even the use of nails, or the principles of the lever. There was, his geological knowledge told him, iron everywhere in the land, yet only hoes, spearheads and arrow barbs were made of it. 'The people are worn out for want of contrivances,' he observed. 'Old men and old women are rare.' He dealt smartly with grass fetiches by setting them on fire with a magnifying glass, calling them 'a mouthful for a cow'. He built a loom and demonstrated a lightning conductor. Mutesa, however, expected the Pandora's box on the lake shore to produce at the rate of a Birmingham factory, and MacKay indignantly complained that he had only two hands while two million Baganda were idle. That had no effect on the monarch, who considered that his kingdom was as powerful as Britain; if what he wanted did not appear he assumed that his foreign engineer, whom he openly called his slave, was being sulky and unco-operative. MacKay toiled far into the night mending dane-guns with which the Baganda shot the other tribesfolk. He gave Mutesa a musical box (Coillard went one better and gave Lewanika a phonograph). MacKay even made copper coffins for the Kabaka and the Queen Mother.

The clergy were particularly hopeful of the effect of the first railways. 'The civilizing effect which must be produced on the minds of the natives around us when they see these signs of the genius and greatness of the glorious country from which we come,' said a bishop at the Cape, and urged it be extended northwards, noting, however, that he had had to dis-abuse some native notions that it proved completely that the white men could conquer death also. Livingstone taught the use of irrigation and dams at Kuruman Mission. But Africans sometimes doubted any direct connec-tion between technology and theology. To the unmechanical missionary, Ashe, Mutesa said: 'MacKay we want, but what can *you* do?'

THE MISSIONARY WIFE

The missionaries hoped to win the Africans also by the example of their own lives, dress, modesty, eating and other habits. Here the wives played their part in impressing the native women. A wife was an almost essential adjunct to successful proselytism. In West Africa they died as quickly as the men, if not more so. They sewed, they cooked, they kept house under the surprised eyes of the African women. The wives taught these to sit at table instead of on the ground, and to eat with spoons from plates instead of with their hands. 'A missionary without a wife is like a boat with one oar,' remarked Moffat, and noted that natives clustered round his wife's kitchen table gazing at her dress.

Only missionary women could easily raise the delicate question of getting native women to cover their breasts, though most missionaries took a profound interest in this problem, and in the fullness of time found that the brassière was a boon to Christian decorum. A Baptist told one of the authors that the introduction of the tartan brassière had helped enormously to popularize decency in the past fifty years of the current century. There is no doubt that missionary dress, plain as it naturally was, started female fashions in much of southern and central Africa. Naturally, at first missionary wives required that African girls should be dressed as English servant girls. The missionary wife too was always an extra teacher. But she was also a pioneer and a helpmeet. Mrs Coillard was proud of her efforts to make her husband's wagon a home. 'People can't believe it is a travelling wagon, it is so fresh and Mignon, with its pretty curtains, its elegant pockets hung on either side, the leopard skin, the plants, the whole forming, one would think, the eighth wonder of the world. In Africa people make marvels out of very little.'

Some of the best missionary wives were, of course, the daughters of missionaries, but unmarried ladies who volunteered for mission work in England often found husbands in Africa. Rivett told his friends: 'I flatter myself I have chosen one of the best ladies who came out with the bishop. She is most amiable, thoroughly domesticated and I have reason to believe will make me a most excellent wife. You will be surprised to learn we were engaged less than a month.' She ran an orphanage which duly produced some useful young women to do their housework. It was not always plain sailing for the women; we have a pathetic picture of Mrs Coillard, wretched with homesickness, reading her old journals and letters, tears streaming down her face – until she suddenly destroyed the lot and turned to her husband and religious duties without a further backward look for thirty years. Other clerical ladies, in the comforts of the colony, found life more like an English diocese. Mrs Gray did the diocesan correspondence and accounts, and urged her husband on to victory in his theological battles with Bishop Colenso.

Missionaries believed in the lives of strict religious routine inculcated in them at home. They have left notes of their timetables. Rivett, who began as a teacher of white children in Pietermaritzburg, sets it out as follows: '7.00 Rise. 8.00 Morning prayers. 8.40 Breakfast, followed by school, Latin and Greek. 1.00 Lunch. 2 to 4 School. 4.30 Evening prayers. 5.15 Dine. 6.15 to 7 Training chorister boys at my lodgings. 8.00 Tea. 8 to 12 Reading.' On Saturdays for his health's sake he went riding. Colenso's regimen upcountry was similar: 'Get up with the sun. 7.30 Divine service for whites and natives followed by breakfast. Attend to the cattle. 9 to 12 Work. 12 to 1.00 Surgery. Dinner and rest, "with light book" till 3.00. Followed by afternoon school (sewing for the women). 4.00 to 4.30 Study, followed by riding. Then tea, followed by study till 9. Supper and reading till 11.00 or 12.00.' Colenso's 'study' was largely translation into Zulu.

THE HEALING MISSION

The other power that the missionaries brought was medicine. It early on suggested itself that the twin pillars of missionary work ought to be education and healing. Medical missionaries were appealed for by the societies in the 1830s, and a growing number qualified by taking the medical degrees of the day. Unhappily that experience, limited as it was, sometimes resulted in the inability of the newly-qualified doctors to subscribe to the literal verbal inspiration of the Bible, and they were turned down by the societies. Nor did the wards of the London or Scottish hospitals provide a complete basis for practice in the tropics. Little was known about the diseases which killed the white visitors faster than the natives, and only Livingstone and a minority thought the Africans had much to teach them – Richard Burton dismissed in a contemptuous footnote in his book on his expedition to Harar a Somali superstition that a prevalence of mosquitoes in the wet season was followed by outbreaks of malaria, and that the insect bites had something to do with it. Wise to their limitations, many missionaries were in no hurry to prescribe for any but the simplest ailments. It was dangerous to fail. Livingstone was, again, an exception; the blacks crowded to him but 'as I believe the expenditure of much time and medicine is not the way in which in this country I can do most for the Redeemer's glory, I usually decline treating any but the most serious cases.'

Judicious treatment of native chiefs, however, often opened a road or won a piece of land for a mission settlement. By the end of the century the mission hospital was recognized as an essential part of the dual process of winning souls and saving one's own through service. Yet, outside the towns, well into the twentieth century, such hospitals were treated with widespread suspicion. It is perhaps only in the past twenty years that Africans have taken strongly to Western medicine, largely because of the obvious but unseen and magical efficacy of antibiotics and suchlike drugs. The methods of the past, and missionary insistence on their own type of hygiene as the only sure methods available for conquering disease, made much slower progress, while government medical work, aimed at epidemic diseases, was authoritarian and, if anything, widened the growing gulf between black and white.

Until the partition of Africa, the other recommendation that the incoming missionaries carried was, of course, their political support. Like Philip, they were concerned to preserve the Africans' living space and livelihood, as an essential basis for the work of moral and spiritual reform.

Missions on the Kaffir border had sometimes to be used as forts for refugees. Moffat recruited Griqua riflemen to defend his people against invaders. Though in the Kaffir Wars the missionaries occasionally got slaughtered because they were white, in general they were treated by the Africans as neutral, sometimes as benevolent neutral, a wise if instinctive

77

policy which brought the missionaries more to their point of view. Early on, men like Moshesh perceived that they must use the split between missionaries and trekkers to preserve their people. Khama was schooled by Moffat and others to become the perfect gentleman on his visit to England where, almost the first of a long line of black dignitaries who have proved totally unimpressed by British society and might, he naturally made a good impression and won protection for his country, denying it to the local settlers whose leader, Rhodes, burst out: 'It is humiliating to be beaten by those niggers. They think more of one native at home than the whole of South Africa.'

In South Africa mission influence continued to be strong with government until the Cape and Natal got self-rule, which meant settler rule, in the 1870s. But by then, further north, the missions, faced with the Arab slave trade, had swung round to the view that the lesser evil was colonial government. When Ashe surveyed the bones of little children along the slave caravan routes he demanded 'that the most powerful appeal is made to civilized nations to take the African tribes under their fatherly care ... to England to do for Africa what she has so triumphantly done for the peoples of India.' At first the Arab slavers had been impeded by British operations, naval and diplomatic, along the East Coast; they then moved inland and showed every indication of setting up their own states based on slave export under Islamic empire builders like Tippoo Tib. Other problems contributed to this change of view – closer acquaintance with the native, the effects of adventurers, gun-runners and liquor dealers, in fact the combined evils of Western and Islamic societies with little of their good points.

The mere introduction of the Scottish mission into Nyasaland in 1875, and its creation of an area of security to which natives flocked and chiefs came for allies, raised the question whether the mission was a colony and had to exercise jurisdiction. The first mission to Nyasaland in 1861, in fact, went to war and was much criticized for so doing, but Livingstone had freed slaves at gunpoint and Bishop Mackenzie bluntly declared: 'We have vindicated the English name and have shown it is not safe to attack an Englishman.' The next mission had only to indulge in target practice to protect its converts and allies, but drew the lesson that the civil power, especially to defend oneself from the Arabs, was necessary. The first missionary group to Buganda in 1877 presented a letter from the Foreign Secretary to the king, which upset the Consul in Zanzibar so much that he repudiated it, and caused Mutesa to accuse them of being impostors. Africans often assumed missionaries were envoys of the Queen.

Colonization that could be influenced by the churches in Europe became the need; and the Congo conventional treaties, which banned imported alcoholic liquor for Africans in a large part of central Africa, were deemed a fair exchange for colonial rule. Arnot even said that the drink trade was more demoralizing than the slave trade. The Convention involved the missionaries in struggles against forced labour which had always been the settlers' alternative to outright slavery. The plan had been to replace slavery and slave-dealing with commerce and Christianity, with roads, mechanical porterage, legitimate trade; but this could only be achieved when the apparatus of civil government, with its network of white District Commissioners, was introduced. When it was, the missionaries found their own functions shrank from the initiatory and heroic to the drudgery of education, sanitation and uplift. They became, in some degree, agents of the government after the pacification was largely complete. The political influence of the missions, unrealized by anybody, took a new path; the training at school and orphanage, of the generation of African leaders who would dissolve the whole structure of colonial Africa within seventy-five years of its proud erection.

MISSIONARY AND SETTLER

Relations between the missionaries and the rest of the white population remained far from cordial through the whole period. Moffat on arrival noted: 'I find missionaries are greatly despised here and indeed it is not to be wondered at after the conduct of some.' Until the second Anglo-Boer War, there was ceaseless friction between missionaries and Dutch farmers, and later Rhodesian settlers. The missionaries were blamed for the Hottentot rebellion, if not for the Kaffir Wars. The Boers threatened to attack the Kuruman mission at one stage, and, in their own republics, hindered them in every way possible. Arnot recalled that in 1880 Boers caught him on trek, stole his clothes and mule and left him to shift for himself. Leys noted in 1925 that the Kenya settlers preferred Roman Catholic missionaries because they did not circulate the Scriptures, which might too readily suggest to Africans that the white farmers and officials were the pagans and Romans of the Bible, and provide handy quotations.

The evil example of the rest of the white community was a constant worry to the little bands of evangelists, who often had to offer them hospitality, and endure their conduct as neighbours. The trader, it was admitted in West Africa, was more powerful than the clergyman, while the farmer was a patriarch whose Old Testament authority could not be challenged by the clergy. The call was even to 'send out converted settlers'. 'Fearful are the wreck of the English people in this land,' despaired one report to the S.P.G. 'Our own countrymen require our first and greatest efforts. A mere labourer has little chance of success; he receives degrading treatment; they wander truly vagabonds from village to village, no shelter but a canteen, no refreshment but Cape brandy and bad wine with dry bread.' The profanity and swearing of the settlers was a continual problem for the cloth. When the Chartered Company moved against the Mashona in

1893, the troops' language was very painful to the bishop who accompanied them.

It was not long before the missionaries in South Africa were in trouble over the 'determined opposition of the English artisan class to the training of the natives in skilled labour', as Moffat and Coillard saw it. 'Talk about missions,' said one colonist in Mashonaland, 'I'm a member of the Congregational Church in Bulawayo ... I believe in belonging to the Church. I've a brother who is always asking me about the mission in N.W. Rhodesia. I tell him we convert the natives with the sjambok – teach them the gospel of labour – that's what they want! My brother lives only for the next world – why, we can make a heaven of this one if we like, and we pioneers of this great empire have got a duty to posterity.'

As the missionaries were forced more into the native reservations or tribal areas, they saw matters more from the native viewpoint; but at first they were perplexed over how the natives were to be put to work at a time when the Church had not yet put over the gospel of labour. Calloway noted that the settlers went out to break new ground, to be frustrated by an abundance of lands and no labour. 'The white man is irritated when he sees these men apparently doing very little yet coolly refusing to labour for him for money; he sees his cattle suffer, his harvests in danger of being ruined, and this in the presence of an abundant supply of labour ... how are 8,000 whites to compel 200,000 to work against their will?' The problem recurred and the settlers expected the Church to help, since what could be morally worse than the idleness in which they thought Africans lived? In Kenya the bishops in the twenties declared they were 'strongly of opinion that compulsory labour, so long as it is necessary, should be legalized.'

John White was told in a Salisbury Store that 'these damned parsons ought to be kicked out of the country.' It infuriated the Rhodesian settlers that the *Methodist Times* was sent accurate reports that the settlers bought African girls from their fathers, in accordance with tribal custom, whom they regarded as private property like their own cattle.

So, in south, central and east Africa relations something between hostility and alliance grew up between the missionaries and the other 'civilizing' authorities.

4

ADVENTURERS, TRADERS AND BUSINESSMEN

The businessman's life in Africa began on the heaving decks of slaveships in the triangular trade, and in the castles built along the West Coast for bartering goods for slaves. In the main it was a maritime life because of the health hazards on the shore. The mortality on the ships seems to have been at times almost as great for the white sailors and factors as for their African captives. Merchant-adventuring to Africa was a risky business; it remained so until late in the nineteenth century. To find the trade, the trader had to be, like the missionary seeking converts, by turns explorer, pioneer and sometimes administrator. He played a large part in the process of 'opening up' Africa. At the same time, if he did not survive, he could not expect to enjoy his profits. On the West Coast, therefore, traders tried to make their pile as expeditiously as possible and retire to Britain. In the south, they could spend a lifetime trading, before retiring to Capetown or to England. From the first conditions were very different, though all over Africa business, politics and development were closely intertwined.

JOBSON AND OTHERS

The first difficulty was to find a trade worth the investment and the risk. In West Africa, slaves provided it. One of the first English merchant adventurers, Jobson, during his visit to the Gambia in 1621, when he wrote his celebrated report, repudiated slaves as merchandise when they were offered to him by the African chiefs he met. His hope lay in gold, not in the exchange of commodities; although he explains how the Africans most of all desired the Europeans' iron and salt, and he took ivory, hides and cotton in return. Because the West Africans had gold ornaments in some profusion, the Europeans were convinced – as they were all over the world – that there

81

must be some 'infinite store of gold' which would rival the discoveries of the Conquistadores. They did find it in Africa, later. Jobson was not so lucky. Though he was told of 'houses covered with gold', such West African gold was probably an accumulation over the years from river panning. In exchange the British traders offered copper in bar, gold and silver, cloths, calico, glasses, mirrors, cutlery, axes and tools of all kinds, pewterware, spirits and brass rings for arms and legs, 'and they will turn over a whole cask before they find two to please them'.

As the gold proved evanescent, the English traders turned to the 'triangular trade' where profits were reasonably assured, and on that trade built a substantial part of the prosperity and progress of eighteenth-century Britain. If they had found gold and failed to get slaves history might have been different. But slaves it was, and trading life was confined to the slave ports, as the chiefs in the interior, supplied with guns by the traders, brought down the merchandise. Life in the forts or hulks, as we have seen, was unpleasant, often riotous and often dull; the traders waited only to clear the barracoons, fill their ships if they could, and be off.

Such a trade set few traditions for normal business. It led neither to colonization, nor to the founding of substantial commercial communities. When it was abolished, the problem of finding commodities to exchange returned. The Africans wanted almost everything that a newly industrialized Britain had to offer in the early nineteenth century. But on their side they still had (notwithstanding the great civilizations they were reported to have enjoyed) little to offer except gold dust, ivory, the pelts of wild animals, camwood and a few plants. Their own big trade in cola nuts did not appeal to the Europeans, whose stimulants were liquid. It was not until palm oil was found to be an excellent cheap lubricant for the growing variety of machinery in Britain that a substantial trade could develop in the 1850s. The 'oil rivers' then became a centre of African business life. But it was on a small scale: 'a parody of the practical hard-thinking mercantile life in England,' wrote a business visitor. 'A pantomime of business,' he complained. Dutch margarine in the 1890s created the large export market for which the Coast was waiting.

It was a leisurely life saturated with heat, but sustained by black underlings. John Whitford, an English trader in the 1860s, gives the most detailed picture of business routine on the coast. In Sierra Leone, he writes:

The business hours are from six to eleven a.m. when most of the stores close for breakfast and repose until midday. Breakfast is most enjoyable. Friends assemble and talk business or colonial politics. They partake of good country beefsteaks, Madeira potatoes and onions, turtles' eggs (rare delicacy) and the contents of various tins of preserved provisions, mellowed by Allsopp or Bass, or claret, followed by a cup of tea when reclining on easy chairs in the verandah outside the dining room. All doors and windows are opened to admit the sea breeze. When the sun goes westward another bath and change of clothes is desirable, after or before which some go riding on horseback, others walk on the green by the battery. When the band plays, thousands assemble to hear the music.

Most of these were black: the white population was then about a hundred. 'If the green is not occupied by troops,' he continues, 'young men play cricket. Sun sets at six . . . Europeans then hurry home to dinner, which is the same as breakfast with the addition of soup. Friends drop in after dinner . . . It is a very weary existence.'

At Freetown, and at some other ports, merchants inhabited houses close to the shore, often in unhealthy places. Whitford was critical of their lethargy in supinely taking on the houses of their predecessors.

They live on the first floor, overlooking a garden. In this garden, in many cases, exists a pump drawing water from a well. Within a few yards of this well is a cesspool carefully housed over but never emptied. It is a horrible abomination; quantities of chloride of lime are thrown into it and strewed about, will not drive away the foul stench emitted. Everything thrown into the cesspool is consumed, or it percolates, perhaps to the well . . . You lower a lantern through the hole and observe a mass of reptiles and foul insects gorging on filth and offal and on each other . . . but unless householders are compelled to pay for and use the good water they stick to the wells. Is it any wonder Sierra Leone is the white man's grave?

And not just the white man; 'a self-respecting English terrier', he reported, succumbed to the climate in a few months.

But stores further down the Coast were more carefully designed for use, and one at Bonthe is described as 'a large and slated store, two stories high, on its right the powder magazine and on its left strongly constructed stores to hold palm kernels, palm oil in casks and salt in bulk. On the land behind the beach 25 feet above the river is an enclave 200 yards square containing the agent's house gracefully shaded by trees.' This store cost £6,000 to build. The agent lived as well as he could, but had in smaller dwellings four or five white clerks under him, whose lives were less pleasant, and generally shorter. These clerks were for the most part 'gaunt and sickly men, some of them wearing the stamp of alcohol, and the faces of the rest the impress of many fevers.' No less unhealthy were the stretches of idleness between trading. One clerk told Bindloss 'we make every cent we can and I would sooner be worked to death than idle here. All you have to look forward to is the arrival of the quarterly liquor supply. Then we have a carnival for a week and forget it all. Afterwards it is worse than before and we hold on until the next arrives.'

In the Gold Coast Whitford reported that the trading stores or factories as they were still called in the 1860s, each occupied:

several acres of land enclosed by a high wall with only one gate, where a policeman keeps watch day and night . . . an entire block, square or oblong with streets on every side, presenting only the appearance of high blank walls, excepting the dwelling building which rises from groves of acacia trees, rose trees and palms high enough for the inmates to enjoy the sea breezes. Inside the walls are buildings facing inwards. These are blacksmiths' shops, coopers' and carpenters' places of work, stores for produce, cookhouses . . . In the front stands the trading store, and on the first and perhaps second floor above it, are the living rooms. Inside the store natives stand before a long counter and receive payment in cowries, guns, cloth, or any thing from a fishhook to a cask of rum, for palm oil, palm kernels, cotton or other produce delivered. In the open space formed by the courtyard, beneath the shade of graceful trees, the natives who have come long distances in canoes lie about and talk . . . meantime the cotton they have brought is undergoing the process of ginning . . . the palm oil is boiled in huge coopers and . . . run into casks. Palm kernels are packed in bags or left in bulk and furnish continual cargo for homeward-bound steamers.

But at Lagos, the trading houses were until the 1860s largely situated in hulks on the lagoons, as the town was not yet built, and the lagoons were, perhaps rightly, considered more salubrious and, at an earlier period, safer from African attack. The hulk was described as 'a huge Noah's ark, anchored in a swift current, it swings with the tide. A wide ladder staircase reaches to the water's edge. Gigs bring visitors alongside.' It had possessed 'a sheltered cool and clean white upper deck, the living and entertaining hall, to take 1,000.' This was furnished with wickerwork chairs and sofas introduced from Madeira. It had comfortable bedrooms and offices including bathrooms built on deck for the senior agents, while the juniors occupied the cabins below. The former saloons were converted to the trading store with its counter. The hulk like the ports was a scene of vigorous activity, with canoes moored all round it, coopers making casks on deck, Kroos melting kernels for refining, Europeans supervising.

Trading life was thus hot and monotonous, with everybody counting the days to go home. What sort of men were the traders? The archetype, who achieved his niche in literature, was the half-legendary Trader Aloysius Horn, who, living in his old age in a Johannesburg dosshouse, told his yarns to Ethelreda Lewis. As a stripling he went out to the Cameroons and Gabon with Hatton & Cookson; charted the trade rivers, established posts at gun-point, came to terms with German traders. He described scenes of slavery, piracy and cannibalism (he relished cannibals with as much gusto as Mary Kingsley) and finally, and improbably, rescued a half-caste 'goddess' of noble English lineage on the paternal side from a 'josh house, where no white man has ever been until I came' – as a member in good standing of the secret Egbo society. (It became the basic theme of many films with an African locale.)

Perhaps more representative, and certainly more historical was John Holt in the same period. In his memoirs Holt, who achieved eminence, described himself as typical, since he said Liverpool was full of young men like himself who had emigrated from rural areas to escape from poverty. He was, in fact, exceptional – most remained clerks in that city. Holt, with others, like him, decided to move on, often in response to newspaper advertisements by the firms. 'Mankind is like a lot of hungry pigs fighting over a trough of milk,' he wrote to his parents, in the heyday of *laissez faire*. 'Everybody seems to be trying to pull the piece of food out of his neighbour's mouth . . . what am I to do? If I stay where I am I have the prospect of a £60 salary which to my nature is beggary. No! It is money I want and money I must have if I go through fire and water for it.' What he got was a post as assistant on the Coast to a merchant through his Liverpool employers, a brother of Macgregor Laird, a steamer pioneer. He borrowed £70 to go – the fare from Liverpool to Bonny was £20 10s. 6d. – and initially joined the commercial community at Fernando Po. He had heard that supercargoes took home £10,000 to £15,000 in three years. Luckily for him, his employer's affairs there were in a mess, which he was able to straighten out, and when his employer died in a year or so, he was given the senior management post by his widow at £200 a year. Three years later he bought the entire business from her. In 1867 he built new premises; in 1869 he opened factories at Bata and Gaboon, and others elsewhere later. By 1874, Holt employed eight or nine Europeans, including his own two brothers, and had three stores, a schooner and up-river factories. He was the successful Victorian businessman; and Trader Horn said he flogged his natives for not pulling their weight.

Such a businessman's relaxations on the Coast were limited. There were some comforts. By the 1860s freezing machines were reducing the temperature of the claret and beer to 7° Centigrade (45° Fahrenheit). There were the games of cricket and billiards, and whist parties. Old-style banqueting began to die out in the 1870s because competition made a hangover bad for trading. The easy-going Coaster lost out to the sterner man of Methodist or Presbyterian faith, who prayed aloud before trading or dining and did not mind being overheard doing so; such men helped the missionaries to develop profitable small industries with African convert labour. They permitted no liquor to their white staff or themselves and led the church parade on Sundays in toppers. Among them were the eccentrics, like 'Daddy Jim' who threw his peg-leg at customers who annoyed him. As late as the 1920s a trader could write, 'the object was to keep alive if possible, but to keep detached from sentiment and self-pity in any event. Wet blanketry and the maudlin kind of sobriety on sufferance were the unforgivable sins.' But the new century brought the Coast new diversions – lawn tennis, shooting, croquet, cricket, skittles – above all bridge and practical jokes. The books from home often lay unread.

Holt gives a description of a trader's household in Fernando Po, which was probably fairly representative of the Coast generally.

Our establishment consists of Mr and Mrs Lynslager, a son of the late Governor Beecroft, for whom Mr Lynslager is guardian, nine wenches, three boys and myself. These sleep in the house, outside is a cook and two or three men. Besides these, we have a clerk in the house shop whose assistant is one of the above girls and in the other shop, in another part of the town, two girls, also some 18 Kroomen who do any kind of labour. The girls who live in the house are too thick by half; they do nothing but wash clothes, look after the three bed-rooms and wait on Mrs Lynslager except when Mr Lynslager is at home when, I am told, it is usual for them to lend him a hand in his bath and dressing. This seemed rather too delicate for me but although Beecroft cannot get into his room when the 'old man' is dressing, the girls have a free passage and have to wash him all over. They sleep in the same room with Mr and Mrs Lynslager but it appears to be nothing thought of. The three boys are for the purpose of cleaning the large room in the office, and for waiting at table, etc. If I had an establishment of this kind I fancy I should make about a third of our number of boys and girls do for me; however, I suppose it must be fashionable here, perhaps it may be a sign of aristocracy as our powdered flunkies are at home.

Holt went out with black girls, some of whom had been back to Liverpool and dressed as Europeans, took quinine regularly and were capable of superior conversation; but the generality of African girls were sneered at when they pretended to be white ladies. 'On going to dinner,' Holt wrote of such a party for Christmas, 'the gentlemen politely offered their arms but what a farce it all was for they have not a bit of lady about them in the sense that word is generally understood; they may play at ladies but will never be.' He soon deplored the lax morals of the black 'ladies' and virtuously reports that he meant to have no connection with the blacks, although 'nothing is easier', for in Fernando Po: 'There is hardly more than one virtuous girl to be found in the place and in spite of their constant depravity a child and especially a mulatto child is scarcely ever born.' Nor, he reported, did marriages take place. He noted that the blacks had effective medicines to prevent conception and cause abortion. Finally he did meet a black virgin, who was the envy and butt of the other women, but realized that 'it is not the white man that a black woman likes; it is his money and the distinction of the connexion.'

The black girls gave the Coasters companionship and solace, as indeed native girls did elsewhere in Britain's spreading network of trading posts round the world. By the 1890s colour prejudice even in commercial circles had become as strong in West Africa as in the American south. Bindloss observed that 'while the white man may purchase a dusky helpmate for some £5 unreproved, if he espouse an educated negress as is sometimes done, he loses caste at once.' When Henry Martin, a new clerk of Frank and Andrew Swanzy, arrived in the Volta in 1902 he was warned by the Agent never to allow his servant to bring a woman into his room 'even if he says that his sister wants to see you'.

The coastal trader's life was very different from that of the man who ventured into the interior. In Sierra Leone it was possible to walk, but the major trade routes were the rivers, once small steamboats and launches became available. Such steamers could out-run canoes, and defend themselves if attacked, and with them the trader could avoid the high cost of the African intermediaries by dealing direct with inland producers who were perhaps less sophisticated customers, though the accounts hardly bear this out. A big steamer carried three hundred tons of cargo, did thirteen knots downstream, and had several six-pounders.

There were many prospects of adventures. On the way from Onitsha to the sea one twelve-ton steamer, for example, was attacked and grounded, losing one of its twin screws. It was pushed off under attack, struck a rock and sank, and its crew, led by two white traders, were captured, and had to be bought off with a heavy ransom by other traders. The ransom amounted to £206 7s. 6d. in trade rum, cloth and matchets; but once they were safe, and the victors carousing ashore, the rescuing vessel shelled the offending village. Mary Kingsley reports how in 1875 one young up-country trader, when local agitators stirred up the villagers around him, defended his store with a gatling-gun. When cornered with only his revolver in hand he cried, 'I have six men's lives in this gun. Those six I *will have*. Then you may have me.'

But at other times the local potentate was entertained on deck with champagne. 'He was dressed as a naval engineer,' remarked Whitford, 'and his wife in corresponding finery. But the lady soon sat naked to the waist and ate thus.' Many coy references to the 'charms' that the dark-complexioned Venuses were so ready to expose adorn the descriptions of Victorian travellers. However, 'you never see beauty beyond *beauté du Diable*,' remarked an engineer in the Gold Coast sourly in the 1880s, 'and the piquant plainness which one admires in a pug-pup.'

Later it was possible to establish permanent 'factories' high up the rivers, connected with the coast by the steamers. Whitehouse saw it in 1865 as a great new opportunity for the young – for 'juniors possessing sound constitutions combined with a knowledge of Manchester, Sheffield and Birmingham goods, also able to handle a rifle, cook food, do anything rough and enjoy doing so, as well as eating heartily.' They had, however, to know above all the baneful influence of the rum, guns and powder which were to be bartered for the palm oil and ivory. New products were found – such as shea butter, which was promoted in England as a hair restorer.

The stores up river were built of equipment brought up in the traders' own steam launches – sawn timber, uprights, nails and corrugated iron to form a roof and a shop. They might become the centre of a new village. 'While the shop is building,' Whitford observes, 'the steam launch plies to and from the ocean steamer. British goods are received, shops opened and produce purchased on such remunerative terms that in a few years the original squatters will be well able to retire into private life and leave the hard work and exposure to an unhealthy climate to others.' Even so, they often returned, wondering why. 'Perhaps,' remarked Bindloss, 'the entire absence of outward restraint had something to do with it, as well as un-limited influence; for in this region every man does what is right in his own eyes, and obeying no law but his own pleasure, is accountable to none – so long as he makes the factory pay.' It was a life that had charm even for British aristocrats.

Habits were a little different inland. Traders wore the local 'tobes', fez and turban, with baggy 'trews' under, and sandals. They dined off buffalo meat, muscovy duck and palm-oil stew, and spent less of their money on European imports. They half believed, as indeed Europeans had from the seventeenth century, in the potency of fetich and were no more ashamed to wear charms and pay protection money to ju-ju men than Horn was too high-and-mighty to call in the witch-doctor to prescribe the 'red berries' that brought on heavy sweating and relieved West Coast fever, or to drink water from water-vines as a specific against dysentry.

Bargaining was an art. A trader soon learned that to expose his whole stock to his black customers only excited their envy, and caused them to hold off the market to raise the rates of exchange. It paid:

to expose only a few bales of Manchester prints and merely samples of Sheffield and Birmingham ware, guns, brass rods, German looking glasses and Venetian beads ... Then the vision of what they coveted being limited, their ideas followed suit; but still they haggled over the price of tusks of ivory ... It is calculated what we can afford to give to make a good profit and then the repre-sentative quantity of goods is placed before the seller; but he is dissatisfied and stickels for more, and sometimes they whine piteously and clutch our garments ... Such childish conduct in trading matters is undignified, and we express our contempt ... We place a few looking-glasses, fish hooks and jack-knives over and above the merchandise offered 'for top'. Yet more articles are asked for. We then refuse to trade and the goods are replaced for the next customer.

Often the tusks appeared day after day to step up their value, and in the end the bargain would be reached.

Other ways of dealing with customers were used – such as 'wardens' with hippo whips to keep them from pilfering.

The brightest articles command the best returns ... they adore utensils of brass, Madras kerchiefs of glowing red and yellow colours, Turkey-red chintz and twills, red blankets, patterned cottons. Delicately-made boxes artistically illus-trated on the outside, and inside filled with neatly packed and ravishing soft silk-velvet robes for the aristocracy – beautiful green, brilliant magenta and scarlet – small German looking glasses, matchets, knives, foghorns, whistles, needles – produced screams of frantic delights ...

There were also the Birmingham guns that cost 7s. to 9s. wholesale, powder and shot.

We have a picture of the model salesman, McCoskry, who presided over these turbulent Victorian bazaars on shipboard or in tin-roofed shanties.

Nothing disturbed his equanimity. He would buy a dozen tusks, wave his hand to the servants in attendance to produce the merchandise required for payment in the midst of jabber and wangle, and he would then turn to the next customer in regular order even if he, or she, only brought a single jar of shea butter . . .

The white traders were normally licensed by the chiefs – they gave them free goods or dashes to open shop. After the trading, there was entertainment and even carousel; in trade white and black were social equals, even if the white man laughed behind his hand (as did the black). But friendships did exist, services were exchanged. A trader would attend a dying customer and pray all night on his knees for his recovery; and even Coasters' prayers were sometimes answered.

By the 1900s the travelling sub-agent of a big firm like Frank and Andrew Swanzy would carry a company staff – a six-foot malacca cane with a nine-inch silver unicorn on top and a nine-inch silver ferrule – when touring inland as a *laissez-passer* to the local chief. Harry Martin recalls that he was met at Addah by the local African agent who gave him a dinner of roast chicken, boiled yam, white bread and Dutch tinned butter before he sailed up the Volta in a launch with a temperamental engine. He lived in a mud-walled communal lodging house equipped with a netted poster bed, unshuttered windows, earth walls and floor, and crude furniture. Marching through the interior with six boys and a hammock he traded for the company, and promotion finally elevated him to a seat in the Legislative Council; the fun and 'stingo' of trading life in the nineteenth century was finally gone.

F. & A. Swanzy was a not untypical West African family firm, which was duly absorbed by the Lever colossus. The first Swanzy on the Coast was James (b. 1767), second son of an Irish family. He went out as a surgeon in 1789. He was thus a fairly typical example of the penniless youth of middle-class education, who went out in a constant stream to replace those that died, an average of five or six a year. The recruit was generally a Writer at £200 a year, who would, if he survived the 'seasoning fever', get promotion as a Factor with a salary rise of £40 within the first year, and then launch out into private trade after three years, in the intervals of official duty, at an Out-fort or in the Accountant's office. If he were lucky, he might go on to become a Senior Factor, and a Chief in an Out-fort, with pay amounting in all to a sum considerably over £2,000 a year. Everyone except the chaplain wore military uniform, for it was an establishment devoted to violence.

James Swanzy lived on the coast for ten years. He worked as a surgeon in two places, then as Governor at Dixcove and British Sekondi. Then he returned to London and carried on trading with the West Coast from there. Meanwhile two of his brothers were at the Coast. John, in his factory near Cape Coast Castle, and Francis Lucas. Then James returned to the Coast. He had four sons, two each by two marriages. The two by the first marriage were John, a lieutenant in the African Colonial Corps who died in battle, and James, a trader with a Creole wife, who was a magistrate in 1841, the year before his death. The sons of the second marriage, who were not on very good terms with their half-brother James, were Frank and Andrew, the founders of the firm F. & A. Swanzy. Frank was a soldier and a magistrate, who spoke Fanti fluently and loved the country. He married the mulatto daughter of a governor. Andrew was the main architect of the firm. The personal link ended when he returned to England.

TRADERS IN THE SOUTH

Natal also started its existence because British sailors, exploring along the coast, landed or were wrecked there and built settlements and ships on the shore, where the Africans at first thought them monsters thrown up from the deep. Henry Francis Fynn, who failed to make much of a living in Cape Town in the 1830s, took the sloop *Julia* to open the first trading store at a dubious harbourage later to be called D'urban, then Durban, after the governor. Their object was to make contact with a king called Chaka, whose immense power was rumoured further south. Fynn recorded in his diary the impact of the huge mass of an *impi* marching past him on the shore: 'My view extended over several miles of the beach, but I could not see the rear of this dense black and continuous mass of natives, all armed and in their war dresses.' His status as a sea-monster saved him, and Chaka received him and gave the British permission to trade for ivory.

Business in Cape Town was at first largely a matter of ships' chandlering, but gradually traders moved out, and found their markets both in supplying the Dutch farmers with their limited needs, and buying ivory and skins from the Africans – often a dangerous way of life. The trader lived partly as a hunter, sometimes as a courtier in an African king's kraal, partly as a prospector. In Cape Town, the British arrived to find that as trade was forbidden, owing to the East India Company's monopoly, smuggling and trade were synonymous. When the monopoly ended, and a British currency was introduced, trading and minor manufacture began. By 1811, there were forty-two retail shops, and the shopkeeping element in British life was established. Snobbery flourished from then on.

Shopkeeping at the Cape could be profitable. John Bardwell Ebden, for example, began as a clerk in a victualling office and retired as a well-to-do merchant in England in 1818, founder of Ebden & Eaton & Co. Men like Twicross, De Wet, Ross and Hertz were well-established merchants; Pero was a tailor, Isaac Manuel was in hides, Rot Hefoord in real estate, John Colison in wine. By 1804 the traders had their chamber of commerce which met at George's coffee house, where they met the ships' captains, took in the newspapers, and discussed whaling, remounts for India, ivory and wool prospects, besides regulating weights, measures and auctions. Later they had their own building where they gave what were described as 'brilliant receptions'. The businessmen gave the unpopular Governor Somerset a great send-off, drawing his carriage themselves, causing the journalists and wits to note with what hypocrisy they made 'asses of themselves'.

It was a comfortable life. The balls were enlivened by the Indian army officers, and there is reference to 'that period of the evening when on ball nights papas begin to look obdurate and speak severely about keeping horses and carriages waiting, and daughters, who care for neither, beseech papas for "just one other little waltz, no more".' Only a handful of merchants had their own carriages as late as 1880 in Port Elizabeth.

The Mental Improvement Society was soon in full swing, and in 1840 came the Institution for the Diffusion of Knowledge. Knowledge came in ever more quickly after 1836, when everyone trooped down to the harbour to see the first steamship arrive, and move about the bay to demonstrate its independence of the wind. Steadily a mercantile culture was created. In 1830 insurance broking began. Until 1834 securities were kept in iron-bound chests in Cape Town, but in 1836 the Cape of Good Hope Bank was floated successfully. By 1850 the merchants were agitating for railways, and even before that for a parliament.

Nevertheless, it was a small town, and the merchants could see that it needed a hinterland. Some of them became explorers, but they preferred to finance exploration. George Thomson explored Bechuanaland early; in 1833 there was set up the Cape of Good Hope Association for exploring Central Africa. In fact, the missionaries and itinerant traders moved far ahead, backed by firms like Mackie, Dunn & Co. or Ebden & Co. Westbeech, for example, was already installed at King Lewanika's court when the missionary Arnot arrived there, and was experimenting with locks on the river on the Thames' design. The first trader to arrive was sometimes unlucky; Thomas was probably killed by the Ovambos when he encountered them.

The back-Veld trader became a key institution in the development of the colonial economy, extracting such little wealth as it could produce from the self-sufficient worlds of the Africans and the Boer farmers and patriarchs respectively. They provided expert services that ranged from mending gunlocks to castrating sheep. They hardly led a social life, and they have left few records of themselves. They seem rarely to have had families, though they no doubt took African concubines (Fynn had three).

The 'trek boer' trade was limited. The Karoo farmers brought in springbok skins for bookbinding, boerseep made from sheep's tallow, biltong and wheat. Jackson sold American canvas, or white duck, for tents and wagon canopies, powder and lead to the men. To the women he sold checked ginghams, patterned cottons, prints, *nainsook* (underwear) sateen, silk ribbons, woollen stockings (mainly outsize, twelve inches across the top), corduroy and crepe. A major line was patent medicines, notwithstanding the vaunted Boer women's skill with simples and herbal medicines, learned from the Hottentots. Jackson stocked chlorodyne, red lavender, peppermint, paregoric, Chamberlain's cough remedy, Mother Seigal's syrup and Holloway's Pills.

Eight to ten children tumbled out of a Boer wagon, and for them the store stocked peppermints, sugar-sticks, and butterscotch – and in the 1870s Fry's Cocoa (chocolate came later). 'Colonial mixture' cost 4d. a pound. The older Boers bought sardines, ginger and sugar biscuits by way of luxuries.

Much trade was done by traders in their own wagons. They sold dried fruit, often conveniently packed in coffins which were also in demand in treeless country, bush tea and even *dagga* (hemp). They bought sheep and goats which they could drive to the town markets, often riding on donkeys which could be fed on old newspapers when fodder failed.

Trading with the Africans also involved long treks by wagon, which took the place of the launches on the West African rivers, and the trade goods were more like those sold in West Africa. In addition, brandy was a staple diet, although it was prohibited to Africans and a licence had to be procured to sell it to the Boers. But traders sold it to the Boers by the bottle and the Africans by the tot, just the same. By mid-century money was circulating, but barter was still usual – trade goods for cattle, ivory, ostrich feathers and corn. Mrs Heckford took to trading, first with the Boers and then the Africans, after she found she had not enough working capital to develop a farm. She did so well that she bought a farm and a house in Pretoria – only to lose her business when the British were driven out in 1881. As a 'smouse', or wagon-trader, she relates how African interest in trade was keen, and:

men, women and children literally besieged the wagon, chattering and screaming like so many monkeys, clambering up on the wheels . . . I never saw so grotesque a caricature . . . of scenes I have observed at Swan and Edgar's. Some absurd-looking savage in a blanket would ask to see a shirt, or a coat, or a pair of trousers or a hat. The assembled multitude would become all attention. He would be turned round and round, the critics would fall back a pace or two, while he watched their faces anxiously: no, there was a bulge at the back, or the brim was too narrow – he must try another . . .

The wagons piled high with goods, or produce bought in return, the traders slept in the veld or bushveld under canvas or in the open, and eked out their expenses by shooting game for the pot. They went from one Boer encampment to another, or among the tribes paid the chief (as in West Africa) for the right to open shop. They thrust, like the missionaries, ever deeper into the heart of Africa: in a real sense they were the frontier, as the land became relatively settled behind them. For several years getting concessions, for subsequent profitable resale, from native chiefs in the north became a risky but worthwhile enterprise. Henry Ware, a trader from

Kimberley, for example, induced King Lewanika of Barotse to grant him exclusive rights in 1889 for £200 a year and four per cent royalty, which he resold to Rhodes and the Chartered Company.

THE RIDERS

Transport riding became an important occupation as settlement proceeded, until railways and telegraphs were built. Everything for the mines (Kimberley and the Rand) had to be dragged by ox-wagon from the coast, and the Rhodesian settlement depended on wagon transport. One wagon sufficed to carry out the country's first annual exports. The old transport road, a broad track of veld, ran northwards through Palapwe, Bulawayo, and Victoria Falls; it created new towns and new communities. Conditions were bad; skeletons and corpses of oxen, mules, horses and other animals and broken equipment lined the route, which in the 1880s was devastated by rinderpest, deep in dust or mud, the stench appalling, the flies torment-ing men, women and beasts terribly as they moved and worse when they outspanned. Even the donkeys succumbed. The railways arrived only in the nick of time. The skilled transport rider, or teamster, hiring his services, and usually (but not always) owning his own wagon and teams, was a free man, who combined hunting, trading and prospecting with his trips.

He was a figure of Victorian romance, in his dungaree trousers, his flannel shirt open at the neck, and 'disgraceful sombrero', which was imitated by many a young man who (Andrew Melrose remarked cuttingly),

could neither ride nor shoot; he would have lost his way had he gone three miles from the nearest township, yet he invariably wore riding breeches, puttee leggings and a hunting stock, whilst a stranger hearing him talk to a barmaid would have taken him to be one of the original band of pioneers.

Many young men took to transport riding and found it a gamble; Sir Percy Fitzpatrick learned from it his uitlander politics, journalism and poetry alike, wandering in backwaters of lawlessness along the Rand and into Portuguese East Africa. Fitzpatrick extolled the trek-wagon as 'a master-piece of the primitive, loose and limber, yielding and tough, borne on the beasts that alone could haul it'. A wagon then cost about forty pounds new. He described the transport rider's easy life in the reef towns – 'a lunch at Colquhouns, a stroll through the bar, a drink or two, toss the papers about, a cigar on the *stoep* with one's heels on the railing, and an "aw, I think I'll be going now, get my horse, boy".'

THE KOPJE

The hope of gold burned in the minds of the British almost as soon as it was possible to move inland. The lonely prospector was known to trekkers and missionaries alike. One of them, J. H. Davis, found the first traces of gold at Wilpootjie in 1852. The discovery of diamonds in the 1860s, however, first transformed the Cape Colony and the prospects of businessmen. J. B. Robinson decided to be a wool merchant, and like other traders moved with his trekwagon through the Orange Free State, and lent a hand in the fight against the Basutos, when in July 1868 he heard of the finds in the 'fields' and picked up diamonds in a drift. He tested the stones' cutting powers on a glass tumbler which he borrowed at a Boer homestead, and at nightfall held them up in the dark to see if any threw off phosphorescent light. One of them in a handful proved to be a diamond. Then, on the Vaal River, his panning brought in more. He sent his partner to England to make arrangements with dealers, and create the New River Diamond Syndicate; and the news of the find leaked along the world's growing network of ocean cables. It became a great sensation, like Ballarat, California and Yukon; and diggers began taking every train, ship and trekwagon to the new adventure. Diamonds were found everywhere – in fowls' gizzards, in the wall of Boer houses, in tree roots: every tale grew with the telling. It cost £100 to hire a wagonette at Pietermaritzburg, and the four hundred miles to the Vaal took nineteen days' hard travel; the ox-wagon with the equipment followed and took six weeks. In two years 25,000 tons of equipment were conveyed to the fields, at the rate of 40s. per 100 lb. The building of wagons became a booming business.

In a few months a motley diggers' republic was set up, while Britain and the Orange Free State quarrelled over sovereignty, and dispossessed the unfortunate Waterboer, a coloured leader who probably had the best claim. A committee in a tent made the rules; disputes were settled by fisticuffs, as the white tents went up and fleets of wagons dotted the plain. When a Boer patrol tried to assert its authority, the diggers made it drunk and shooed it away. Lord Kimberley, the colonial secretary, disliked the name New Rush, or *Voorsitsicht*, for the diamond fields, and much preferred it to be called, simply, Kimberley.

Robinson's story is paralleled by that of a few score who not only struck it lucky, but knew where the real money lay. After his Colesburg kopje claim had made him rich, his transfer to buying from digging made him richer still. He built an office, bought a newspaper, organized the law against illicit buying, got himself into the Cape Parliament, and in 1877 married a famous beauty, Elizabeth, the daughter of a merchant in the fields, James Ferguson. By then Cecil Rhodes was buying up the claims and creating the De Beers monopoly, upon which his dream of British expansion in Africa was to be built.

In the camp, the diggers lived high. The buyers did best of all, and the merchants did well too, even making bread for the diggers brought one family a fortune.

Illicit buyers, who received from the Africans who smuggled stolen stones, sometimes had their tents burned, but usually retired to the coast

Mining and Commerce

The big hole – the source of the diamonds and of Cecil Rhodes' monopoly and fortune. Kimberly in the 'seventies by Henry Seppings Wright.

The diggers, whether of diamonds or gold, had their own vigorous social life – and indeed once proclaimed a 'Digger's Republic'. Scenes from Kimberley.

Cecil Rhodes on trek, rather more luxuriously than other travellers, through the new 'Rhodesia' in 1896. Cape ox-wagons were soon to disappear as the railways advanced.

Diamonds were the basis of greater fortunes made later from gold. J. B. Robinson, the greatest Randlord, seen at Kimberley with S. G. A. Shippard, and Dr Rutherford Harris, two of Rhodes's intimates.

Markets had to be large when the ox-wagon was standard transport. Transport riding was a thriving trade for young men until the railways linked cities. Kimberley in 1888.

Early gold-mining was a matter of prospectors, outcrops of 'banket', panning and native labour. Mines began to go deep and require heavy machinery in the 1890s – and then they also needed capital, shareholders and London finance.

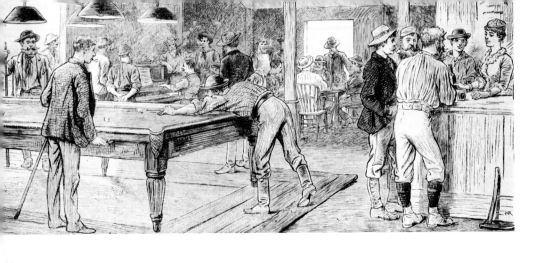

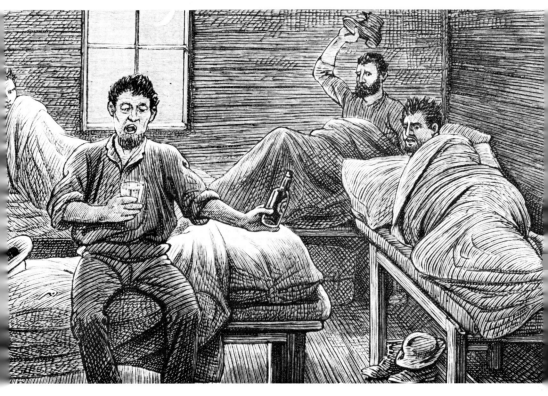

Life in a typical Transvaal mining 'dorp' in the 1880s. Miners dancing to piano and squeeze-box in a Barberton canteen; a billiard saloon with white barmaids, and the interior of a bedroom at the local hotel.

Early trade in West Africa was conducted from ships' boats, or by leaving trade-goods on the beach. From the 1840s traders often operated from converted ships' hulks, a combined floating shop, factory and residence, like the *George Shotton* at Degama, Nigeria, about 1880. But with the security of colonial rule, shops were opened throughout West Africa to create the demand for the products of civilization (including gramophones) which would bring down groundnuts, rubber and cocoa for world trade.

with a competence and became substantial middle-class citizens whose past was not investigated. The Africans, by their own standards, also did well, putting their money into 'an old gun, a canister of powder, a bar of lead, a bullet mould ... a glorious equipment for robbing and killing white people', one visitor noted grimly. The diggers probably did less well than any. Twenty thousand of them and their Kaffirs toiled by day, removing the diamondiferous gravel in casks ready for washing in sieves, tubs, cradles (rocking wooden boxes) and finally rotating drums; amid all the noise a loud shout would signal the discovery of a diamond. Their tents, lined with green baize, were pitched anywhere. There were no landlords, rates or taxes; frame houses with canvas walls followed the tents, which were often blown down by gales or washed away in the rain – and a young woman was killed when her tent pole was struck by lightning. The Vaal River served for water supply, ablutions and drainage, and camp fever would have been more serious but for the cold, dry atmosphere of the veld. Scorpions posed a larger problem than dysentery, for which a one-bed hospital had to suffice.

The bars were heavily patronized, pianos were sent up in crates, and in the gambling tents white women presided over the roulette, and miners played fly-loo, staking money on lumps of sugar to see on which a fly would first alight. Bread and sugar cost 1s. a lb, tea 5s. a lb, milk 2s. 6d. a tin. The diggers, however, were a passing breed, as the earth walls between their claims fell in and the costs rose.

Melina Rorke described the camp in the late 1870s as 'a wild primitive place where fierce bearded men gambled fortunes away, fought over the possession of a Kaffir wench, drank and stole and murdered for the sake of diamonds or women.' By then the diggers were living in corrugated sheds, festooned with overhead wires to carry electricity; the days of characters like Yorker Bill, Lanky Tom, Stiff-Collar Ted and so on were over. Rhodes, Beit and Barney Barnato were consolidating the diggings, and Kimberley was on the way to becoming a prim company suburb. A visitor from the Cape wrote:

The kopje is one immense circular basin, dug out to the depths of 100 feet in its deepest part, about 50 in most and 20 feet in the higher parts, but there are now very few blocks left standing; the whole extent is nine to ten acres and 1,800 people are generally at work at once. The top is encircled by a close wall of windlasses erected upon high wood staging, and hundreds and hundreds of wire ropes run from these stagings to different claims so that the kopje looks like a huge spider's web. I do not think I ever heard such extraordinary sounds ... the rattling of the carts, the shaking of sieves, the rustling and rattling of wheels and buckets, the hum of thousands of voices, above all the shouts and howls of the kaffirs ... keep up an incessant noise which is excited into something diabolical when anything fresh occurs, such as a larger cart than usual on the kopje, a party of riders, but above all *a lady*.

'Nature, the Jew dealer, and the uncontrolled Kaffir killed the individual diggers,' concluded the engineer, Ransome. With, of course, the aid of Cecil Rhodes.

GOLD BUGS

Many who had intended in those years to prospect on the Rand, where by 1868 the London and Limpopo Mining Co. was working the reef at Tati, and who offered the South African Republic £50,000 for exclusive rights, turned aside to Kimberley, and to defeat. Robinson heard of the struggles of the Stuben brothers near Barberton, but was not moved until he received a tip from two exhausted small prospectors, Harrison and Walker, that there was solid gold in the reef at Langlaagte Farm. Rhodes' own prospector's report was unfavourable. Robinson bought the farm for £6,000 and became one of the wealthiest men in the world when the first two tons of banket realized 22 oz. of gold. It signalled another rush, and Johannesburg, which in 1886 had six houses, began its meteoric career, and the Standard Bank operated from a mud hut guarded by men with revolvers. Rhodes followed hotfoot on Robinson, who was however ahead of him all down the reef; hence the story of Rhodes talking business with the farmer at the front door in halting Afrikaans while Robinson settled matters with the wife at the back.

The new crowd, from all over the world, poured into Barberton, Kriel Lydenberg, Pilgrims Rest; the Boers found their starved treasury unwontedly full but with a large new polyglot population led by the English, but including Jews, Americans, Australians, Europeans, and the sweepings of the City of London. The local Boer farms found that they had a good market for their produce, selling mealies at the unheard-of price of 7s. 9d. a bag and firewood at 28s. a load. Traders hurried to the reef from the rest of the country: Sir Harry Grauman, who started life in a wholesale merchant's but made some capital out of spare-time trading in ostrich feathers, went to Barberton as a young man and toiled up and down the reef making a fortune out of the miners. At Barberton he found 'a great scarcity of titled men, although in later years they became plentiful', and noted that the miners had black girls to keep house, and life was largely lived on hope, music, and supper parties at which the champagne flowed, and evening dress was improvised. Barmaids were tipped with shares standing at £800 on the market; when a French hotel-keeper's wife arrived, miners poured in simply to look at her.

Barberton, complete with theatres, hotels, two stock exchanges, shops, and three newspapers, sprang out of the ground in 1885-6, to spread optimism all along the reef, and to become noted for its bogus flotations. It was quickly eclipsed by Johannesburg, which in 1887 acquired its first white woman, its first newspaper and its first curb share market. As streets and stands (blocks) were laid out values soared.

It took thirty-three wagons three weeks to drag Robinson's milling machinery to the Rand. The Rand Club was formed almost at once on a site costing seventy-two pounds and became the stronghold of the British, particularly Rhodes, Robinson and Beit. By 1888 coaches from the south were arriving every hour. Tented brothels were brought in complete. The 'Venus of the Veld' was put up to auction at the 'Black Cat', and standing naked in a top hat on a billiard table, 'went' for £3,000. The first murder took place that year and the uitlanders demanded an increase in the twenty-five-man police force. Daylight robberies at the Central Hotel indicated that 'Goli' was to be a place of crime and romance. In 1889 the Boers gave the city a thirty-acre sports ground, while refusing it the franchise, and in 1890 a steam tramway was laid down the length of the reef. The railway reached the city from Cape Town two years later, reducing the journey to two days, fourteen hours in a fast train. But there was no municipal water, which in a time of drought cost 1s. a bucket, 'and even "decent men" did not bath for days'. They washed their faces in soda-water. Then, in 1890, the bottom dropped out of the boom. Many wished they had taken the advice of J. B. Taylor who said to Grauman when £1 shares rose to £100 apiece: 'Look here, my friend, I have seen more of the game than you have. I know about high hopes falling as fast as they rise, and I am sure the same thing will happen here. Take my tip, sell all you have and clear out.' Along the 'Wallaby Track' to Pretoria sick and starving diggers threw themselves on the mercy of farmers and officials. Not until a new process was found did the city recover fully; meanwhile to Rhodes's fury the British declined to revolt against Kruger's exactions, and left Jameson in the lurch; they duly had to see their own leaders jailed. It was not a good omen.

CHARTERED RANDLORDS

Out of this hurly-burly arose the same monster that emerged from the welter of collapsing walls within the Kimberley pit: big business and big businessmen. The paying gold lay deep within the reef, which meant that it was an opportunity for capitalists, not for the small adventurer, prospector or trader. Initial finance was needed to buy the small men out as well as the Boer farms; there had to be flair to see where the gold lay, and contacts in London or Paris where the shareholders who could be excited by prospectuses could be found; and there had to be the organizing ability to amalgamate and interlock repeatedly the smaller into ever larger groupings. A variety of men disposed of some or all these skills, and in the Rand Club they worked out in a dozen years the frontiers of the big ten – while smaller men worked for them, dwindling to clerkly status, or made money by providing services.

There was the Robinson group. There was also Wernher Beit and Co. Beit, later to be Sir Alfred, came out to Kimberley to buy diamonds for

Lippert and Co. (Lippert later had the explosives monopoly for Kruger) whose canvas office was always thronged with diggers; he prospered, set up on his own, met Rhodes, and then brought back the Lipperts into the great adventure of the Chartered Company; he persuaded Rhodes to go into gold (Consolidated Goldfields), after he had helped Robinson to go in first. This produced permanent enmity between Robinson and Rhodes, a festering jealousy that died only with the men. There was room for both and both duly got into trouble with finance and shareholders. Bailey, the great Sir Abe the sportsman, derived his start from Rhodes, and also profited from Barney Barnato's advice to abandon Barberton for Johannesburg.

A high proportion of the rest were foreigners or Jews, who exploited the English, and were insistent on their own Britishness. Barnato came from the East End of London and began, according to the legend, with a few boxes of cigars and a turn on the variety stage, finally to fight it out for control of Kimberley with Rhodes and to lose. He became instead a member of the Cape Parliament, a member of the Kimberley Club and a man of immense wealth, none of which saved him from a growing conviction that he was a nobody, so that returning to England he jumped overboard and drowned himself. George Albu began his climb as a counter assistant in Stuttaford's, the Cape Town drapers, and rose by way of Meyer and Charlton to affluence. Sigismund Neumann bought diamonds in Kimberley and assembled for an assault on gold a brilliant syndicate which included Major Goldmann, soldier and journalist, and Carl Hanau who made and lost his fortune 'with the celerity of a juggler producing rabbits from a hat'. Goertz was a mining engineer who went out with the backing of the Deutsche Bank and the Siemens family to which he was related. Sammy Marks was a Russian by birth, almost incapable of writing or even speaking English intelligibly, but who did speak the Taal (Afrikaans), and made a fortune both in mining and in land and other investments which extended to breweries, collieries, plantations, mills – everything the growing Rand community needed and would pay for.

The new millionaires were soon prominent in the Edwardian society which seemed to its critics so deeply decayed, and helped on that process of class decomposition. But big businessmen, with the ear of Royalty and ministers in London, were not a phenomenon produced only by diamonds, gold and Rhodes's imperialism. The final stages of African colonization required men with dreams of empire, springing from country parsonages or Scottish counting houses, who could create chartered companies to acquire territory by treaty and gunpoint, using soldiers, traders, missionaries and even hunters as their agents. Thus the British Imperial East African Company was the brainchild of Sir William Mackinnon, founder of the British India Steam Navigation Co., who, with his partners, got an inkling of the riches of the interior of East Africa in the course of buying cloves and ivory in Mombasa and Zanzibar, supplying goods to the Sultan, services to missionaries like MacKay and to explorers like H. M. Stanley.

In West Africa a man of destiny with dreams akin to Rhodes's founded the Royal Niger Co. George Goldie, destined for the Royal Engineers, fled to Egypt when he inherited money, fell in love with an Arab girl, and lived with her for three years till she died 'in a Garden of Allah', returned to Britain and was redeemed from a life of dissipation by the imperial vision, which in his case took the form of the creation of a British dominion from the Niger to the Nile, as a contribution to the all-red Cape-to-Cairo route, which he later discovered had been the resolve of his childhood. Like Rhodes, he saw that he had to bring together all the competing interests of the little men – in this case the Delta traders – and like Rhodes gathered round him a devoted staff of young men. 'Don't tell me that anything cannot be done, go and do it,' he said to them, much as Rhodes said 'I am Rhodes', which finished the discussion. Like Rhodes's company, Goldie's company made war on the tribes and Goldie was in the square commanded by Lugard when with maxims stuttering it seized Bida.

After the commercial Napoleons had forced the London government to think imperially, move in and take over the claims they had staked out in Kenya, Rhodesia, the Rand, Nigeria and so on, and also to pay off their shareholders more or less handsomely, came the era of the great commercial magnates, who did not fight wars, but confined themselves to adding interest to interest and millions to millions, like Sir Ernest Oppenheimer and Lord Leverhulme in West Africa. It was quite a new breed, which did not produce politicians. It restricted the activities, however, of the lesser men, who found themselves simply officials in the resultant organization, with a career in Africa that began with cadetships and ended with divisional managements and the like, and was socially inferior to government mandarins and to the officers of the armed services.

5

SETTLERS IN
SOUTH AFRICA

The efforts of British people to find and populate suitable homelands in Africa was a continuous, if spasmodic, process from 1820 to 1900. But it took a different course from settlement in other new countries, and it had a very different outcome. Its initial inspiration sprang in large measure from official convenience. The officials acted for the best, but in almost total ignorance of the conditions on the spot. They had the permanent official conviction that whatever the facts, decisions and judgments could best be made at all times in London.

New Zealand was the only temperate colony established after settlement in Africa had begun, and accordingly the attractions of Africa had first to compete with the alternatives offered by Australia and Canada, by South America, and above all by the United States. But for official necessities, it seems doubtful if British farmers would ever have taken up much land in Africa. This would have delayed the advent, or at least the success, of traders, merchants, prospectors and industrialists in southern and East Africa. The development of West Africa, where white settlement was impossible, was notably slower.

As in Canada, British settlers could move into one area – the Cape – where there was already a small white settlement, though as in Canada it was a settlement of people of a different language and culture. The basic conditions which settlers first met were much as in New Zealand or Australia – a totally strange environment for man, beast and plant. The big difference was the presence of the African tribesfolk, in greater or lesser numbers, and the missionaries already working among them.

THE CAPE

From the first, British settlers in the Cape had to accommodate their thinking, personal and political, to four ever-present factors in their lives:

the Boers, the Kaffirs, the missionaries and the officials. A pattern of thought developed in response to these factors which was wholly unlike the conditioning of British settlers elsewhere. Basically, of course, the settlers' prime thought was for his land, as his wife's was for the future of her children. As in America and Australia, the growing settler community was the driving force against the frontier, the community whose efforts wove the infrastructure of roads and commerce which created and overran the frontier between wilderness and 'civilization'. Missionaries and soldiers could not animate that development. The Boers, who basically lived more like Africans than Europeans, enjoyed an ambiguous role on both sides of the frontier until about 1880. The British settler, without quite understanding his position, always felt, with some justice, that he was the real force for change: that he was the real subduer of Africa's natural intransigence, and the one who took the risks and pledged his economic security. And it was the British settler whose interests and growing power proved to be the obstacle alike to African and Boer ambition. For this the British were destroyed as a force. They never generated the numbers or power to outmatch the other communities, except in Rhodesia.

When the officials decided for settlement they little knew what an explosive force it would be, what land-hunger or land-lust would mean – though there was plenty of evidence from the other continents of European settlement. Moreover the officials in London never learned from their successive experiences of planting out white men in Africa. The settler repeatedly proved to be a genie from the bottle which they could not control.

That was not the officials' intention. They wanted him under their thumb. At the Cape, the plan was to create an area of small-holdings in the Zuurfeld which would produce a sturdy race of yeomen who would provide a more effective and cheaper defence for the all-important victualling station for Indiamen against the marauding Kaffirs than could the small military garrison. The officials, and notably Lord Somerset, the Governor, steeped in the classics, the only training in sociology then available, thought in terms of the Roman Wall, the legions being in fact half agriculturalists, half regimental warriors. It was a reluctant decision. When Britain took over the Cape in 1806, there was no intention to do more than keep a garrison there; but sovereignty meant, of course, some obligation to protect all British subjects in the vicinity – some hundred British who had been there since the port and town was captured from the Dutch East India Company, and an unknown number of Boers in the hinterland. But already the Bantu tribes were moving southward. Although the British forces had cleared them out of the Zuurveld the Boers had not the nerve to return to their ruined farmsteads, and Colonel Graham, who built there the fort that bears his name, called for a cohesive British colony. Lord Somerset, at first opposed to settlement, changed his mind when the invading Xhosa nearly took Grahamstown in 1818. But the 1820 settlers were not told of their high destiny.

The second wave of settlement was to Natal, where again the officials discovered the need to hold a trading base from which the Boer trekkers had departed, and on which the Bantu were pressing; but their minds were alive to two other problems – the supposed need to relieve surplus population in Britain, and the prospect of growing cotton in the new colony for the Lancashire mills.

The third wave of settlement was into Rhodesia in 1891, in this case organized not from Whitehall but by Rhodes's Chartered Company. Again the object, jointly subscribed to by the settler government at the Cape, the Colonial Office in Whitehall, and even the missionary bodies, was to head off the Boers from further expansion northwards, to contain them and to prevent their depredations against the natives expanding. (Before long the Company was slaughtering the Matabele.) Soon after, it was Whitehall that thought up settlement in Kenya, as a means to make the Kenya–Uganda railway, built to break the power of the slave trade, and head off German expansion towards the Nile, pay for its cost and operation. There again, the settlers found themselves destined to a Roman and imperial quasi-military role. By the end of the nineteenth century, however, this had become a welcome thought, satisfying to self-esteem.

THE VOYAGE TO AFRICA

The prelude to settlement was the voyage out. Until in the 1860s the Castle and Union steamship lines could offer regular and relatively cheap passages the voyage to Africa took three months, decreasing to two by the 1850s, in varying degrees of hardship, which provided vivid experience that cut the umbilical cord with the homeland. The mental agony of crossing the bar in open whaleboats, or battened-down lighters at Port Natal, was said to destroy all idea that a return voyage was possible.

The emigrant ships of the 1820s and 1830s were small and crowded, often no more than 250 tons burden. To the passengers, at least, they often seemed ill-found and dangerous. They were merchant ships with additional decks put in, partitioned into tiny cabins and living areas, with glazed skylights let into the decks. Life was communal. There was no hesitation about taking children, or as Philips put it, 'ladies in the forward state'. The children who died on board would be partly replaced by new arrivals, and often half the passengers in fact were children who in fine weather attended school on deck.

Cockroaches swarmed below decks. 'It was not unusual for people to find that during the night their finger and toe nails had been gnawed to the quick,' Barbara Buchanan recalled. In stormy weather the hatches were battened down on the passengers, and the resulting mess and pandemonium were terrible, children yelling, mothers exhausted. The male passengers might have to help the crew. The officers sometimes drank to excess. On occasion fires broke out. Writing in 1835, Dugmore remarked:

I know nothing about the regular emigrant ships of the present day; that is, so far as respects the quality of the food, or the accommodation they supply; but I remember the close packing 'between decks', the 'banyan days', and the hard salt junk and harder biscuit of 1820. I have not forgotten how salt the outside of the puddings used to taste which the old weather-beaten cook had boiled in sea water in the general 'copper', nor how the passengers sometimes quarrelled with the steward for cheating them out of the supplies ... Then came the tantalising 'variables' – the calms of the 'line' – the rough shaving operations of old Father Neptune, the lather of whose brush, and the edge of whose razor stuck, the one to the chin, the other to the memory, for some time afterwards. Nor have I forgotten the one or two fearful storms we encountered, when the hatches were battened down, the heavy seas were shipped, and while the torrent poured down among us in the midnight darkness, the mothers clasped the children to their bosoms, exclaiming, 'We'll all go together.'

Emigrants were advised, by those who published rather than acted, that they should travel steerage to Natal, both to save money, and because a two-month voyage in which a person had to look after himself 'is good preparation for life in the colony'.

In the 1820s settlers had to bring with them virtually everything that they would need to support life for a few years until the colony began exporting and importing. Philips took out his carriage, and others took pianos. Later, as stores accumulated, this advice could be changed, and by the 1850s it was said that 'emigrants should encumber themselves as little as possible with luggage. A sufficient stock of clothing for the voyage and the first year is all that it is prudent to lay in. Clothing suitable for the climate is now abundant in the colony and costs only a little more than it would do in England. Boots and shoes are the more important exceptions to this statement. It will always answer to bring a good supply of these ...' Settlers were told to take a tent to live in while building a house, fowling pieces, medicines – and books on practical subjects as there were no booksellers.

After 1845 or so steamships shortened the voyage, gave more cabin space, and reduced illness and mortality. Victorian ship routine took shape: games, concerts and theatricals. Once established they quickly became traditional, and accounts of voyages to South Africa by Victorian travellers varied little save for their *facetiae* – details of the practical jokes which were the standard way of enlivening existence everywhere.

1820 SETTLERS

Lord Henry Somerset made his plan for the settlement of Albany with military precision. A speech by the Chancellor of the Exchequer, Mr

Vansittart, publicized the venture, for which the budget provided £50,000. It was suggested that, if necessary, paupers should be forcibly sent, but in fact some 3,736 persons came forward from all classes of British society, high and low, with an assurance of land in the deserted Boer farms – 1,610 men, 659 women and the remainder children.

It was foreseen that families and groups must come out under leaders, and their reception and accommodation must be planned. Their heavy gear must come out in transports, with pre-fabricated wooden sheds and tentage going in advance. They deposited their money with the government to be claimed on arrival, although there was little to buy except Boer transport. There were depots for implements, and the need for surveyors was realized. The troops were there to provide labour and give assurance. As the twenty-one ships arrived between April and June 1820, surf boats brought the parties ashore. Algoa Bay was a large transit camp under canvas and bright sunshine. The scene, in the recollection of the settlers, was like that of an invading army. Some were in family groups, like the Philips, who came out with a relation of Southey, the Poet Laureate, farmers from Gloucestershire and Warwickshire, and a group of labourers. Another group consisted of twenty-four Scots, led by the lame Thomas Pringle, who emigrated from Scotland 'to collect again into one social circle my father's family, which untoward circumstances had broken up and begun to scatter over the world. To accomplish this, emigration to a new colony was indispensable . . .' It consisted of twelve males, six women, six children; Pringle had a letter of introduction from Sir Walter Scott to help him find an official job.

In the camp were also to be seen elegant marquees where ladies and gentlemen were observed reading or rambling in the shrubbery.

It was obvious [Pringle noted] that several of these families had been accustomed to enjoy the luxurious accommodation of refined society in England . . . I could not view this class of emigrants . . . without some melancholy misgivings as to their future fate; for they appeared utterly unfitted by former habits, especially the females, for *roughing* it (to use the expressive phraseology of the camp) through the first trying period of the settlement.

Few of the settlers realized how trying it would be. Somerset, and especially his officers, could get them there and provide a reception camp. But the area had been examined with a military rather than an agricultural eye, and the advice of the few local Boers on the size of holdings needed to support life was not sought. Somerset was determined to have a closely-packed patchwork of smallholders, as though Albany were Kent. In fact, the settlers' first and best instructors as they took up their plots were inevitably Boers, from whom they learned the art of ploughing with oxen, sowing, the construction of mimosa-thorn paddocks for their cattle at night, which they learned to call 'kraals'; the best type of local woods for building, furniture-making, and other purposes; and how to adapt ant-hills to ovens for their wretched bread.

The settlers took up their little plots in their family, clan or party groups. There are several first-hand accounts of how the early days were passed, partly as a picnic, partly in encampments, partly in the pioneering euphoria of cutting the first sods. They saw the future in terms of the English or Scottish mixed farming of the time, where a hundred acres was quite a big farm; what nobody appreciated was that one thousand years of colonization and improvement had already gone into English farms and farmland – though a study of Adam Smith might have helped them to foresee the trouble ahead with Africa's virginity. They were buying space and earth, not tilth. Even so, in five years, a colony existed in the grass veld.

Thomas Philips and his family of wife, three sons and three daughters were exceptional rather than average settlers. He not only had grit and intelligence as well as culture, he also had some political pull at home and at Cape Town, which he exerted whenever he could. But his account, being full and literate, in the form of letters home which were widely circulated as a sort of news-sheet about African conditions, gives perhaps the most intimate picture of the daily life of the settlement. From the military tented camp in Algoa Bay he proceeded to his location, carrying all he started out with in five ox-wagons, each with a payload of just under a ton. It took five days at a speed of 3–3½ m.p.h. He was lucky in finding a ruined Boer house on his location on which he based his first home, 'Lampeter', but otherwise he felt doubtful.

The soil [he reported] is universally sandy, but in most places wonderfully adhesive, in some situations it is mixed with black soil, and in others, bright red, the latter is considered by some as the best, there is a little chalky limestone, but I have none of it. We could give but one ploughing, and in August and September we sowed our wheat and barley, choosing for the latter the most sandy soil ... the seed soon appeared above the ground, looking very fine indeed, but it appeared for a length of time afterwards dormant, and did not stool as we fondly expected. In October there was no amendment, this month it has grown a little from the fine rains, but in many places it is coming into small ears with only half a dozen grains, and the stem hardly twelve inches high. We now begin to find that all the tales of luxuriancy of the land are false.

This was to be the experience nearly all over the colony as the British tried to farm; the Boers looked on with grim doubt, the Hottentots with amazement at the iron ploughs pulled by only two oxen, and the wandering Kaffirs with cupidity at the cattle. Philips, Pringle and their countrymen were contemptuous of the Boer plough with only one handle, the triangular harrow with wooden teeth, and the total absence of rollers. Pringle cried, 'I long for a good farm-yard and sheds.'

In two years the colony was bankrupt, the settlers abandoning the land for town jobs, or living on rice rations from the Government, furious with Somerset who controlled the press, and passing round hand-written attacks on him. The wisest among them had, like John Goldswain, already taken to trading and had built the basis of merchant houses on wine and wool. But Philips and others hung on, trying new varieties of crops and increasing their herds. 'I got about an acre of Bengal wheat, during a shower, or rather after one in the beginning of July, and it is now in ear!!! Absolutely in ear!!! But, hush, say not a word about it for we have had no rain since . . .'

Thomas Pringle describes the wooden frame cottages which were erected and thatched by his Highlanders in ten days, clad with reeds to the ground, in which they lived for three months while buying stock, digging drainage and irrigation trenches, removing tree stumps, getting in slips of apples, pears, apricots and plums, and planting English seeds which failed like everyone else's. Pringle comments that he found himself 'performing the novel and somewhat improbable functions of a sort of civil and military officer, of a medical practitioner, religious instructor, engineer, architect, gardener, plasterer, cabinet-maker, and, might I add, *tinker*'.

Within a few years the settlement was on a half peace, half war basis as the Bantu advance guards arrived. Somerset's plan was called for, and all the men had to register for military service to repel invaders. But they were still few and campaigning drew them from agriculture; yet the more reinforcements arrived the greater the need for land. Pringle himself wrote:

The future colonists, be they Dutch or British, must of necessity continue to be semi-barbarians so long as the commando system – the system of hostile reprisals – shall be encouraged or connived at; and so long as the colonists are permitted to make encroachments on the territory and natural rights of the natives the colony can never have a safe frontier.

But the colony had to expand because the settlers found that to farm successfully they needed huge acreages. In the early 1830s it was discovered that some grazing areas would produce fine merino wool, and the colony, having an export, could not only become self-sufficient but draw in new settlers. By 1835 Philips was quite rich, and indeed had an estate at Glendour, having given his first farm to be added to that of other settlers. When William Napier visited the Pringles in Baviaans River in 1838 he remarked in his journal:

It is really a pleasant sight to see people who eighteen years ago left their native country without money and nothing to assist them except their knowledge of sheep farming, now possessed of large herds and flocks and having all the appearance of wealth and comfort around them . . . Caffers do not steal sheep as the difficulty and danger of driving them off does not compensate for the trouble.

But most settlers had cattle and sheep and, as their herds increased, the natives decided to raid them because their own resources were being squeezed; and a bitter controversy on black and white rights developed, never to be settled. 'Oh, what a relief!' cried Philips when he got his 4,000 acres from the government. But his sons had periodically to leave the plough. The father's anxieties were eased by the reflection that 'a savage with only a spear cannot stand against powder and ball, shrapnel, shells, etc.' All men under sixty with mounts were, however, always liable for call-up, to retrieve stolen cattle, or to deal out punishment or death to the blacks.

Their dress is a light blue jacket and pantaloons with a plain military foraging cap, their Horses with tails sweeping to the ground like cossacks. On their shoulders are their own guns enclosed in a case made of tiger [leopard] skins, before them is their blanket rolled up, and accompanying Hottentot with led Horse on which is placed light saddle bags inclosing some wardrobe, also a little brandy, biscuits and any other little luxury their sisters may have thought for them for much baggage is not allowed.

The settlers' attitude to Africans can be traced from the earliest contacts. On the one hand there was the sense of threat – the vast hordes that might press down on the young colony from the north and east. Such hostility feelings were in part contracted from the Boers. As the colony took shape and civilized ways of life were established – which everyone hoped would make him a 'gentleman' with an estate such as he might not aspire to at home – a sense of self-righteousness set in. The land was theirs; or it ought to be; the blacks did not use it, or only wastefully . . . and when they stole, primitive feelings took over. On the other hand, there was always an awareness of the 'good' black – not perhaps a noble savage, but a biddable, helpful, hard-working person, knowing his place but faithful to his master's truest interests, and grateful for his education into civilized ways.

The British did not see blacks as house-slaves as the Boers did, and they felt pleasantly superior in rejecting the Boer doctrine; they simply saw them as the agricultural labourers and domestics of England, perhaps a little nearer to feudalism than the oppressed rustics they had left behind in the early industrial revolution. The problem of getting the work done was always with the English in every settlement.

The great want and difficulty of procuring servants and the very high price of labour renders it impossible for us to get on with the improvements on our new place [Glendour]. But we shall now be better off, Government having brought down a great many people belonging to a more distant nation . . . distributing them among us as servants . . .

said Philips. These men and women, the Fingoes, were found delightfully tractable; while stories of their persecution by other tribes developed the settlers' sense of self-justification in their punitive raids – even though these often killed the wrong people. Chaka, chief of the Zulu nation, soon became a monster in the English mind, driving before him the Sotho and the Mantatees. The ineffectiveness of government as the guardian of law and order became a firm article of faith by the late 1820s. Soon the settlers were setting spring guns at night, and importing iron roofs in place of the thatch which the Kaffirs could set alight. There were gloomy reflections that the Africans, with their pastoral economy, were likely to prove a far longer trial than had been the redskins in America who were merely nomadic. 'All our feelings to treat them leniently have vanished,' noted Philips after a cattle raid. 'They are not to be trusted.'

The community grew steadily. In thirty years the British had settled fairly closely on larger areas than the Dutch had occupied in one hundred and fifty. Its social life became important in and beyond the few towns so that it might reproduce itself. Farm life was lonely. Few villages formed, for roads were few and in wartime unsafe. Local newspapers held the community together, and before long the accounts of balls, entertainments, weddings and births became their most important items of news. In the 1850s the wedding ox-cart became a feature of the colony, 'its sides rolled up to display blushing bride and maids'. The men followed on horseback raising clouds of dust, and the wedding breakfast was spread by black servants in the open air. There were no church bells at first, and for the earlier colonists few wedding presents, settlements or jointures. These came later. Meanwhile unmarried women were snapped up on arrival.

The picture of the South African farm changed steadily from one of embattled penury and pioneering, to respectability mingled with robustness in the last quarter of the century. But hospitality with a purpose was always the keynote. A border colonial's house was described by mid-century as more like an hotel than a home.

You pay no reckoning for your entertainment, but the doors are always open, a fact which is taken advantage of to the utmost. A family in any town on the border lives but little within itself and relies still less on the entertainment and amusement that its own members can provide ... anyone and everyone will drop in casually, providing they have some previous introduction.

By 1850 the Home Government was actively encouraging reinforcements to the colony. But, by then, most of the agricultural land was taken up. The building of roads, public works, communications had begun, and it was no longer farmers who were needed. The Cape Town newspapers were full of advertisements for skilled labour. Apprentices were needed for grocers, bakers and blacksmiths; bricklayers were wanted (at 5s. a day); coopers were needed as transport increased the requirements of casks; notwithstanding the availability of coloured labour, there were calls for coachmen, grooms and errand boys, cooks, coachbuilders, wainwrights, wheelwrights, printers, carpenters, dressmakers, white female servants (country girls were preferred), farriers, gardeners for gentlemen's estates, millers, nurses and governesses, painters, plumbers, plasterers, masons, tinsmiths and upholsterers: the list of trades in fact maps the growing complexity of the colony. Many people of the lower orders for whom 'any change must be for the better', frequently took coloured labour and set up themselves in Cape Town or Durban or any of the small towns servicing farming or the military.

To the tyro in colonial affairs [wrote Mann in an early account of Natal] it is at first a somewhat amusing sight to see the mechanical labourer, who has been used enough to hard work and hard fare at home, calling to his personal kafir attendant to pick up for him the saw or hammer which he is about to use. The workman in Natal rarely thinks of carrying his own basket of tools. He walks along the road on his way to work with one or two laden kafirs behind him.

Thereby was started a tradition. Thomas Baines, who found employment as a cabinet-maker easy to get 'at a low wage but with plenty of free time', trained himself as a portrait and marine painter and rose in society. The market for skilled white labour remained restricted, and Moodie in 1848 thought that 'the colony would rather lose than gain by the acquisition of considerable additional population.' Wages were low, living was costly, but there were opportunities, and there was leisure. Mrs Ward in 1851, for example, found that when you went into a shop to complain after broken promises to deliver an article, 'it has either never been thought of since you bespoke it, is left half-finished, or what is more likely your tradesman has gone out riding, or is driving his family out in a well-built English carriage with a good pair of Cape horses.'

NATAL, SUGAR AND COOLIES

The disappointments of the Cape settlement discouraged ideas about colonies in Africa for some years. A small group of traders were established near Delagoa Bay, however, and in 1823 Lt Farewell urged colonization and tried unsuccessfully to form an advance party. The eventual success of Albany on the basis of wool production did teach one lesson, and when some experimental crops of cotton planted by two hundred German settlers in Natal in 1847 produced exaggerated hopes for an export crop there, rather than simply a community based on agriculture, plans for a new colony began to be made in Whitehall by the Colonial Land and Emigration Board. By 1848 private enterprise was in the ascendant, and the prospects of making a profit out of land encouraged Joseph C. Byrne to establish his Natal Company.

The conviction that Britain was overpopulated was even stronger in the hungry 'forties than in 1819. Lord Grey approved Byrne's scheme. The government's cooperation deluded many settlers into thinking it was as much a Government scheme as that of 1820. In fact, Byrne, a shrewd Irishman, was more a master of publicity than of farming, and his knowledge of Africa and Natal was obtained from official books and the works of other writers who described the 'colony' after its separation from the Cape in 1847. His prospectuses and handbills promised a future in cotton, a comfortable journey out and a retinue of native servants for everyone.

The Government was responsive – and once again because the indignant departure of the Boer trekkers had left only the few English traders under the flag to repel Zulu attacks. The land seemed, as always to European eyes in Africa, empty and yearning for European tillage. Byrne was thus able to paint his glowing prospectus. By his agreement with the Colonial Office, he deposited £1,000 for some 3,000 acres, worth hardly 1s. an acre, on which he could recover half as much again from the settlers on the basis of twenty-acre plots – far too small to be economic. In fact even Byrne miscalculated the capital needed, the Government took too much, and the settlers could not hope to survive: but as before, some hundreds went out to be duly disappointed – many to be beggared – but nevertheless eventually to succeed when, a few years later, Natal's real future as a sugar-producing area was discovered.

There was no harbour at Port Natal, where the settlers disembarked, and ships were sometimes lost, quite apart from the difficulties of disembarking by lighters over the bar. Young girls were humped ashore by African porters, their skirts tucked up, their maidenly cheeks aflame. The Bay and shore were soon littered with broken furniture, soaked chests of clothing and even a piano that was ultimately cleaned and made to play. The scene is described by Mrs James Arbuthnot in Hattersley's, *More Annals of Natal*:

That first day in Natal, we and others were enquiring where the town was. A large flat below the fine Berea bush was all that we could see, save one wood and iron building which we were told contained Mr Moreland's (the agent) Office. Thither went my husband but he got no satisfactory information about Mr Byrne's affairs. Gradually we came to understand he was insolvent and all the ship's cargo taken possession by his creditors, and nothing could be got to represent the money we had handed to Mr Joseph Byrne. The land was there all right . . . Looking back to that time, I know that many have prospered . . . However at that time after strolling about we found people living in all sorts of queer little huts, some trying to sell a few things they brought out with them, some finding employment from those who had means, and on all sides rising the framework of houses like large basketwork . . . Our wagon driver on arrival turned out to be a real gentleman of education and ready to practise as a physician when people took sick, and, as they seemed to be in no hurry for his aid, he had purchased a wagon span . . . I arranged to have my sea-born babe christened in the place called the Church, the Government school really. After a short time my husband, accompanied by several gentlemen who had been shipmates, shouldered knapsacks, and, with stout stick in hand, proceeded to take a pedestrian trip up-country to look for their future farms, leaving me in the tents with my children and servants . . .

The land was duly found and claimed, but there was no money to be got to stock it or convey the family, which became destitute like the rest there. Mrs Arbuthnot recalls the Saturday evening when there was just 1s. 6d. left; but they got credit, being – like the Philipses – people of some influence, and they started their farm. After only three months of market gardening they took to sugar as a crop and thus did not have to endure the long privations of the Albany settlers.

Durban first consisted only of the post office, the customs house, Cato's landing establishment, and an emigrants' barracks. Huts of wattles cost two pounds to build; three of them formed a square as the 'hotel'. Trenches were cut for drainage and trellis-work preserved some modesty and privacy. Natives removed nightsoil. Beds were slung between stumps hammered into the dung-covered earth floors, and plank shelves were hung from the roofs. Lamps were oil, and roofing was of tambootie grass; British thatchers plied a roaring trade from the outset. Gradually improvements were made – dadoes and ceilings, bricks for walls, slates, and finally iron for roofs after the 1851 exhibition had demonstrated its use. The sugar warehouse of John Roberts was said to be an actual portion of the Crystal Palace. Cabinet-makers were soon putting in shop fronts and making furniture. At first there was little money to pay workmen, but as one Yorkshireman said, 'Ah thowt if them blackies could live, ah could do t'same.' The Boers were angry if the English paid their black labour in money, when it did begin to circulate.

The settlers were soon learning to eat conger-eel, monkey, cane-rat, porcupine and iguana. Beef, when available, cost 2d. a lb. The Dutch showed them how to cook and serve mealies. The Africans brought milk in clay pots. Flour was imported from Cape Town in coastal brigs, and rice came from Carolina in casks; soon the port was handling tea and ginger from China, coffee from Rio, dates, tamarind and sugar from Mauritius; salt was made from sea water; bottled beer came from Britain, lucifers of phosphorus and sulphur from Germany. Baking and cooking in the open produced a good deal of dyspepsia it is recorded.

The settlers included many people of substance, as well as the usual mixture of unemployed mechanics after the Hudson railway boom, crofters driven off the Highlands to make room for the shooting, and tenant farmers ruined by the Corn Laws. There was Highbert Baker, for example, a friend of Isambard Brunel, and John Basely and Strapp who were engineers. A Scot, John Sanderson, founded *The Natal Pioneer*, while George Mackeroy became wealthy after escaping from consumption contracted in a cotton factory. William Campbell, later one of the sugar magnates, started off with a kirk and its collections, while Scottish settlers like the Trotters and Mackenzies Marans brought the latest Scottish farm implements. Between 1849 and 1850 about five thousand settlers went out. Cholera and unemployment in Britain drove some solid Yorkshiremen to Natal, among them

Samuel Lamb, an auctioneer and printer, Charles Mayne, a tobacconist and snuff-maker, who found himself sited on his own raw material, Isaac Canning, a draper, and shipbuilders put out of business by the competition of the Yankee clippers which ruled the seas until iron steamships beat them in turn. Many gentlefolk determined to live as squires were among the first arrivals; Natal was recommended as a colony where distressed gentlemen could keep up appearances. For those with capital, however, 'anybody may make from 12 to 16 per cent by finding money for other persons to employ'.

The settlers succeeded not only because, after the failure of cotton, sugar proved profitable, but also because of the trade in ivory and hides which existed with the African tribes, a trade which actually called for a market town and emporium. This need developed both Durban and Pietermaritzburg, which the British took over from the voortrekkers when the Boers settled down in the Transvaal; and the towns went on growing.

The first cane was harvested in 1850, thirty-five miles north of Durban, crushed by wooden rollers made from ships' masts, and boiled in iron pots. By 1858 production was five hundred tons and the farmer-settlers turned planters were demanding Indian labour to do the hard work, as the Kaffirs would not. 'Coolies' began to arrive in 1861, and the British soon got used to Indian servants.

George Lamond describes how he was robbed of his cash on the emigrant ship, but was advanced money to go to Pietermaritzburg to seek work, where he first did some government clerking, and was then invited to work on Morewood's estate 'Compensation', where sugar was being grown, often, in some places, at fifty per cent profit on outlay.

The estate was managed by George Jackson with some half dozen ploughmen and a strong force of Kaffirs. We had six acres under cane; and every conceivable fruit and vegetable peculiar to the tropics, besides large plantations of trees . . . Buffalo used to come out of the bush at sundown . . . the flat swarmed with riet buck and paauw, not to mention pig. We had very rough times at Compensation, but I was in grand health and enjoyed the life thoroughly. The main drawbacks were lack of books and proper associates . . . I actually discovered coal in the bush at Morewood's cove. The discovery created the greatest excitement and enthusiasm in Durban. Almost all the inhabitants rode up to inspect, and I used up more than one horse in riding to and from the site to exhibit the find . . .

The Mechanics' Institute, that Victorian community centre, was created, where dancing, fencing, concerts and above all instructive lectures were held but for a long time there was no public library to supplement it. Amusements were few beyond the races, impromptu concerts and 'refined soirées'. Schools and churches were built during the fifties, and Durban grew as trade developed in the harbour and as market gardening proved profitable on its outskirts. Large businesses were founded on the supply of butter and milk to the townsfolk. The building of groynes and breakwaters began in the 1850s, taking fifteen years to complete. But at first there was no mayor or city government, and no rates; people set up businesses where they found space. Water was taken from wells and was often contaminated. Boys were put to school immediately when the Rev. Nesbitt, elderly and unmarried, and under government licence, set up a classroom in a thatched store, and acquired an excellent reputation as 'a sound whipper of boys'. For small children a Dame School was instituted early in the settlement, and a child's weekly treat was to be carried on the shoulders of a native to see the sea. Transplanted Victorian settler children created their own amusements. Wrote Francis Carey of his Natal youth:

In my spare time, I often played about with little native herdboys. Sometimes we roved in the Veld and killed little birds either with bows and arrows or with sticks and stones. We then made wood fires and after grilling the birds in the coals would devour them with enjoyment . . . sometimes we shaped from lumps of clay miniature cows and oxen even attempting occasionally the human form divine.

They also played pebble games and had sham fights. Elsa Smithers records that little girls chased each other in the veld like tomboys – and then fashioned swathes into crinolines and used orange blossom to pretend to be brides.

Social life developed earlier in Pietermaritzburg, which had stone houses by 1844, than in Durban because of its garrison whose band played in the afternoons. The children there could fish for crabs in the sluits, or open watercourses that served until pipes were laid in 1882, which drove the bakery mill.

We used to have a philharmonic society [wrote Mrs Lamond] under first Mr George Sweeney, then Charles Lascelles, a gifted but eccentric musician . . . I remember a fancy dress ball given by two young officers – Munro who wore his highland uniform, and Wilkinson, in the Old Theatre Royal. The invitations were in rhyme, and the answer requested to be in rhyme too. I thought myself beautiful as the 'grand duchess of Gerolstein' in black velvet dress, scarlet satin hussar coat, profusely trimmed with gilt braid and buttons, and a white wig of long curls . . .

There were the races, bus trips to Durban, amateur theatricals, riding, parties, lectures – and church on Sundays. The Turf Club was formed in 1844, and the Natal Society for literary and scientific instruction, in 1857. It was occasionally possible to watch the soldiers being flogged. There was a big turnout for the first public hanging.

By the 1850s, Durban and Pietermaritzburg were hard at work trying to change themselves from fontier outposts, colonial dumps, or 'dorps', into replicas of Victorian cities and suburbs, with coffee houses and assembly halls for meetings where the townsfolk closely followed the news of court, society and fashions in the weekly newspapers and in the serious reviews arriving regularly, and only six to eight weeks old, by steamers from Britain. By 1872 a daily postal service by Cape cart ran between Durban and Pietermaritzburg, a service of once or twice a week to other towns in the colony and a monthly service to Britain via the Cape; unperforated stamps were available from 1857. Dare's buses operated between the dorps in 1860 (Dare had driven shillibears in London), and a bus service ran between Cape Town and Rondebosch as early as 1855. Equipages became elegant despite the roads, and families used gigs, buggies and spiders within the colonies, only taking to the ox-wagon for major moves over long distances. Coaches, with twelve inside, six on top, slung on buffalo hide, jolted violently over longer distances. Contact between Cape Town and Durban improved with the coming of coastal steamers and port developments.

Social structure as the Victorians knew and valued it had to be synthesized from the elements of pioneer society. Some of the materials lay at hand. People of all social classes came to the Cape and to Natal, and there were some groupings based on origins in the home country. But many colonists were dispersed into the interior; and many of the most socially advanced lived largely on farms and estates, as indeed they still did at home in England, only visiting the towns briefly for shopping and sales. Much more important, right from the first, were the distinctions drawn between officials, military officers, and people in varying degrees of trade. In Britain, the officials would have been nobodies, apart from the Governor, who would himself have been a nobody at Court; this became the fixed quality of British social life, which certainly existed, with relatively minor modifications until the 1950s.

The word 'emigrant' became derogatory quite early in South Africa, as it did in Australia; 'settler' was a title of dignity only when associated with substantial land holdings. In the 1860s, Hattersley reports, an English visitor thought Pietermaritzburg 'the most clique-ridden town it has been my lot to live in ... a well-disposed stranger, not over-nice about social lines and grades, runs a risk of being left in the cold altogether if she tries to make herself agreeable to all'. Cape Town was no different; the fact that a Cape magistrate got along on only £250 a year in the 1830s abated not a jot from his sense of consequence. James Findlay, who opened a tobacconist shop in Cape Town, looked down on his cousin George, who had only a hardware store. In 1820 Moodie divided Cape Town, which was of course an elder society,

into six classes: I. the civil and military functionaries, including military officers of all ranks, and the clergy of the established churches. II. Lawyers, medical practitioners, merchants, retailers and those who live by letting out their slaves, and by receiving boarders, who form a large portion of the householders, and, in short, all the other white inhabitants above the rank of servants. III. European and Cape Dutch artificers and labourers who form a very doubtful class between the other white inhabitants and the freed blacks and Malays. IV. The free Malays. V. The Hottentots . . . and VI. The slaves . . .

But inevitably colonial society could only be patterned on the homeland, as its class-consciousness developed between the 1820s and 1890s within the little towns. South Africa was growing outwards for seventy-five years, and the frontier spirit was a great leveller – and one that the Victorians generally accepted. They had a real sense that what was acceptable in Natal or the Transvaal was fit only for a humorous narration in the drawing rooms of Belgravia or Cheltenham. Personal adventure was a quality, an experience, which was profoundly prized, and the small-town societies were in contrast with the up-country rugged individualism of 'men with souls above shipboards, carpenters' benches or ploughtails' who sought riches in their own way:

There was ivory in the kloofs of the kooms and the Fish River, and a bold shot from a daring hunter might put him in possession of $500 worth at once . . . and there was a more adventurous career still for such as had courage to enter upon it. There was, among the Kaffers 'over the border' ivory already collected, as well as cattle ready reared. And for those who did not mind risking 'the penalty of death', which governmental unwisdom had attached to a trade it had made contraband, there seemed to be the chance of getting rich rapidly . . . There was another class, less daring indeed, but of great importance to the formation of the future character of the province [the Cape]. The young men of mercantile tastes soon tired of 'the location' and soon found that money was to be made by becoming commercial travellers on their own account . . .

BRITON AND BOER

The British who came to the Cape, like those who went to Canada, found they had to adjust to an established white society. In both countries they began by intermingling with it to a limited extent, and in both presently decided to despise it and to regard it as an inferior. But the Boers were, after all, Protestants. Furthermore, they alone understood the country in the first period of British colonization. Relations were a mixture of friendliness, suspicion and hostility from the first. Intermarriage occurred, just as it occurred between Catholic Scots or Irish and French Canadians. When it did, the Boer culture dominated the European, except in Cape Town and Durban. The Cloetes, de Villiers and de Wets sent their sons to Europe whence they brought back British and Dutch brides, but they kept themselves to themselves socially. Only fresh injections of European people and ideas could keep the exotic Western culture alive in the arid environment. In any common enterprise, or in professional liaisons, relations were often excellent. It was the politics of Whitehall and the liberalism of the British press that proved utterly irreconcilable with the Afrikaner view of life.

The early British settlers examined the ways of Boer life with an anthropologist's sympathy and respect, which they would have done well to apply to the Africans. Philips, who presented a Bible to the voortrekkers, a group that, it is sometimes forgotten, included many British subjects who disagreed with slave emancipation, wrote of one of his early encounters:

They are distant and reserved in their manner, like all people who live out of the world and not subject to a mixture of society to each other even their approach seems cold, they do not give the hearty handshake of the Briton, but simply grasp each other's hands and touch their hats universally. I like them much, it seems they have been fearfully wronged and misrepresented ... the Arbitrary government of this colony disgusts them.

The early British settlers did not, however, adopt fully the Boer attitude to the natives, even though they themselves put them at the lowest social level. When the Boers came to the Britons' church services, Pringle reports that they were invited to sit among the Hottentots, who were preached at in Dutch; this duly kept the Boers off thenceforward.

Boer household arrangements were endlessly, and frequently cattily, commented on by their British guests, hospitality being the Boer article of faith. The Boer patriarchal system was more biblical even than that of the nineteenth-century British, who noted how the slatternly *vrouw* sat at one end of the great hall 'with the tea and coffee before her, a pan of hot coals under feet', while the slaves did the cooking, domestic and farm work, and the husband presided over the family. The Dutch *vrouw* 'fast developed that necessary amount of fat which renders a Dutch wife beautiful in her husband's eyes'. But she also had a sewing-machine, which she did not know how to use, a drawer for loose coins, and was always consulted in economic affairs by her husband. It was noted that a small Dutch family was a 'disappointment'.

The English noticed that the Boers were endlessly interested in their neighbours' and visitors' origins, lineage and family connections, which is also a British characteristic, at least among the upper classes. The Boers carried it further, and this was awkward when so many British came to the colonies for their families' riddance. The Boers needed this tribal institution as much as did the blacks, being a dispersed people. Through its network they obtained news and organized marriages, meeting in their *Nachtmaals*, an institution that intrigued their first British guests. The English envied the Boers' large farms, usually two to a family, largely self-sufficient, based firmly on a cattle-pastoral system, an idyllic life (*die lekke lewe*), that could be recognized from the Old Testament.

It was a system that the British could not wholly copy, because the Boers would not produce for the market, but the British could not produce a revenue and a colonial government without production for the market. In due course, Boer economics kept the Boer republics in a more or less permanent state of bankruptcy, gradually convincing the British that their cash nexus system alone was right. Yet they adopted much from their Boer contacts – above all the attitude to natives, to the right to dispossess the natives of land and suspicion of home governments. At first they even copied the Boer manner of dress which made a man look like 'the very counterpart of Robinson Crusoe'.

The platteland or high-veld Boers did not change as fast as did the British settlement, and by 1875 they were thought of as a 'quaint' or 'antediluvian' community with 'old world ways', at which point the English had ceased to learn from them or in any way imitate them. It was noted that the Boers in the south had become as educated and clever as the British – especially in politics and the parliaments of the Cape and Natal.

There is, indeed, ample evidence that personal relations between Boer and Briton were good until the end of the century, and sometimes even when their respective governments went to war, and the men of each tribe had dutifully to shoot briefly at each other.

In the 1870s the economic distinction between the peoples had so far changed that the trader, Mrs Heckford, could write:

A Dutch farmhouse is very different from an English one. It is merely as a rule a wretched hovel, stuck down in the middle of a waste of grass. The Free State farmhouses are particularly desolate, owing to the Free State being unfit for agriculture and given over to pasturing cattle, sheep and horses. The cottage where we stopped, however, was a rather good specimen and the people – a young man and a pretty woman, his wife – were very hospitable, and gave us a good supper, cleanly served, and, to me at least, a clean bed. There was a nice basin and jug, with a clean towel in my room; but they never thought of the water!

Elsewhere she repeated that she lodged with dirty families, some of whom even demanded payment 'but not getting any because I had only gold and he no silver'. The Boers were learning from the British. She found that 'they were rich in flocks and herds, and yet all but the father, mother, and two eldest sons were barefooted; none had stockings, none appeared to be possessed of a brush and comb, or any soap!' However, ultimately a basin with soap and water appeared, in which Mrs Heckford washed, and the same water, soap and towel were then used by the eleven males of the family in turn – the girls being left out; and when giving their English (or rather Irish) guest food, she was provided with a knife and fork as well as a spoon, like the father – the rest had spoons only. Finally she got a bed in which she lay down dressed, noting that the Boers never undressed for bed, regarding it as improper to do so. Mrs Heckford, like other English travellers, complained that Boer hospitality often loaded them with fleas.

She was aware of the gulf between the attitude of the English settler and the Afrikaner: 'a gulf made wider when the European settler has been bred among all the refinements of European life, but which exists even when he is of the lower middle or even of the labouring classes.'

To the European, life here is an excitement – it is a race after wealth. There is something of the spirit of the gambler in all who try their fortunes here. They may work in the fields sowing crops, or they may tend their herds and flocks – unexciting occupations you would say – but this represents the portion of a game on which they have generally staked all they have; and to all there must be something of excitement in such a game, whether it be dice or oxen, cards or seeds of corn, that are the counters. Then further; until a settler here becomes demoralized, he always looks forward to something beyond what he has – it may be to home; it may be to bring some dear one out to him; it may be to become rich . . . How different are this man's thoughts, as he glances over his cultivated lands, and at his livestock, from those of the Afrikaner farmer, who, standing perchance at his side, thinks of all his possessions as things that he has perhaps won by toil, but which now that he has them, he is contented, looking for nothing beyond. His crops will realize a price which will enable him to live as he is living. If they fetch a higher price than usual, he can perhaps get a new wagon, or indulge in a half-bred English horse; or perhaps if he be a very enterprising character, he may think he will sometime take his children to Natal, and let them behold the sea, and the great ships that he would be afraid to trust himself on, though, may be, he has faced the lion . . . they are as far separated from each other as the gamester is from the man who plays a quiet rubber of whist. Of course, if joined to this there be in the one the remembrance of all the artistic culture – the refinement – the romance – the historic remains, which can be the portion only of him who has lived in the older countries . . . the gulf is enormously widened.

The British, in short, could be rude and underbred, or they could come from the flower of the homeland, but they developed a new attitude to the Afrikaner, and gradually felt him to be almost as backward as the cabin-dwellers in Ireland, apart from his guns and his ability to shoot. To Mrs Heckford the Afrikaner was even untrained to appreciate beauty – in the sentimental form of which the Victorians approved. Yet she loved her Boer friends dearly, and taught their children conscientiously. She was perfectly ready to sentence an African to be whipped almost unconscious for theft, but she would not allow the Boers to lay it on as thickly as they would have wished. In Pretoria, under British rule from 1877 to 1880, it was not only Shepstone's arrogance that alienated the Boers. The English women snubbed the dowdy Dutch ladies, and the Boers openly showed their contempt for the affectation and helplessness of the British officials and hangers-on, and their bedizened wives.

The British prided themselves on giving the African justice in their courts, whereas the Boers assumed a native's guilt; but the British were perpetually revising their views of Africans in a Boer direction. The permanent source of enmity between the two white tribes was of course the reports of the missionaries on the consistent ill usage of the Africans by the

Boers in their trek northwards, and their nomadic search for new pastures. The missionaries duly told their London offices that the Boers, outside British jurisdiction, kept and still took slaves and committed murder with impunity. This ill report, however, was repudiated by the English farmers, who generally declared that they were opposed to the civilization of natives, acquitted their neighbours when summoned for flogging natives, and gave little support to the missionaries.

In Pretoria the Boers and British traders were equal critics of colonial civil servants. But a certain similarity of views on social problems still left the two white communities up-country alien. The British were trying to become refined. Atcherley described a gathering of high-veld Boers:

perfectly at home in their waggons with their wives, children and household goods. From all of them we experienced the usual hospitality – a cup of coffee and a series of flabby handshakings; for when you meet a Boer with his family you are not supposed to shake hands with him alone, but to extend the same form of salute to his vrouw and to everyone of his kinderkins present, often ten or twelve in number; so that, as pocket handkerchiefs are the exception and leckers [a kind of sweetmeat] the rule, your hand at the finish . . . has something of the adhesiveness and consistency of a glutinous fish.

COLONIAL GRACIOUSNESS

There were 26,000 Europeans in Cape Colony in 1805; 185,000 in British South Africa on the eve of the diamond strike and 250,000 in 1875. Gold and diamonds, as we have seen, imparted to the country a new dynamism, a source of wealth which pleased the Colonial Office, sick at heart of the cost of Africa, and produced a tremendous bustle at the ports; but it left settled British patrician life in rural areas and in small towns unchanged. By the 1890s tradition had set in. The natives were tamed, servants gave life smoothness and regularity. The Boer set the example of spacious living. 'Months and years flow smoothly on,' noted Bryce with acerbity, 'they are not in a hurry as in most new countries.'

Melina Rorke, whose father had been British consul at Delagoa Bay, evoked the background of British town life:

The ox-carts rumbling along the dusty road, the elegant carriages whirling past with glimpses of smartly-gowned ladies making their afternoon calls; the black nursemaids bumping perambulators along the uneven pavement; black boys herding their small charges away from the danger of galloping hoofs; the new houses under construction with the smell of fresh timber and paint and the busy sound of hammering; the dignified old Dutch mansions trying to draw their green lawns about them in outraged disdain of encroaching newcomers; the store windows filled with all kinds of tempting merchandise; the black rickshaw pullers in their grimy shorts, their sweating backs and gorgeous headdresses of feather . . . the pavements crowded with fashionably bustled ladies, whose billowing skirts swept the dusty ground and whose slender necks swayed beneath the weight of flowered ostrich-plumed hats.

Everyday existence in the one-street dorps was duller still: Thelma Gutsche noted laconically, 'We have a court and a prison, policemen and criminals, two medical men and scores of patients; law agents and endless litigation, a dozen shops and people head over heels in debt.'

But the excitement was the land, the sense of space and ownership in Africa which entered British eyes and nostrils. As one newcomer put it in 1887:

How splendid the veld looks! It was a fine thing to be your own boss, to have no train to catch, not to have to wear a stiff collar ... what was that picanin saying? That there was a duiker standing just by that clump of bush, an easy shot! Plenty of fresh meat now, and tomorrow the wagon would be amongst the mealie lands which would mean plenty of guinea-fowl ...

It was a happy, leisured, country-house life, in which work was mere supervision, and much of the time was spent in hospitality, riding, shooting, going to gatherings, to huge house parties and dances where courtships could be begun and advantageous marriages arranged or encouraged. 'Pride of race asserts itself in children brought up with kaffirs,' said Fuller at the turn of the century, as social conventions hardened. 'The boy and girl alike acquire a sturdy independence. Hence it is proverbial that the girls need less chaperonage, and the boys have less tendency to the grosser vices ... The colonial farmer can ride any kind of horse; the colonial horse is smaller, less trained, more enduring ...' This was the new British breed.

6

THE DOMINION
THAT NEVER WAS

At the end of the 1940s settler politicians began to think again about a dream that had lived on fitfully ever since the death of Rhodes: a new African dominion for the British Empire, the revival of 'the ceaseless march of British progress'. Suppose Kenya were to link up federally with Tanganyika and Uganda? Suppose 'Huggie' pulled off a federation with Northern Rhodesia and Nyasaland? Suppose furthermore that the two consequent federations were to unite? Then there would come into existence a state larger than South Africa and richer than the Congo, run by white men, but not by the insane Colonial Office; and there would be room for immigrants from Britain by the hundred thousand; and security for everyone, because to Rhodesian autonomy would be added Kenyan toughness.

They felt the time was ripe, as they studied affairs in Salisbury or visited farms in Marandellas. True, vital links between the Central and East African railway systems were yet unbuilt. There were other gaps, too, and break-of-gauge problems. But this would not matter now that aircraft could link up the cities, and the booming copper industry could pay for motorways. The Boer War and the two European wars had stunted the growth of the settlements, but there were 200,000 whites in Southern Rhodesia, 15,000 in Northern Rhodesia, 5,000 in Nyasaland, a few thousand in Tanganyika, and 40,000 in Kenya – and more coming in weekly. As for Britain, wallowing in post-war blues, did she not need a new frontier for gutsy enterprise to make up for disaster in India?

In 1952 the Central African Federation was indeed created, though without excluding the despised Colonial Office; and soon afterwards Mr Oliver Lyttelton (Conservative Colonial Secretary) propounded the idea of a Kenya–Tanganyika–Uganda union. In the face of the Kabaka of Uganda's objection that this would infringe his country's 1900 treaty, the Tories, to the settlers' disgust, promptly retreated, as they had done in India before

Mr Nehru. Thoughtful Kenyan settlers began to wonder what a servantless life in Western Australia would be like.

THE PIONEERS

F.C. Selous, who had obtained a hunting licence from Lobengula, King of the Matabele, told Cecil Rhodes in the late 1880s that Mashonaland had a climate and soil that could support a large British settlement. The Boers already knew it. It was this prospect that clinched Rhodes's formative decision to seize the entire area bounded by the suddenly clamant Portuguese in Angola and Mozambique, the Boers in the Transvaal, and King Leopold who was grabbing the Congo basin. To give himself a free hand Rhodes made use of a Chartered Company, the basis of which was the Rudd Concession, and later others granted by Lobengula and Lewanika further north. Rhodes was also in active consultation with Harry Johnston who was making treaties with the Angoni and other chieftainships in Nyasaland. Lord Salisbury approved, provided that no taxpayers' money would be involved, and that trouble with Portugal and the Boers would be avoided. The prospectus of the Company, for the purposes of the City, was not based upon wars of conquest or upon farming, but on gold. Kimberley was Rhodes's creation, and he had a firm stake in the Rand; there would be mineral discoveries wherever he pioneered. The ancient kingdom of Monomotapa had been renowned for its gold; Selous and others had reported seeing the ancient workings. There were sure to be dividends.

The missionaries had to be considered, but it was again Rhodes's good fortune that the societies had been converted to the view that Christianity could best be spread under colonial rule. Reports of the Matabele, from Coillard and others, were wholly bad. Their Zulu military system was crushing the life out of the tribes beneath their sovereignty. They used them as game to blood Matabele youth, who took their women at will, made torches of their aged, and roasted their toddlers over slow fires. These tribes were retreating to the tops of the stone kopjes. Any criticism of the Chartered Company or its concessions and wars could be countered by citing this barbarous state of affairs. The Mashona were to be saved from the Matabele to do the work on the mines for which they were naturally destined. The Chartered Company's work could thus be aptly compared, by newspapermen duly tipped off to do so, with that of the East India Co. in putting down suttee and thuggery in India. Bryce entirely approved. 'The English race,' he wrote, 'is more likely to serve the interests of civilization than any other [in Rhodesia and Nyasaland] . . . The Portuguese have neither the energy nor the capital. The Germans have not the requisite experience . . . The Boers are a backward people.'

The occupation of Mashonaland was a military operation, again reminiscent of ancient Rome. The column was heavily armed, with maxim guns and artillery, and a portable steam engine for making electricity for a searchlight, when the column camped in hostile territory at night. There was to be no repetition of Isandhlwana. The column was officered by regulars. The privates, drawn from every walk of life in South Africa, were described as a 'fine body of men'. They were led by Colonel Pennefather with Sir John Willoughby as Chief of Staff, and consisted of five hundred men with two hundred pioneers who were to build a road and lay telegraph lines as they advanced: a force 'large enough', it was said, 'to hold off the Boers and Portuguese, small enough not to frighten King Lobengula into immediate resistance'.

'Farmers, miners, prospectors, crack shots, good riders, in a word the flower of South African manhood' moved with a mass of ox and horse transport building forts as they advanced, drilling regularly, practising skirmishing, outpost duty and bayonet drill. Among them went 'Rhodes's Apostles', a group of adventure-seeking Englishmen, of whom one, Hugh Marshall Hole, wrote:

Hitherto they had mostly been working in offices in Kimberley or Capetown, or in the de Beers compound. Now their chance had come and almost all of them were destined to make their mark in the years to come. One of them – Pat Campbell – the youthful husband of a lady then making her debut on the English stage – was to fall in action ten years later in the Boer War; another was Bob Coryndon, who lived to be the Governor of Kenya and other African Colonies.

Another pioneer was Monty Bowden, an English county cricketer whose death was mistakenly reported, so he read his own obituary. Communications were bad, so this sort of error was not uncommon. Colonel Pennefather's death was also rumoured, and a young subaltern who had appropriated his superior's boots received a nasty shock when the rightful owner appeared to claim them. There were the usual sprinkling of eccentrics, like 'Harry the Reefer', a prospector who could not work because of an arm injury, but for the price of a drink would tell a good story; and 'Captain' Bullock, an accomplished horse thief, who, because he carried crested ivory hair brushes, was reputed to be a nobleman, and who eventually went out of his mind with delusions of his own divinity. Besides Coryndon, two other 'Apostles' became colonial governors – Fiennes of the Seychelles, and David Houston of the Windward Islands.

Lobengula sent cattle regularly to the column and warned his own people on no account to fight the white men. The Makalala and Mashona welcomed them, as did Khama of the Bechuana, who had long feared more attacks from the Matabele. It took the pioneers three months to cover the eight hundred and fifty miles from the base camp at Macloutsie River to Mount Hampton, whence they moved to the site of present-day Salisbury and raised the flag.

Wrote a commentator at the time: 'Thus we have as the result of one

year's work a magnificent country occupied, forts built, and excellent communication by a good wagon road 440 miles in length established, 140 miles
of railway and 480 miles of territory conceded.' The natives, it was felt,
would from the first provide the means of opening up the country. 'Besides
making very good servants (nearly every member of the police force has a
"boy") they are proving useful labourers in Fort and hut building. Their
manual skill in the manufacture of various iron implements will no doubt
be turned to good account.'

Their fear of the Matabele, beside whom they described themselves as
'mere women', justified the Britons' conviction of their own mission and the
inevitable fate of the natives to be their servants. From the very beginning
the acquisition of an experienced houseboy not only ensured personal
comfort, but, as Hole recalled, 'carried indirect advantages of a social
character . . . Many a time a letter inviting me to a dinner party has contained a postscript such as this: "Would you be so kind as to bring Alfred
with you to help our boys" – a request that I cheerfully complied with, as
it meant that I, at all events, would be well looked after.' Rhodesia was
founded on British middle-class attitudes to servants. It was built upon the
wars – the whites conquered outright, and the submission of the natives
denatured them.

Early Salisbury was a street of one thousand yards of mostly native-type
huts, and a hotel in a marquee which charged 2s. a head a day, and had
a billiard room. The population consisted of

Four or five hundred sunburnt young men, clad for the most part in flannel
shirts, weather-beaten corduroy breeches and broad-brimmed slouch hats – the
type beloved by lady novelists . . . There was said to be a white woman somewhere in the camp, but she must have remained in *purdah*, for we never saw her.
The only local 'institutions' were the English church and the weekly newspaper.

Everybody lived on the Chartered Company's rations, and when stores
were in short supply a Saturday auction was held and payment was made
by cheque for lack of currency. Once again, the atmosphere was that of
a picnic.

Problems of food and housing occupied us far more than abstract questions of
government . . . our only cares were the minor inconveniences of living at the
back of beyond – a temporary shortage of coffee, perhaps, or candles, or soap . . .
or a delay in the arrival of the English mail, or the collapse of one's hut, which
was a small matter, after all, as one could build another in three days.

The prospectors at once moved out to find gold. One of them returned to
Salisbury with pebbles which he said were diamonds, and started a 'rush',
but the pebbles were mere crystal and the Administrator explained that in
any case all diamond rights had been reserved to the Chartered Company
which, of course, had an arrangement with de Beers. In 1892 groups of
traders, missionaries, speculators and company promoters arrived, many of

whom had been in trouble in the South African mining boom. Rhodes sent up a column of Afrikaner farmers, which made a small beginning. Stores were erected, and life was run on credit; for the first two years a cash purchase over the counter was almost unknown. 'At the hotels one signed cards, and the proprietors thought themselves lucky if their patrons settled their accounts monthly. This led to extravagance and debt which few escaped . . .'

Big game hunters also arrived in the second year of occupation, among them Lord Randolph Churchill, and scientists like Theodore Bent studying the new land. In 1892 the settlers who were to form the core of Rhodesian society began to arrive 'together with a few enterprising women, whose presence soon exerted a refining influence . . .', like the Dominican nuns who nursed the men at Macloutsie camp. By 1895, the year of the Jameson Raid, white settlement had reached three thousand. Prospectors had pegged thirty-five thousand claims, and building lots in Salisbury reached fifty pounds each.

A good few of the early arrivals were young men from the Old Country, who seldom had any more serious reason for seeking fortune away from their native land than the mischance of having failed at Sandhurst or run up too many bills at Oxford, and there was, of course, a substratum of qualified professional men – doctors, lawyers and engineers – who saw the advantage of starting business early in a new field.

The calibre of these early settlers was recorded by a visiting lady novelist in 1913, who through the eyes of her heroine saw

bronzed muscular young pioneers whose ranks are swelled in greater numbers every year by the wellborn Britisher. The colonist . . . is out like the sappers 'where the strange roads go down' making the paths, building the bridges, at hand grips with deadly wilderness diseases, that there may be safety for those that come after him. One great feature in the future of our race will be that great band of colonists.

Many, however, were adventurers from South Africa, whose origins were diverse, and whose talents were varied. But both prospectors and farmers met with bitter disappointments. Farming, which began in a small way with patches of mealies, only got going with the grant of six thousand acres of native land and ten thousand pounds in cash, as well as looted cattle, after the Matabele and Mashona rebellions. Even after the native rebellions had yielded plenty of farmland, Jameson had no difficulty in recruiting experienced officers and men for his raid against Johannesburg.

The settlers felt the land was finally theirs after the rebellions of the Matabele and the Mashona had been put down by 1896. They had paid for it in blood; some hundreds of white men, women and children had been killed, the natives had had to sue for peace and withdraw to areas allotted to them. The feathers of the *impis* gave way to tattered European clothes.

Their behaviour had forfeited their claim to any sympathy or consideration. Great was the indignation when Olive Schreiner attacked the revengeful brutality of the settlers in her novel *Trooper Peter Halket of Mashonaland*. Rhodes snarled at the attack upon himself, but was able to rise above the criticism of even such a distinguished lady novelist.

As in other settlements, the pioneering years were spent vainly looking for a staple cash crop. The first setback was rinderpest and cattle disease in what looked like ideal cattle country; scientific aids were on the way, but in the meantime losses were heavy. As one report put it: 'Mr B. arrived in '94 with £5,000; lost all his cattle with rinderpest. Started again and in '98 lost all with east coast fever. He tried mules which died of horsesickness, then mules who all died of malaria. He bought a steam plough and now has assets in excess of liabilities of £12,000.' To start in Rhodesia, a man had to lay out pounds in thousands rather than hundreds. Men with much less came out as the result of the blandishments of the railway company, and duly failed – but in so doing enriched the traders.

The trouble in Rhodesia was not land acquisition – settlers were given more than they needed – but the means of working it. Because mining hopes were not realized – gold was found only in very small quantities and asbestos and chrome produced but modest returns – the problem was to find the working capital to buy oxen, wagons and ploughs and concentrate on farming. The white population grew slowly and acquired a stubborn streak, refusing to be daunted by constant setbacks. By 1908, however, one settler spoke of 'the healthy satisfaction with their lot' of the early settlers in the Mazoe district. 'One tells of success with bee-keeping as an adjunct to agriculture, another of Mr Ewing's successful work with angora rabbits . . . Rhodesia is no longer a mere experiment . . . Bulawayo with its four or five thousand inhabitants, and Salisbury with its thousand, are solid proofs . . .'

Even so stories of failure after costly experiment were many. A typical settler wrote the diary of his first crops as follows: in May he ploughed for maize, expecting 10s. 6d. a bag. He put down six hundred acres anticipating eight bags an acre, and saw himself netting £2,520. As tobacco prices had slumped he planted only twenty-five acres, expecting 700 lb an acre at 1s. a lb which would net him about £800. He hoped thus to get over £3,000 for an outlay of £2,000. 'Analysed soil and added fertiliser, disc ploughed, palissaded against winds, resorted to hand watering.' The rains fell at the wrong time, locusts swarmed unaccountably, drought set in, army worms attacked the maize, and angular spot and red rust appeared on the tobacco. The price of maize fell to 6s. a bag, and he only got three thousand bags, or £900 for his investment of £2,000; and no tobacco at all.

Rinderpest wiped out Southey's dairy farm near Johannesburg in 1896, so in response to a company advertisement he made up a party of nineteen men, women and children, all, as it happened, descendants of 1820 Cape settlers, and set off for Rhodesia in four wagons and spans. Passing through Bulawayo just after the siege they found a market for their eggs at £1 a dozen, but when they settled on their land they could find no native labour, and even the women had to do manual work. They found a permanent home in Mazoe in 1901. In 1903 Southey lost all but six of his one hundred and twenty cattle from East Coast fever. In 1905, heavily in debt to the Company, which was prospering, he started growing tobacco, and his fortunes took a turn for the better.

In all their trials, the settlers placed their trust in Rhodes. An Umtali pioneer said – and it was a typical feeling – 'It may be wrong to say we worshipped him, but one had only to hear the disappointed and despairing ones say "Wait till Rhodes comes up", or "If I can only hang out till Rhodes comes, things will be all right." He was our Moses and law-giver and he never went back on us.' This may have been true, but his advice to the farmers was hardly practical and could usually be summed up in his famous remark, 'Don't grumble.' He did cut red tape in matters like claims, and when he died the bureaucracy of the Chartered Company soon proved as infuriating to the settlers as that of any colony secretariat. Of Rhodes's sayings, doings and eccentricities there are legion, lovingly pre-served and embroidered by Rhodesians, as the British have done Churchill's. He gave the colony a basic cultural tone, which did not come from Whitehall; from the first they were, in this sense, Rhodesian-British.

Gradually large farms developed and with them the social life of a farm-ing community. White homesteads with their thatched roofs and deep eaves spread over the land, looking down over cultivated fields, where the Africans laboured. Success came from shrewdness and organization, and the right touch with the natives. Many wrote of the art of settlement, but few successfully explained it. The ingredients were capital, good farming and grit. The abiding dangers were credit, fast living, and, worst of all, consorting with native women.

The author Rawden Hoare drew a contrast between the successful farm, where he was met by the householder, his cheerful wife, trained servants and the barking of dogs, and the neglected, overgrown homestead further down the road, where the owner was sodden with Cape brandy, and proved to be living on the proceeds of the sale of his sporting prints.

He came out about ten years ago with plenty of capital and his prospects seemed bright. He hit the pace pretty well though, and after losing quite a lot over tobacco began the usual game of living on credit . . . Then we heard things were going very badly with him, that his creditors had taken most of his farm and all of his cattle . . . There is no doubt that the gossips of the country were greatly to blame. He was naturally shy and weak, so he shut himself up more and more and started to drink . . . It was hopeless from the start. He felt that the hand of everybody was against him. And then to make matters infinitely worse he got entangled with a native woman who is living with him now.

K   127

A substantial coloured population attests to the fact that some Rhodesians did consort with native women, but it seems that miscegenation was short-lived, dying out with the early arrival in some numbers of white women who fought ruthlessly to discourage inter-racial liaisons and punished offenders by social ostracism. Another contributory factor was a certain change in the English character by the end of the century: 'good form' had come in, and it was 'not done' for young men to succumb to the temptations which had overcome the Boers and the West Coasters. Inhibitions flourished naturally, and no Mixed Marriages Act was necessary.

By 1900 the white population of Rhodesia, nearly all British, had risen to 11,000; by 1914 it was 34,000, but it rose to only 36,000 by 1923 when 'responsible government' was achieved, partly because of losses in the war, but more because of slow development. This at least enabled the Rhodesians to prevent a serious 'poor white' community from developing. First-generation Rhodesians were being born in some scores before the end of the century.

LORD DELAMERE AND PEERS

The settlers of Rhodesia were headed by Rhodes's Apostles; the settlers of Kenya followed one man – Lord Delamere. Kenya in the 1890s was still British East Africa and was administered by the Imperial East Africa Company which was forcing the Foreign Office to take over its assets on due compensation. Lugard, who had explored the railway route, had declared in 1893 that the highlands were almost uninhabited and possessed rich pastureland that could sustain dairy farms as productive as those of New Zealand. He conjured up a new Dominion to rival that colony as easily as Rhodes had done; and he saw it as a land of rich ranchers. Through it ran the railway o Ugand , built to abolish the slave trade and its caravans – and to keep out the Germans.

Sir Charles Eliot was sent out to try to make the country pay, and saw that every train, subsidized by the British taxpayer, was indeed running through rich but empty countryside. As rinderpest had caused three-quarters of the Masai to starve, and other tribes were hard hit by smallpox, this was not inexplicable. Since a few natives living in Stone Age style – and, incidentally, stealing the telegraph wire – obviously could not make the railway pay, Eliot decided that white settlement was necessary. 'We are not destroying any old or interesting system but simply introducing order in blank uninteresting barbarism.' Kenya had its native wars like other colonies. The Nandi fought the railway itself. Later the Masai and Samburu revolted, and finally the Kikuyu rose in 1953 because of deep-seated feelings about the land that the white man had taken and transformed.

Delamere, who had visited Kenya on several hunting trips, returned to stay in 1898, when he heard that a settlement scheme was to go ahead. The authorities for political and military reasons envisaged a settlement of small farmers who would take up an initial 160 acres, and another 160 after improvements had been shown; further land could be acquired up to a maximum of 640 acres. Delamere at once exploded with wrath. The Foreign Office, he said, wanted a man to risk his capital under a yoke of petty bureaucracy which retained all rights of water, grazing and timber to the Crown. Small tenant farmers, he said, could never make headway in Kenyan conditions. Eliot finally agreed that land must be made available in amounts and on conditions that would bring in men with capital and City connections. Delamere himself bought hugely. He was criticized, but others did the same, and after some resistance from Governors, who felt, as Sir Harry Johnston had done in Nyasaland, that native interests should be considered, men like Sir Percy Girouard, a later Governor, strongly backed the creation of a landed aristocracy stiffened by a squirearchy of ex-soldiers. They encouraged officials to own land in order to identify their interests with the white, rather than the black, community, and 'followed the simple rule', as one critic put it, 'of making one's friends happy by land and railways'.

A tropical territory at a high altitude on the equator was only in appearance an easy country for white men to farm; it proved as tough to break as the other areas had been. Delamere, carried to his new estate near Nairobi on a stretcher because of a back injury incurred while hunting, erected two huts. He mortgaged his English estate and committed his income. At first, paradoxically, the difficulty was to know what would not grow on the rich loam soil. He decided on large-scale mixed farming on the Australian pattern, and was against plantations (though these came later with Brooke Bond and others) because he clung to his vision of an aristocracy of Kenya-born whites entering their great inheritance by primogeniture, as in the shires.

He sank £80,000 into his estate, which he saw as the model, social and technical, for White Kenya. He brought his stock out from England, and experimented with every possibility, keeping up with expanding agricultural research at home. The real breakthroughs, however, lay fifty years ahead. Worms attacked his sheep because the pastures were too wet for merinos. Until a vaccine was found his cattle went down with pleuropneumonia, and the imported stock died. East Coast fever and ticks wiped out his dairy herd. Later he discovered that the use of paddocks and dipping, once the necessary labour was trained, was the answer. His first successful crop was potatoes.

Life was spartan for himself and his wife. The cows peered through the unglazed windows of his hut, which had floors of unlevelled earth on which good English furniture settled at all angles, while expensive china and plate were used to serve meals consisting almost wholly of game shot on the estate. Incongruously, music was provided by a gramophone. Delamere's failures and triumphs were later recounted in every homestead to build a national history to be handed down to successive generations.

The campaign for attracting settlers started in 1903. The Englishness of the colony, which later became a cult, was stressed. Joseph Chamberlain (Colonial Secretary), who visited British East Africa unofficially on his way to South Africa after the Boer War, said:

I have learnt at school, and have always thought that a tropical climate was associated with a heavy hot atmosphere, where it was very difficult for Europeans to even breathe, but my visit here has dispelled that illusion. When we reached the high level up-country it was very difficult to realize that we were not on the Sussex Downs in the height of a perfect summer . . . we were very much struck by the bonny English children we saw, who had been born in this country . . . we have seen and enjoyed splendid English fruit and vegetables grown here, and, seeing you have the railway, all that is necessary is a population and traffic to ensure your future. This country I have no hesitation in saying will one day be one of the greatest and best Colonies of the British Empire.

Some six hundred settlers followed Delamere within a few years, most of them middle-class or professional people, with a sprinkling of skilled land grabbers, and a number of aristocrats, seeking sport and adventure. One of these, Lord Cranworth, wrote: 'Why did we first decide to go to East Africa? My memory puts the answer in a two-fold urge. Love of sport, more especially of big game shooting, and shortage of cash. The former had been whetted by a trip to India the previous year, and the latter looked like being a permanent fixture.' With the arrival of Galbraith and Berkeley Cole, sons of the Earl of Enniskillen and lady Delamere's brothers, the Nakuru Hotel could appropriately be nicknamed 'The House of Lords'.

President Theodore Roosevelt, the Duke of Connaught and a wealthy hunter, Sir Northrop Macmillan, came out on safari. The latter so liked the tone of the colony and its prospects that he bought an estate there. Lord Portsmouth, the Hon. Denis Finch-Hatton, Lord Francis Scott, Raymond de Trafford and other top people followed, attracted for reasons similar to Cranworth's. By contrast there were also illiterate Boer transport riders, trekking in from Rhodesia in ox-wagons, Australians and New Zealanders, Scandinavians and Americans. A circus strong man arrived from India with only a packet of opium in his pocket, which he sold to buy a camel and start a transport business. It flourished, he bought land, and became a highly respected resident. A simple Scottish shepherd ended up with 30,000 sheep of his own.

It was a standard procedure for the Kenyan settlers and their families to arrive at their farms with their buggies or ox-wagons and pitch their tents; within two days they had a grass hut ready lit by paraffin lamps tied to the poles. A simple house, built of local limestone and timber, sometimes with an iron roof but more often thatched, could be put up for fifty to one hundred pounds; only later on when the farm was paying its way came the solid stone farmhouse with its great fireplace and spacious rooms that was the dream. A Dr Marsh brought out a pre-fabricated iron house in 1906. Some walked to their land, as did Colonel Grogan and Captain Fey and his family, bringing their entire belongings and equipment on the heads of porters. The first European to settle at Ngong came on foot even before Delamere, arriving in 1896. Elspeth Huxley wrote of those beginnings: 'Having built his house, the new settler must get on and work his land. Should it be cattle and sheep, or potatoes and maize? Should he try coffee, keep ostriches, grow flax or experiment with fruit-trees? Such decisions he must make alone. He had no one to turn to for advice . . . all farming then was guesswork.' African labour was completely untrained and, before African fecundity began to fill the gaps left by pestilence, slavery and tribal war, it was so scarce that settlers were always demanding more taxes to force the blacks to work on their farms. No African knew how to plough, how to drive oxen, use pick or saw; many servants were natives who had come out of curiosity to see the new civilization in the making; they were also able to observe the failures – the birds and pests that ate the crops, the lions that purloined cattle, the endless breakdowns of machinery.

After the 1914–18 War, the first of the soldier settlement schemes brought in more of the ex-officers who distinguished Kenyan life. As one of them said: 'Like many others at a loose end, moving about from pillar to post and still full of fire and energy, we wanted to settle down somewhere with a good climate and less overcrowded than England, with something to do and a sporting chance of making a living . . .'

From the first the climate ensured that the settler could bring his family with him. Before Englishwomen arrived as a matter of course, however, a few Kenyans took the same view of black girls as the first Rhodesians. Some well-landed men, living in remote areas, openly chose black women and enjoyed affronting the rest of society. Captain Popkess tells the story of Hyson, a planter on Mount Elgon, who boasted that his Somali mistress's shoes from Paris cost more than she herself had done: 'I bought her and her kid sister up-country for six quid the pair.' To a visitor who refused the sister's services he retorted, 'So you don't like native girls, eh? Well, some people like mustard with their beef. Others like horseradish. Some again like both. There's no accounting for taste, eh?' Kenya remained relatively more liberal than either South Africa or Rhodesia, but gradually the social colour bar became rigidly enforced by the white wives and spinsters. Junior officers who procured native girls as concubines in the West African manner were pulled into line. The East African Women's League was founded in 1917 by Mrs McGregor Ross 'to promote the physical, moral and mental welfare and happiness of all women and children'.

Relations with African labourers and house servants were often bad. The settlers had no experience, no models to imitate except the few Afrikaners, and the East African blacks were wholly unused to white ways – 'as raw as the bush', the settlers said. Delamere had a certain touch. He dealt forthrightly with the Masai, who took a professional interest in his cattle, and they with him; they told him he needed their skill. Their smell was to him simply part of the atmosphere of the new dominion; he respected them and their nakedness never shocked him as it did the prudish, who forced the Nairobi Council to pass a law decreeing that Africans might only appear in the city if wearing blankets. According to Elspeth Huxley the Kavirondo obliged by wearing them round their heads.

Because the Africans first came to them knowing nothing of Western life and having to be taught everything, the settlers formed the indelible impression, lasting until 1960, that Africans could not grow coffee or tea hygienically, or run businesses, or drive cars or locomotives reliably or combine successfully for any purpose, least of all for running a state.

African servants could be hired, by 1910, for between 6s. and 30s. a month with board and food, but they were 'incurable thieves and extremely cunning,' declared Mrs Boyd.

What the native wants he takes – if he is clever enough to do so unobserved . . . constitutionally lazy, entirely ignorant, inconceivably stupid and completely unambitious . . . Not only have you to supervise all the work out here, but you also need at least a working knowledge of every branch of the science of living, from house-building to boot cleaning . . . garden boys will have to be instructed how to dig and trench, make paths and plant; the cook required to be shown how to make bread and cakes and pastry, how to fry and how to roast. You've got to know how to build dams, work rams, wash and iron clothes, clean silver and polish floors, make beds and shine shoes, mend your car or your cream separator or your mowing machine, even tune a piano . . . When you know all this, as well as a hundred other things, you will require in addition the patience to teach them, and then the patience to see they are carried out.

Patience was, unfortunately, a commodity in heavy demand in Kenya, and it often ran short. The settlers wanted things done their way, and quickly; the Africans only existed for their convenience. 'Hence the daily irritation, exasperation, infuriation that hardens the hearts and blinds the minds of their masters,' wrote Norman Leys, who had watched the process for thirteen years and was a determined critic of the government that had allowed such a settlement. 'The great mass of settlers make admirable and successful efforts at self-control, the prevailing attitude is one of strain.' It was one of strain because the Europeans did not understand the African way of life, and insisted on his conversion to settler ideas of routine by clock and clockwork – necessary enough when crops are grown to timetable and development must be carefully phased. To do these things, and create the English community that the highlands became in a mere three decades, the harassed young British supervisor or farmer had to bully, coerce and insult the mystified and unbelieving African. One suffered, it was said in both Kenya and Rhodesia, from 'muntitis', depression and despair at the mere thought of Africans.

From anger and shouting, it was bound at times to be a short step to violence. There were cases of Africans shot, and yet white juries insisted on acquitting even the man whose guilt was admitted. Minor assaults were, in relation to the small size of the settlement, quite high; and excuses were always found for any farmer whose wrath boiled over at the end of a trying day. Yet any reduction of sentences against Africans on appeal were resented as softening 'discipline'.

Africa could get one down, it was admitted, and de Janzé observed that

those who return too often to the bottle, slowly soak, and soaking, sink. Soon in the house boys' huts native women will sit and soak; one more enterprising will speak to the white man. He, with convincing faith, will take an interest in her children, tell them to mend their ways, and one tropical night . . . a bodily desire takes shape . . . The weeds will choke the garden, the cactus grow through the verandah floor, boards become disjointed; he'll wear khaki – it shows less stains – the white ants one night in a carelessly opened tin box will eat his evening collars, and so he rots.

The English had, perhaps fortunately, other ways of letting off steam, other means of keeping tribal discipline. The festival of the early settlers was race week, an event which was ensured by their social origins or pretensions. Started in 1900 by A. S. Cooper, it became a tribal gathering – what the *Nachtmaal* had been to the Afrikaners. Drink inspired new feats in unconventionality. Farms were deserted, agricultural disappointments forgotten, everyone attended the gathering, where large hats and revolver fire mimicked the American rodeo. When the race meeting was threatened financially in 1906, the Governor stepped in to save it. Race weeks – one in summer, one at Christmas – became a feature of Kenyan life at which visitors never ceased to marvel. They also extolled Kenya's unbounded hospitality – that is, between people of equal social standing. Games were played with fervour as success in farming provided leisure for the white men – though the joys of leisure in Kenya also led many farmers to leave their land to supervisors and African overseers, sometimes with disastrous results. Football, cricket, tennis, hockey and above all golf and polo, were available for a settler's leisure hours, quite apart from shooting and fishing. Little was made of scientific interests; the ex-officer, extroverted atmosphere rendered intellectualism unpopular, and Kenyan artists were few and 'popular' in genre.

If in Rhodesia the keynote was conformity, in Kenya it was individuality, and the *haut ton* set the pace which lesser people copied on a smaller scale. Farming done for the day, fancy had play; the professional job of breaking the bush completed, aristocratic freedom took over – partly to show the

Colonial Office what sort of men they were dealing with, and make them tremble in Whitehall – necessary since unlike Rhodesia the officials were not appointed on the spot. It was settlement of a special kind, just as life in a good regiment was soldier's life of a special kind. Delamere adored a good rag, and like Rhodes made himself a man of legends, by smashing up the furniture of the hotel he himself owned in Nakuru, or shooting out the town's lamp posts while the native officials looked on helplessly. He feuded ferociously with his neighbours, all as part of laying down the good school, good regiment, unwritten law basis of life lived hard and high but for a common purpose.

The Club, more than the Church, was the centre of the English community, as it was in South Africa and Rhodesia. The old Club at Nairobi stood on the hill, its walls decorated with horns, its billiard room, card room and bar, faintly in the St James's tradition.

Here as the sun went down [wrote Lord Cranworth] assembled the elite from farm and office, from store and counter. Plates of potato chips and monkey nuts garnished the mahogany, and behind it an autocratic Indian marshalled his troupe of smiling natives in their white kanzas. Drinks flowed freely and so did the conversation, of which one could take one's choice of almost any brand. Certainly as the dinner hour approached the babel became louder and the stories taller and even thicker, but unless it was a big night, perhaps six times a year, it was extremely rare to see anyone the worse. And even on those nights intoxication was of that jovial variety which inspires an overwhelming urge to throw a billiard ball or other handy missile at a stuffed and staring kongoni head, and the damage was almost invariably made good. Assuredly I had some good times in the old Club, and never ceased regretting when the process of evolution demanded something grander and more dignified.

This was provided by the Muthaiga Club, started by the Coles, for the sake of exclusiveness and refinement. Aristocratic rowdiness, on the Delamere pattern, produced good stories – and the need to provide stories produced practical joking. Kenyans were delighted with the man who got under the table during a boring after-dinner speech, jabbed the speaker in the leg with a fork, emerged to offer, and have accepted, a gentlemanly apology, and then returned to jab his other leg when the drone recommenced.

Not all those who played hard, however, worked hard. There were plenty of failures, but as Kenya was a colony, not a self-governing dominion, these could be, and were, shipped home and out of sight as 'distressed British subjects': there were few poor whites in the sense of white beggars, such as were frequently met with in Cape Town; to be on the verge of bankruptcy was no shame, and settlers were able to prove, when an income tax was proposed in the 1920s that they could not pay it.

Those who had land and money, and no such devotion to nation-building as Delamere, engendered a fast set, which began to be spoken of with awe, though the quip 'Are you married, or do you live in Kenya?' was not always relished. In the Happy Valley, on the slopes of the Aberdares, wife swapping and orgies were said to have taken place. At least one man was horsewhipped by a cuckolded husband, and Elspeth Huxley tells of a married lady who was consoling herself for her husband's infidelity with 'one of the playboy pseudo-settlers who appeared after the war, dressed in bright silk shirts, richly coloured corduroy trousers and wide-brimmed hats, driving box-body cars with rifle racks inside, and lions' claws as mascots on the bonnet'. Lady Idina Gordon, who had several changes of name, was alluded to obliquely in many books, and became in contemporary imagination the prototype of untamed emancipated woman, shouting 'to hell with husbands' at the thin Kenya air. Mrs Huxley, as a child, remembers her presiding at her house named Clouds:

Everyone called her simply Lady Idina because her surname changed so often it was impossible to keep up. Now and again, at polo tournaments perhaps, she flitted through the periphery of my life like some gorgeous bird of paradise, brilliant in green or plum coloured corderoys, a gay silk shirt, pearls and pendant earrings, slim as a wood-wasp, the clarity of her complexion and the candour of her fine eyes evidently freshened by the all-night parties and gallons of gin on which she and her circle so manifestly thrived.

The trial of Sir Delves Broughton in 1941 for the murder of Lord Errol, one of Lady Idina's cast-off husbands, and Broughton's wife's lover, provided a grim ending to a hedonistic era which in its heyday enjoyed a romantic reputation. In the twenties Kenya was a more fashionable place for a girl to go to pick up a husband than Rhodesia. Cranworth noted that the race meetings were the chance of a lifetime for an unmarried girl, as the men then were in a mood 'to see beauty in the most meagre charms'. Informality was still the keynote in Nairobi, as one lady visitor noted: 'I should think it doubtful whether any other town in the world sports such a variety of dress, and in the lounge now at the dinner hour there is a pretty average assortment. Here is a group of men and women in safari kit ... then at a nearby table sit two girls in low-cut evening dresses and high-heeled satin slippers, the two men with them in immaculate evening dress. There is also a girl in a chic afternoon dress and hat. Some of the groups again are mixed: one man and girl in slacks and a shirt sitting drinking with two others in evening dress.'

The Mount Kenya Safari Club provided a useful back-drop for stories in women's magazines, and for films – it was founded by William Holden, a Hollywood magnate. The white hunters, some of whom were titled, became a sort of sex-symbol, and Hemingway gave them the accolade. The hat trimmed with leopard-skin became the emblem of their appeal.

After the Second World War, a new ex-serviceman's scheme was launched as though nothing had changed, though the motive was undoubtedly some anxiety in thoughtful settler circles that even if the white

population was growing, the number of farmers was still extremely small –
barely three thousand. Meanwhile, the African population was soaring, and
few could doubt from their surliness of mien that black-white relations were
deteriorating. This was put down to the attitude of Africans who had come
back from serving in the war, and, even more, to decadence in Britain; to
the insidious spread of communism, particularly to the turn of events in
India. Few recognized that African desire for more land was a cause.
Looking back, Blundell meditated:

I sometimes wonder whether the impact of the European mind, its restless-
ness, its energy, its knowledge, its dynamics, has not created an insoluble problem
for the people of Kenya ... Without the European the African scene in Kenya
could have been tranquil, slow and largely as unconcerned as other countries in
Africa. The restless energy of the European settler, his insatiable demands for
new knowledge, for new techniques in farming, for better roads, for better
administration, for better communications, raised the standard of the whole
country beyond that which the indigenous people themselves may well wish to
maintain ... What might have been good enough for a simple immature people,
without much technical knowledge or education, was completely unsuited to the
type of man who came from the western world intent on making a new
country ...

In 1952 the settlers found themselves faced with the Mau Mau rising'
and those who had so criticized Britain found they needed British troops·
They rose to the emergency, and a few young men, their faces blacked,
went with non-Kikuyu Africans into the forests to hunt out the gangs.
But when the British Government decided to accept Tom Mboya's order
to 'scram out of Africa', the British community found itself powerless to
hang on, unable to call Sir Roy Welensky to its aid. It surrendered at
discretion, squabbling bitterly within itself. The Great White Dominion
spanning central Africa finally faded into thin air.

7

MEN OF THE ESTABLISHMENT

'To a Colonial governor two things are of supreme importance. One is Government House, and the other is the government yacht,' wrote a vinegary colonial judge early in this century. He added that Governors were ready to threaten to leave their posts if they did not get the yacht. Governors, however, had to put first things first, and the gubernatorial memory of Colonial Office stinginess was a very long one. In the early days of the African settlements, every reason existed for concern about Government House, which was frequently small, insanitary and far from weatherproof. As for the yacht, this was the only way to get about along the West African littoral, along the coast of South Africa, and up the oil rivers of Nigeria to the inland settlements.

HIS EXCELLENCY

The apotheosis of British rule was the Governor, though the Consul was often his forerunner and prophet. At times he was the only official; and somebody always had to be acting Governor when fever carried off the Queen's representative. The basic colonial establishment normally included the colonial judge or magistrate dispensing British justice to British subjects of all races, the Governor's own private secretary, and perhaps an assistant; the officers of the garrison – the Governor liked not only to be titular commander-in-chief but also to be commanding officer leading the troops to victory and to his own C.B. – and a doctor or surgeon was also a basic need. The district commissioner, lynch-pin of the African empire when it moved inland, hardly emerged on the scene until the 1880s and 1890s, when roads and railways were securing military lines of communication. Long before the D.C. arrived, the Secretariat took shape in the coastal settlements, as the Colonial Office appointed such specialists as the colonial surveyor – a most coveted, because lucrative post. At the Cape, the establishment was from the first larger as befitted a strategic base.

Government House was therefore a seat of government and general headquarters until the growth of the establishment justified the erection of the secretariat building itself in the capital. In West Africa the slave forts provided ready-made premises, but in Sierra Leone the first Governors sent out by the Sierra Leone Company had to make do with a thatched hut. Later an unsatisfactory wooden-framed building was provided. Fort Thornton had to be built, however, after the sack of the colony by the French in 1797, and threats to the growing community of liberated slaves from 'King Tom', the local potentate, and the indigenous tribes. It grew from a cottage within a palisade to a stone residence with ramparts and bastions, but it was never comfortable, roomy or rainproof and was indeed often described as 'ruinous'. For a time Governors lived in a private house in Gloucester Street, a 'large wooden box' which was barely an improvement. The walls at Fort Thornton were so thin that no private conversation could be held within doors, and an offensive dry latrine was situated by the dining-room door. (Somerset, at the Cape, had imported W.C.s for Government House long before.) In 1860 Fort Thornton was roofed with corrugated iron and then consisted of 'a good drawing room, a good dining room, one large bedroom and five attics. The Governor's office gave off the dining room and the Council room opened off that.' In 1869 it got a new kitchen range and an ice-box, kept refrigerated by blocks of ice brought from Liverpool by mail boat. Governor Hennessy added a staircase and running water from the converted Martello tower incorporated in the fortifications. Fort Thornton was the seat of the Government at various times for all the West African settlements, and a 'government steamer' was provided; in 1879 Sir James and Lady Marshall were nearly drowned when the engine broke down just as the vessel was negotiating the harbour bar at Lagos, and the breakers began to smash over her.

But along the coast, Cape Coast Castle offered better quarters. Its amenities in the 1840s were described by Letty Landon, a literary lady who after a neurotic courtship finally married George Maclean, who had been appointed 'president' of the merchant community which was carrying on after the abolition of slavery had reduced trade to a low ebb, and who nonetheless thought of himself as governor. 'L.E.L.', who arrived in terror of Africa's evil reputation, wrote home that it proved 'superior' to all she had dreamed of:

The castle is a very noble building, and all the rooms are large and cool, while some would be pretty even in England. That where I am writing is painted a deep blue, with some splendid engravings – indeed fine prints seem to be quite a passion with the gentlemen here. Mr Maclean's library is fitted up with bookcases of African mahogany, and portraits of distinguished authors ... All my troubles have been of the housekeeping kind ... I have numbered and labelled my keys. Their name is legion and every morning I take my way to the store, give out flour, sugar, butter etc. and am learning to scold if I see any dust or miss the customary polish on the table . . . The solitude, except for an occasional visitor, is absolute.

They lived unhappily there, for Maclean was a morose, ambitious, pernickety Scot whose hobbies indoors were the collection of navigational instruments and the violin, and out-of-doors, the cultivation, against all odds, of coffee.

Government House, Lagos, by contrast, was a Victorian iron pre-fab with a fearful reputation. Sir Richard Burton described it as 'an iron coffin, with generally a dead consul inside' – and it was so sizzlingly hot that its inmates, according to Governor Pope Hennessy, would 'spend sleepless nights wandering with mattresses and pillows about the cast-iron verandahs, or up and down the shadowy central corridor where the Houssa troops' arms were stacked, seeking a shaft of air'; it was supposed to impress visiting chiefs to find the Governor asleep among stacks of arms. Lady Glover, wife of another Governor, reported that:

His Excellency, as was his wont, having tried in vain to rest before the break of day, compromised the matter of sleeping either indoors or out by lying down with his head and shoulders in the passage and the rest of his body in the room. The dusky constable on duty as guard came across the Governor in that position and attributing it to a physical inability to move [i.e. that he was scandalously drunk], and alarmed lest his condition should become known, shook him roughly by the shoulders . . . till he thoroughly roused him up, and sleep for that night was impossible.

At the Cape the English Governors inherited the comfortable mansion built by their Dutch predecessors, but at Durban, Government House was a little two-storied house resembling an English rectory, with a reception room so small that guests had to go through to the lawn to make room for others.

In Salisbury the first Administrator, Earl Grey, in 1891 had to put up with a mud and wattle dwelling for a Residency, but in East Africa no time was lost in erecting government houses which befitted proconsular dignities. To Sir Hesketh Bell, Government House Entebbe in the 1900s was 'a really comfortable English house' of the villa type, which cost £4,000 but would cost double in Britain owing to the higher wages paid there. He immediately set about building himself an even better one. Imperialist sentiment gave Governors grand ideas: each wanted to see himself as a viceroy, emulating the pomp of Delhi. Indeed, Government House, Dar es Salaam, was built with the idea that it would be a viceroy's palace for all East Africa. It still suggests it.

Work in the conditions of early Victorian Africa was hardly attractive even at the Governor's level, apart from at the Cape itself. Thackeray satirized the level of colonial governorships in *Vanity Fair*, where Lord Steyne (alias Hertford) tries to remove the impecunious Rawdon Crawley

139

to a colony, in order to have his wife Becky as his mistress. In reality even the most obscure governorships were eagerly sought, such was the pressure of unemployment upon gentlefolk at the time. Governorships were at first given to half-pay officers and retired army men – naturally enough since they were partly military appointments and the Colonial Office was at first only a department of the War Office. Even so, the vacancies were few, the list of candidates long; it was essential to have pull – to know a mysterious 'Mr Holland' at the office – to get one of these little plums for onself or a needy relative.

The Colonial Office, it was said, 'lived in ignorance and would die in ignorance'. The clerks there lived genteel lives and never went to the colonies, although very senior officials occasionally went on missions. Their job was simply to dole out money, cavilling at every penny. They could not give a Governor instructions on local administration until the telegraphs came – the copper plate-written and holographed despatches to Freetown took three weeks at least and to Cape of Good Hope up to eight until steamers came. But they could and did prevent him spending money on even the most needed items. Groaning over the 'volume of work', they merely attended to pay, leave, conditions of appointment, passages, medical requirements and, of course, honours. Policy was a matter between the Secretary of State and the Governor.

Salaries were not generous, though they were far larger than those of other officials, colonial judges for example. Nor were they supposed to be long enjoyed in the death traps of the Coast. Hence the story of the Governor to the Niger who asked if his fare home would be paid on the expiry of his term and was told that the question had never arisen before. 'It is dangerous cruelty to send out white men as governors,' wrote John Whitford in the 1870s. 'One of these colonial officials when seeing some friend off in the mail steamer for home remarked "a feller had better be waterman on a London cabstand than be governor of Cape Coast Castle, don't you know".'

The mortality of Governors, and their wives, though heavy, was exaggerated. One ex-Governor told Parliament that he believed a living Governor of Sierra Leone was a rather rare species, and the journal *John Bull* jested that they had to be sent out, like despatches, in triplicate. Insurance companies refused them cover. Between 1805 and 1887 eight Governors died in Freetown, on campaigns, or on their way home. Mrs Maclean took her life at Cape Coast Castle, and three Governors' wives died in Freetown in that period. Others complained of illness – Kennedy, for example, petitioned the Office to send him somewhere healthier, and finally he was allowed to go – to Hong Kong.

Others were eager to take the place of the fallen. Temple, for example, went to West Africa at the age of fifty, simply as a means to support his wife and fifteen children at home. The salary, which varied from £2,000 to £2,500, carried no pension, and Governors were always fighting for allowances for entertaining local chiefs or visiting dignitaries. Additional responsibilities called for larger salaries – when the Governor of Sierra Leone became Governor of all the West African settlements for a time, his salary went up to £3,000. Sir Charles MacCarthy, who was in command of the forces got his salary raised to £2,500 from £2,000 and his 'table money' from £1,000 to £1,500. Governors everywhere fought vigorously for rises in pay. When Sir Bartle Frere was sent out to be Governor of the Cape with the additional title of High Commissioner, to discharge his abortive mission to federate all South Africa to Lord Carnarvon's formula, he bargained determinedly for an extra £2,000 a year before he would go. This early form of trade unionism grieved the Colonial Office, which took to giving titles more often in the latter part of the century in lieu of the rate for the job.

Plain knighthoods for Governors, even in West Africa, became usual in mid-Victorian times. The Order of St Michael and St George, which originated in 1818 to reward the Maltese and Greeks who had helped in the Napoleonic Wars, was extended to the Empire generally, and became the basic African 'gong' until the Order of the British Empire was inaugurated in the First World War. The need to impress the natives with stars, uniforms and ribbons, it has been noted, rose just as the natives had begun to lose their astonishment at British technology. It was like reverting to the trade goods of the slave trade. While the paraphernalia of local titles (equivalent to the *Rai Sahibs* of India) did not come into existence in Africa, British titles were found handy for local potentates, while cheap gilded crowns were bought by the Colonial Office from toy manufacturers for Governors to crown such approved monarchs as Cetewayo. The Africans were not impressed by them.

The attraction simply of being a Governor, even in a West African port, was apparently great even before decorations were widespread. To be 'His Excellency' and have a seventeen-gun salute appealed to men who would otherwise moulder on their memories of battles in the Peninsular or the Crimean Wars. Such governorships were seen, rather optimistically, as the beginnings of a great career. Maclean was delighted to get the presidency of the Gold Coast merchants at £1,000 a year and no provision for leave, and tended to assume the title of governor; he was reproved for giving himself airs.

An African Governor could hope to gain renown and honours by expanding his territory by war or by treaty with the nearby chiefs, but it was a risky procedure at first in the face of the Colonial Office's reluctance. It could earn severe reprimands. But Governors were thankful when minor disturbances took place which they could legitimately suppress at the head of their 'army' and call a 'victorious war'. After 1870 this became sure of a good press at home, much to the anger of the Colonial Office. Expansion, together with public works, was very much a new Governor's natural bent. The first Governors at Lagos were busy building the Marina and cleaning up the town of huts and shanties, partly to be able to go for an evening stroll. Ports and bridges, when opened, gave the Governor an occasion for homilies and a demonstration of the benefits of British rule. But fighting the Colonial Office, the climate, the malice of the local people and the lassitude and incompetence of their local staff, Governors in the West Coast wore out fast even when they did not actually die. This process led Mary Kingsley to describe their administration as 'a coma punctuated by fits'.

THE PROCONSULS

Governors liked to feel their power. In South Africa this was always great, though it had from the 1860s to be shared with local legislatures, and to be subjected to press criticism. In tropical Africa, gubernatorial authority began to catch up with proconsular importance in the East by the end of the century. A man liked to feel he surveyed a large expanse of country of which he was monarch. 'I have,' said Hesketh Bell of Uganda, 'complete authority over three and a half million people and a territory larger than Spain.' He was delighted to be able to change the uniform of a Governor, third-class (which he had in Dominica), for that of the 'more imposing' Governor, second-class, in the new imperial Africa. It has 'a good deal of gold lace on the chest and coat tails, and costs, I find, a pretty penny'. Like other Governors, his brain teemed with schemes for the expansion of the colony's trade and well-being. The idea of being a 'great' governor, who would set his stamp on a young colony, had arrived; these were Governors who had vital imperial policies to carry out, as well as local improvements to press through. Such great proconsuls found their personification in men like Milner, Bartle Frere, Lugard, and Donald Cameron. These were the men who could easily find a publisher to bring out their memoirs, or reports on their missions, for public consumption, and who could become the subject of scholarly critiques. They were the African equivalent of Curzon or Cromer. Even in the manner of their departure there was drama. For the more important the mission entrusted to a Governor, the more likely a political upset at home would lead to his dismissal in high dudgeon. Cameron was told of his dismissal by an office messenger. Milner was the subject of a contemptuous speech by the young Winston Churchill. But of the scores of Governors who were sent out to Africa, where at the imperial zenith some twelve were always serving contemporaneously apart from the Governor-General of South Africa, a mere handful have left in writings, letters, memoirs or serious books any trace of their lives, their triumphs and disasters, their philosophy.

Governorship became a skilled trade after about 1900, when colonial life grew more predictable; the wise man trimmed his sails to the winds at home. In a phase of imperialism, he expanded and sent out expeditions; under liberal skies, he suppressed domestic slavery and was tireless in native welfare. The job went increasingly to the professionals in the colonial service as these moved upwards and less and less frequently to military officers. Plums were, of course, reserved for politicians. The great game was to progress from smaller to larger colonies, with the House of Lords in view.

Africa only became a good hunting-ground for official careers, however, towards the nineties. The classic success story was Lord Lugard's. Lugard went to Africa as an unemployed officer, like so many Victorian soldiers who made good; he was nursing a broken heart and his menial first jobs in Nyasaland brought him near despair. He ended with the reputation of a colonial giant and savant, who invented the concept of dual mandate through native chiefs and governments, and certainly he elaborated and systematized a form of government which British mentality made inevitable in Africa and has been bitterly criticized by African nationalists since. Where it was unsuitable, because chiefly rule did not exist (as it did in Northern Nigeria, or India), public school and army tradition was equipped to cope: prefects were simply appointed from the most likely-looking boys. Any other way of running things was unthinkable and inconceivable.

The social life of the early Governors was limited; and some of them, like Maclean, worked hard – mostly in dealing with quarrels in the colony or in the hinterland of the *Pax Britannica*. Letty Landon sadly noted that 'from seven in the morning until seven when we dine, I never see Mr Maclean and rarely anybody else'. However, the Governor was the leader of society such as it was. In West Africa it was often an invidious task.

It is very difficult for the governor of a new colony like this [wrote John Whitford] to please everybody . . . chiefs, merchants, missionaries all clamouring loudly for their interests. On this coast they part with more money than they can afford, principally in entertaining . . . with the object of promoting good will and good government. Suppose a dinner at G.H. Lagos; time, 7.30 p.m. Oil lamps are lighted in the reception rooms, and also on the verandahs. The major-domo of the Governor arranges the guests in proper order; native chief and merchant with missionary in between; the latter generally acts as interpreter. If there are not missionaries enough, a clever coloured government official . . . takes the place of the missionary. At the expense of the governor a really good banquet is spread . . . Each visitor has got some grievance to declare, but during the entertainment, as a well-behaved man, he only opens his mouth to partake of good food and drink or to talk pleasantly. Meantime the band of the Houssa soldiers plays lively . . . music in the 'Arabian Nights' lighted gardens outside. When the dining part is over, the governor gives the word of command, and all standing up do honour to the loyal toast. Shortly after which business commences and is recorded by secretaries on the spot.

Mrs Maclean was apt to discover that after some such official function His Excellency could not be roused in the morning to say goodbye to his visitors, who also looked unwell, and she herself had to 'do the honours of adieu; I think I never felt more embarrassed'. West Coast Governors who did not drink were apt to become somewhat paranoiac over their squabbles with local people, such as missionaries, and frequently at loggerheads with their staff, whom they abused in long despatches home. Not a few followed the usual custom in matters of relaxation. Governor Alex Findlay of Sierra Leone kept a fifteen-year-old mistress from the liberated slave community and raised a memorial to her after she died in child-birth.

But imperialism made even West African Governors respectable, and everywhere, even in Bathurst, Government House had to set the tone of snobbish society. In Salisbury, Rhodesia, everybody white came to the Administrator's first reception at the Residency, but later it became possible to set social precedence in a highly-mixed society of adventurers. Elsewhere Governors had the gall to complain that social snobbery was forced on them. Government House became a court. Hospitality became a Governor's important duty – but less and less towards the native society and more and more towards the British. Governors delighted in the fact that in their own colony, the military salutes were for them, not for a visiting Prime Minister or Secretary of State, whom they preceded to dinner. After dinner, the Governor led the gentlemen into the grounds 'to water Africa'.

Lord Altrincham recorded that he had a problem of reconciling hospitality to Kenyan society, aristocratic as it was, with entertaining important visitors, royalty of course being pre-eminent. He was particularly concerned with the security of the Prince of Wales, and provided him with a posse of Masai who surrounded him when a lion came near; the Governor also disguised a doctor as a fireman, in case H.R.H. caught malaria (which he did). When Princess Marie Louise toured the Gold Coast in 1926, the Governor and Lady Guggisberg turned the colony upside down for her and her attendants (even so they once had to try to iron their own clothes); a train of six cars and thirteen motor trucks conveyed them when the royal train reached railhead; and happy was the district commissioner whose arrangements were specially commendable.

Down-to-earth matters of clean food were not below gubernatorial interest. Warned that Government House dinners were getting a bad name, Altrincham diagnosed the trouble as the infected finger-nails of his cooks. It was profound satisfaction to Governors to know that, in terms of African society, they had 'dukes' serving as gardeners, and black menials with the courtly manners and bearing of judges. Not all Government Houses, of course, could have the excitement of Nairobi, the centre of big game hunting, and also the target of settler criticism of the Colonial Office. A plot to abduct the Kenyan Governor in the 1920s was only just foiled in time to save the Establishment from embarrassment; it was the threat to defend His Excellency with Askari guards that caused the settlers to think better of their coup.

Altrincham found King George v worried about the habit of Kenyan farmers dining in pyjamas, and Queen Mary was insistent that divorced persons should not be invited to Government House. Kenya was the one colony where the officials were not society's natural superiors. The Governor and the officials felt that they ought to be at the apex of Kenyan society as in, say, Tanganyika, but the settlers, whose lineage and military records were often better, thought *they* were. They kept the colonial men humiliatingly out of the Muthaiga Club for a while.

In these circumstances A.D.C.s and social secretaries became essential to life throughout tropical Africa. Wrote Hesketh Bell: 'The question of precedence is treated with immense seriousness in colonial circles. The unfortunate A.D.C. who at a dinner party places an official – especially an official's wife – in a seat which they do not consider to be the proper one, comes in for a bad time.' The Governor's life became a round of local festivities varied by the administration of the colony. Unlike the pathetic Letty Landon, the Governor's wife became important and certainly never alone. Up to 1880 the Colonial Service refused to pay the fares of wives to West Africa, and even Governors rarely brought them out. Her Excellency, complete with social secretary, book and daily schedule, became an important part of colonial society by the 1900s in all parts of Africa. Governors were delighted when they found that white women lived in their capitals; it meant tone, propriety, solemnity; 'the ladies' brought suburbia to Africa, and Her Excellency kept them up to scratch and in their places. But some Governors' wives were difficult; Lady Guggisberg, who had had a career of her own, would not play second fiddle, and even stepped forward to royalty.

Governors, explorers, soldiers, even traders with official commissions like Alldridge in Sierra Leone, pushed into the interior, made treaties with chiefs, proclaimed zones and protectorates. But officials were required to administer them. The first administrators indeed doubled as treaty-makers, preparing the ground of annexation. Once the officials were on the ground, the Governor's hierarchy extended. Not only did Governors preside over the secretariat and the local society, they made royal progresses through the interior. A keen Governor was a keen tourer. Hesketh Bell delighted in his retinue: two hundred porters carried his tents and equipment, twelve servants attended him, forty constabulary protected him, as he moved by mule, chair and occasionally bicycle. The chiefs constructed camps for him and when he reached the Nile a forty-two-foot steam launch awaited him. He was an advocate of forced labour, but he paid his men threepence a day.

District officials, of course, attended and looked after Governors much as Governors looked after visiting royalty, foreign crowned heads and British Secretaries of State.

THE MEN IN THE BOMAS

The officials themselves, the colonial service, only began to move out into colonial Africa in the 1890s, though the Colonial Office or the Crown Agents had appointed technical officers, surveyors, engineers, surgeons and even agriculturalists before then. For years, however, there was no formal system of recruiting, and many D.C.s in effect were appointed on the spot as administrators were needed. Sir Harry Johnston had to assemble such a scratch service to administer the Nyasaland Protectorate in 1890. R.C.F. Maugham, who was appointed vice-consul, postmaster-general, judge, collector of revenues, custodian of stores and commandant of the Sikh police, reported that 'some among them were not very well educated; their reports and despatches, I well remember, revealing but an imperfect acquaintance with the rules of grammar and spelling but, with scarcely an exception, these men successfully performed delicate and onerous official tasks . . .' In 1902 Dr Aldo Castellani – subsequent discoverer of the vector of sleeping sickness – craving imperial adventure like so many young men at the time, was appointed to Uganda by an under-secretary in the Foreign Office with the words: 'Well, young man, I am going to send you to Uganda, alien or no alien.' He thought he was ready to leave until he was told that a frock-coat was unsuitable for Africa; so he hurried to a tropical outfitter and bought two tropical suits, a huge sun-hat and a rifle from Holland & Holland.

In West Africa there were, of course, qualified Africans and Creoles for many tasks. Afro-West Indians had already held the posts of acting Governor, Colonial Secretary, Crown Prosecutor and Registrar of the Mixed Court. Governor Macdonald was the first to deny their fitness. Lord Grey from the Colonial Office overruled him: 'The aim of the government in all measures ought to be to break down the unhappy distinctions made between persons of different colour.' But Governor Cardew carefully weeded them out; and when in 1890 it was decided to appoint district commissioners instead of Creole agents in the hinterland, it was the Colonial Office that insisted on whites only.

The Colonial Office had then to undertake recruiting for administration. This was done on interviews of applicants – vacancies were not advertised. The famous Furse selection method preceded Major Furse, who subsequently became a legendary figure as a one-man appointment board. From the Furse method emerged a 'service of amateur humanists' in the words of Sir Kenneth Bradley. Preliminary training, of the sketchiest, was not instituted until 1909.

District commissioners were Governors in miniature, just as Governors were the king-in-parliament in miniature. 'In practice a young man of between twenty-five and thirty finds himself in sole charge of a district as large as several English counties, and in a position which partly resembles that of an emperor and partly that of a general servant,' said Sir Charles Eliot of East Africa. In the late nineteenth century they might take three weeks to reach their stations and once there took most of their decisions independently of Government House or the Secretariat. Long files of porters preceded them to their postings, carrying two or three tons of food, crockery, medicines and household goods which had to last for a whole tour. They began life with French canned delicacies but were two or three years later down to 'native chop', revictualling being mostly a matter of beverages. When Kenneth Bradley made a detour of two thousand miles by rail and boat to reach Fort Jameson in Northern Rhodesia from the capital in Livingstone, his superior on receiving him remarked: 'I can't think why you didn't walk. You'd have been here in half the time. You young men must be getting soft.'

Like 'Rusty' Buckle in Nigeria they sometimes refused promotion, pre-ferring to be lord of a remote domain than an official careerist. When Buckle received a telegram reading 'H.E. is so pleased with your report' he is said to have wired back: 'Glad H.E. pleased.' To a further telegram 'For pleased read displeased' he replied 'For glad read sorry'. He dealt with another Governor's rebuke on a steamer trip by diving overboard, and delayed his reappearance long enough to reduce His Excellency to tears of remorse.

Solitude was frequently the D.C.'s lot, though he might have a white trader and a doctor within some miles. Initially he could not have a wife: the Colonial Office would not at first pay wives' fares, and when they did insisted on short visits. He might derive his close knowledge of his district from an African concubine, who would be chosen with care by the local chief to ensure a good throughput of information in both directions. Some D.C.s contented themselves with pin-ups. When the D.C. came to consist of man and wife, the sense of isolation actually sometimes increased, but many couples have recorded their enjoyment of it. J. C. Cairns, who served with his wife in East Africa, remarked that 'Bush living, like olives, is an acquired taste.' Cullen Gouldsbury, in his diary of a D.C.'s year, wrote:

My wife has Africitis, it is an infectious mental disease, approximating to 'the hump' of more civilized lands . . . occasionally an attack commences with violent vituperation of shivering natives, succeeded by lethargy and coma. Sometimes one weeps – that is to say Beryl does; more often in my case at least one curses vigorously the Powers that Be . . . the station and all that appertains thereto . . . until frenzy gives place to sudden calm. [But he added] Africa holds in her bosom marvellous recuperative powers. I have slunk to bed at seven in the evening from sheer, utter and detestable boredom, to awake at dawn radiant with an energy just as wonderful in its way as the overnight depression.

Officials in solitary stations became peculiar at times. They talked to themselves, sometimes in Greek or Latin. Some had themselves carried even from their dining room to their verandah by their African servants. A policeman would carry their cigars and matches. Some collected native fetiches or masks, and even tried to play native games like *bao* (which no European is said ever to have mastered). Of one it was said he 'had a company of Negro warriors under his command, but unfortunately he had nobody wearing a white skin to talk to but himself, and he repeated aloud over and over again the collects and the Lord's prayer so that he should not forget his mother tongue.' Dinner time in West African bomas became later and later in the twentieth century. A visitor described to Robert Heussler, the historian of the service, how he had dined with a bachelor officer 'of the old school' who drove to his office in pony and trap and never ordered dinner till eleven at night, and then 'tested the consistency of the pounded yam' by tossing it into the revolving ceiling fan, and, if it failed to pass the test, ordered another dinner.

Africa offered obvious hobbies for the naturalists (the happiest and healthiest men): birds, butterflies, bugs, flowers, mosses; most colonies had journals to which such men made contributions of great interest, cited with respect in scientific papers. Some gardened happily; for others, Gouldsbury said, 'such trifles as the set of a garden walk or the insecurity of a log fence are matters of the remotest indifference. Indeed, when "X", a solitary D.C., first came to Malale he lived for three months in the dry season without either doors or windows. As there was, and still is, no fireplace in the house, he existed in an overcoat with a dressing-gown on top by way of evening dress . . .' It was a life which suited the celibate, misogynistic, even mystic temperament. Those who lacked it but were exiled to a remote area because of Government House disfavour had to find ways of not going crazy. There were stories of D.C.s running little wars of their own in the southern Sudan to the blissful ignorance of Khartoum, but most D.C.s had policing measures to keep them busy at times. Another story concerns an officer sent to the edge of the Sahara to rot, who decided to take up as a hobby the first thing his eyes lit on in his new post – it proved to be an article on the Crown Jewels in an old copy of the *Illustrated London News* that lay on the table in his residence. He wrote for all the books on the subject and studied it with fervour by correspondence; before long he was writing to the Tower of London – and then to Buckingham Palace. Kindly enquiries from that quarter which were passed through Government House produced a sudden change of heart and he found himself rushed back to the capital and dining with Their Excellencies regularly.

The recruit was first given a diet of files in a hot district office. 'No time was wasted introducing me to my duties,' wrote Sir Bryan Sharwood-Smith, who rose to be Governor of Northern Nigeria. 'On the first morning, at six o'clock precisely, I was taken round the section, and shown the police lines, the prison, the warders' lines, and the prison farm . . . after breakfast came office and court duties, and the workings of the local treasury . . .' Then the

District Officer got to know his district by spending up to two hundred and fifty days of the year touring under canvas. His job was to collect taxes and deal with African disputes, which, innocent of a thorough grounding of anthropology of the local tribes, he did according to his own notions of justice. He might have specialized duties, like stopping smuggling, checking endemic disease, enforcing quarantine (by which means sleeping sickness was largely eradicated), or constructing public works. D.C.s felt towards the improvement of their district the same feelings that the Governor had about the colony; they built roads (which decayed quickly), introduced latrines (which fell into disuse), and generally sought to deal with a situation of rapidly increasing population brought about by the suppression of tribal wars. This pacification was an occasional part of their duties quite late into the new century, for Africa has perhaps five thousand identifiable tribes, and in remote areas small wars and even slavery went on in the traditional way, the tribesmen having only a vague idea of the meaning of *Pax Britannica*.

Officials' living conditions naturally recalled those of the early Governors on the coast. One officer told Heussler of his quarters:

There were no refrigerators, so that food either came out of tins or was what one shot locally. There was little fruit excepting for a few weeks of the year . . . we found it difficult to grow vegetables . . . Everyone was suffering more or less from chronic malnutrition. Then there was the climate. West Africa was the worst, and we, of course, had no air conditioning and no fans; there was no electricity in outstations (where junior officers spent most of their time). Junior officers in addition spent much of their time touring . . . and so in living in tents or in grass-and-mud resthouses. There were few people who did not start their unsavoury dinners without having had an appetiser of whiskey followed by a gin or two. Then there was disease . . . The mortality or invalidity rate was high . . . I doubt if more than fifty per cent of the men appointed to the West African colonies continued for the twenty years necessary to get a pension.

The D.C. was the head of his own little community, partly British, partly native. Even the solitary received visitors and the residence became a home to them, whether they were other officials, missionaries, perambulating scientists or even undesirable traders. 'Government House is a long parallelogram of bamboo,' remarked a mining engineer with pity of a provincial boma in the Gold Coast of 1880. 'The roof is an intricate mass of branches, with a pitch so flat it admits every shower. Under it are built two separate and independent squares of wattle with plank floors lifted a foot or so from the ground; these dull and dismal holes serve as sleeping places. The rest of the interior goes by the name of a sitting room.' A little later, a Central African boma was described by Gouldsbury: 'A high gabled roof thatched with grass, a broad verandah in front with brick pillars, a balustrade of sawn timber . . . the rooms are all in a line, and all too small for a tropical climate . . . there is none of the cool spaciousness of the Indian government bungalows – never a room in the whole country where one can get the restful shadowy effect of distant corners and doorways leading into other spaces beyond . . .'

The Colonial Office lacked the traditions, of course, of India, and its public works employees had the imagination of Balham and Wandsworth. So in these mean little bungalows the life of Africa's new prefects was lived, humorously dealing with problems like 'how to get the baths into the bedroom through the dining room'. There were no *punkahs* pulled by servants outside the house, and nobody thought of local generators to supply electricity for bomas off the beaten track until late in the 1930s, though they existed elsewhere. The boma proper normally consisted of an office hut or building, a row of servants' huts or quarters, another row of 'police lines', and in the centre a square with a flagstaff.

The life of the D.C. and his wife was varied. It had, however, to be lived with the idea always in mind of setting an example to the natives. The officials had a clear idea of what this was, and on the whole disapproved of those who did not conform and so gave the white man a bad name – though it is far from clear that Africans had any such reactions, and indeed there is evidence that they simply loved those who clearly loved them – however bibulous, uxorious or venal. But to the new, post-Boer War breed, the standards were clear:

So long as a man *be* a man, in the true sense of the word, his influence both for good and evil will be tremendous. Personal courage, even though it include the vices of ruthlessness and cruelty, will carry a man further in his intercourse with natives than any amount of sympathetic insight for the simple reason that the native understands the former but has little experience of the latter. It is likely that the sportsman, the hunter of big game, will be more *en rapport* with natives than he who is crammed full of folk-lore and the unwritten customs of tribes.

British D.C.s worked through their chiefs and had their standards of chiefly character:

A chief after my own heart, a native gentleman and a shrewd lawgiver . . . a prosy old customer who likes nothing better than to arrive at my office in state early in the morning (of a mail-day for choice) and wrapping his voluminous draperies around him, to discuss all and sundry matters with true native disregard of time . . . Still, I have learned a lot from these seances – there is no other word for them. Last month, for example, it occurred to him that it would be a good idea if he were to institute a village-by-village visitation among his people on the lines of the district officer . . . I strongly approved . . . when he got back for a whole morning the old man and I hobnobbed in the office. His grip on things was astonishing. In one or two villages it seemed the birthrate was on the downgrade; goodness only knows how he had managed to calculate it out, but I found my office statistics bore him out triumphantly . . . in other villages it seemed there was a rebellious tendency among the younger women, who were less inclined than formerly to obey their liege lords. He seemed to think the only remedy lay in frequent application of corporal chastisement ... though unfortunately I could not agree with him ... officially.

Thirty years later, Sir Kenneth Bradley was describing the same life in *Once a District Officer* – the same teaching of natives through their own prefects, the natural chiefs who could even teach the bright, clear-eyed cheery young white master something – in whose dusky lineaments he sometimes recalled the twinkling smile of his old housemaster. By then it was clear what Major Furse wanted in colonial servants: 'men who had been prefects ... He looked neither for brilliance – men with firsts went into the I.C.S. [Indian Civil Service] anyway – nor for Blues, but he did want people who had learned at school the elements of leadership ... and who had at the university learned to be sympathetic to the other man's point of view and yet to be detached and self-reliant.' Many of the early recruits to the service had been junior officers in the Boer War.

Most of them [remarked Oliver Ransford of those recruited to Nyasaland, but it was true of all] came from 'good' county families; they obeyed a rigid code of manners; and were punctilious about shaving. They believed quite genuinely that those 'lesser breeds without the law' who had been gathered into the British fold were remarkably lucky ... The earliest residents pinned up pictures of the Great White Queen on the white-washed wall of their offices; then they set about taxing their subjects, gaoling those too poor to pay, and sitting in slightly uneasy judgment over the interminable lawsuits that, with the prohibition of internecine fighting, increasingly absorbed the energies of the Lake people ... The Bwanas moved about the shore unarmed, unguarded and with Olympian confidence in the superiority of all British institutions ...

The Colonial Service, of course, was incorruptible, like the Indian and home civil service; it did not take bribes as had happened in the unreformed days. That is not to say officials were never tempted, and indeed a few have left their reactions to temptation on record. In his first post in Rhodesia, Howard Williams was in his office when

an agreeable looking, well-dressed stranger was shown in by the messenger, who told him that he represented a mining company and was prepared to transfer shares worth £5,000 to his name in return for labour permits. 'My hand was resting on a pile of telegrams received that morning. The top one was from the High Commissioner's office authorizing me to issue the necessary permits ... with absolute ease I could have done it ... Then I saw red. I got up and yelled "clear out before I throw you out!" '

It was a passing élite, which changed as the specialists and experts made a team of what had been a one-man development job. Perhaps it lasted from 1890 to 1945; though the Colonial Office thought in 1945 that D.C.s would be needed as far into the future as eye could see. As Kenneth Bradley said, 'none of us doubted our right to be there ... Nobody thought it necessary to justify colonial rule, and there was no idea of long-term policy.' More and more, however, the career in the Secretariat seemed the ideal, as the capitals acquired amenities, and the run-up to Governor became largely a service matter, to be planned and schemed for. In the 1900s, D.C.s coolly told the Colonial Office they would not serve in the Secretariat. By 1930 all that had changed. Indeed, a higher-born Secretariat type had been evolved, and a lower type of regimental officer only fit to push office files or 'sort out' a neglected province. Of such a one, Sharwood Smith said that he 'was a bachelor and Resident of the old school. He would have been miserable and wholly out of place in a Secretariat, but he was the type of man toward whom most Nigerian hearts warmed . . . he would tour widely and without thought of discomfort . . .'

British social life developed, up-country and in the towns, repeating in the tropical colonies the history of South Africa. The informalities of the white man's genre were, however, replaced not by Victorian modes and conventions, but by the pretentiousness of middle-class suburbs aping upper-class life of the Edwardian age.

Africa [wrote one observer looking back from the 1950s] was probably never as rigid as India, nevertheless, the newcomer had to learn the code and abide by it. On arrival the mysteries of calling were first performed, especially in the smaller stations. You called on your seniors, while your equals and juniors called on you. This involved the whole paraphernalia of hats, gloves and stockings, not to mention visiting cards. The most senior officials in any town or *boma* kept a visitors' book on a table at the door which you duly signed; the more lowly had a silver or brass tray for the receipt of cards.

She records that great care was taken not to encounter the persons so called on; it was necessary to wait for an invitation to tea or dinner, or a sun-downer. 'Every dinner invitation meant black ties for the men and long skirts for the women . . . worn with a pair of large clumsy suede mosquito boots . . . The staff list had to be searched like the scriptures so that no mistake should be made in the order of precedence.' A good African head boy, like an Indian butler, knew what the order of precedence was in the station. 'If I sat my guests in the wrong order he would cast a reproving eye at me and ostentatiously serve them according to their rank.'

Colonies, however, varied in custom, and varied in their own social standing. There were three at the top. Kenya, because of its aristocratic white social settler element, was important – you could marry locally there, even into the nobility, and retire on the spot. Northern Nigeria, because of the British passion for local potentates, desert life and polo, had a special cachet (officers had to play polo). The Sudan, with its own service, for which sporting 'Blues' were a necessary qualification, held itself as equal to the Indian Civil Service. The Lake Bwanas of Nyasaland held themselves to be a race apart. After the 1920s Tanganyika had similar ideas and because it was responsible to the League of Nations and so separate from the ruck of colonies, it was a place for liberals – a Reform Club of the colonies. The other West African colonies rated lower, so Governor Burns was much gratified when he got his Order, Knight Commander of St Michael and St George (K.C.M.G.), as it showed that Gold Coast was moving up in the scale.

EDITORS AND POLITICIANS

The British community looked up to Government House as the local expression of British sovereignty and of the Court of St James – but disliked it as the agent of the Colonial Office. Wherever settlers went they vaguely felt that they took with them the 'natural rights' of Englishmen, which implied, at least by the time of the great Reform Bill in 1832, a free press, free speech, and parliamentary government of some sort. It was never long before they had grievances to express in Africa, and a policy to support – the latter being almost invariably a larger amount of land and a freer hand with the natives.

Politicians are *de natura* produced where there are unvoiced grievances and powerful interests needing leadership on which to build personal power. In the early colonies, however, most farmers were too busy to agitate; merchants and miners were too busy doing business; it was generally those who had failed in these occupations who turned to politics, or those who had positions in the towns with leisure to cultivate politics.

Newspapers were, in Africa, the nursery of politicians. The first political battle was to establish freedom of the press, because men who had failed to find employment elsewhere or needed to supplement their income turned to newspapers. Printing was, by then, a simple technology which anybody could learn, and the capital cost of a press and type was (even with transport) low; and at the same time local and London newspapers were making money from both circulation and advertisements in early nineteenth-century Britain. Thomas Pringle, who had brought out settlers but was himself precluded from farm labour by lameness, turned to newspaper production after he had tried schoolmastering. With him were John Fairbairn and George Grieg, a printer. Any editor and printer immediately came up against the fact that a colonial governor was an autocrat even if he had an appointed advisory council, and in the Cape secrecy and strict control over citizens' liberties were the tradition. Furthermore the stamp tax on paper was in force as at home. Pringle's *Commercial Advertiser* almost immediately ran into conflict with Lord Somerset, who was already angered beyond measure by the attacks made on him by posters and lampoons over the hardships of the 1820 settlers, and the prevailing administrative incompetence. Somerset deployed his censorship against Pringle's attempt to be critical, which would have given his paper interest, and therefore advertisements and circulation. Pringle carried his complaints to England and set the stage for Fairbairn who fought successfully for freedom of comment, along with Robert Godlington, owner of the *Grahamstown Journal*.

By 1830 the way was open for men to fight the establishment, or any other promising target, with print. The Government then found it had to help the press – or be attacked even more strongly. As Lieutenant-Governor Keate complained to a sympathetic but helpless Colonial Office: 'anyone was permitted and encouraged to write what he pleased in it, provided his article contained abuse of the government, or of individual government officers, sufficiently scurrilous and personal . . . there being in the Colony more ready writers in this, the easiest of all kinds of composition, than in any other. Newspapers do so well in opposition to the authorities that the authorities have either judiciously to bribe them or suffer attacks – even blackmail – to which they can never fully reply.' Once this principle was established in the colonies, official gazettes became of limited importance, and newspapers depended on news, circulation, advertising and exciting comment. Editors might suffer, but the press as such was bound by its own inner laws to work steadily for freedom for itself and for popular representation.

The process was slow in Africa because of limitations of education and readership, but it was sure – and it happened in the tropics as well as in the Cape and Natal. Newspapers, weekly or irregular at first, burgeoned, and the jobbing printshop with them. The profession of journalist was now established, and many who would have starved otherwise took to it. Among them were Ridley, described by Keate as 'an inflammatory stump orator' and D.D.Buchanan who, after penny-a-lining with other papers, leadered the first issue of his *Natal Witness* in 1846 with the words: 'Whilst it will be a constant aim to conduct discussions with the sole view of eliciting Truth, it will not be necessary to rush into contentious disputations' – which he promptly did. He immediately began pressing for 'free, enlightened British institutions' and declared 'if we have to cope with the whole Colonial Office . . . the *Witness* is prepared for the contest though the opposition were ten times as formidable.'

All that now was required for the emergence of the politicians intent on enlarging their power in a legislature and executive was a major public issue. This was provided by an ill-advised proposal by Whitehall in 1848 to dump a few convicts in South Africa, rather than carry them on to Australia, where the colonists, through their own legislatures, were becoming obstructive. There was an immense outcry, the newspapers gave it expression and amplification, and in Cape Town a boycott of the government was organized to deny the officials food and services. The army frustrated it; but Whitehall gave way – and the power to organize (and to use intimidation) for public purposes had been demonstrated. It became impossible to deny first the Cape and then Natal elective representative institutions, and with great gloom the Colonial Office submitted, only hoping that the colonist, having got a say in public affairs, would raise taxes and remove the burden of defence from the imperial exchequer.

Although Sir Garnet Wolseley, when Governor of Natal, complained that members of the legislature were men who had failed in every avenue of life and taken to politics as a last resource, leading colonial politicians proved to be experienced settlers of an origin and type that was reproduced from Molteno and Sprigg in the 1850s to Huggins, Welensky and Blundell in the 1950s. At seventeen, Charles Molteno went out to the Cape to be the local librarian, but finding the salary did not keep him alive, joined a commercial firm. He was successful first in the new wine business and then in wool; from the proceeds he bought an estate in Nelspruit, served with distinction in the 1846 Kaffir War with a burgher commando, and becoming a 'leader of opinion' was nominated to the Legislative Council, then elected. He seized the convict agitation to make his name, and went on to the problem of the recalcitrant native, strengthening his popularity by pushing through the Master and Servant Act, possibly to be seen as the foundation of apartheid. He attacked the salaries of officials, and jobbery by the British appointees to Government House and deprived the Governor of control of the burgher forces. A patriarch in private life, with ten children, a house open to all visitors, the tables littered with reviews from England and Scotland, he became the grand old man of the Colony, and its Prime Minister as he gradually forced Whitehall to concede cabinet government from 1865 onwards.

Settler parliaments and politics were leisurely, yet formal, based on Erskine May and Westminster punctilio and points of order. Both in Natal and at the Cape parliament only met for a few weeks at a time, and it sometimes took a member almost as long (on one shilling a day expenses) to reach the House over the still wretched roads and tracks. Elections were quickly over, the handful of voters having also to be collected and entertained; often there was no contest, though sometimes sloganizing. Parties and election agents scarcely existed until Hofmeyr began to organize in 1879 the Bond as a Dutch language group. Election meetings would consist of twenty voters in a thatched schoolroom listening in enigmatical silence to the candidate's address, then departing after dinner and drinks in equal taciturnity. Even when roads improved after 1880 it was hard to find a member for Kimberley because, as the *Cape Argus* noted, 'time is money in the fields'. In King William's Town the local folk were likewise found 'to be much richer in mercantile energy than political activity'. Though most members continued to be solid agriculturalists who spoke little in the House, parliament did provide a niche for more flamboyant characters willing to serve. When one member was found to be a bigamist the *Argus* said 'it ought to be a warning to colonists how they take up with adventurers'.

Cecil Rhodes and his millions helped Hofmeyr and his regimented

Dutch vote to modernize the Cape parliament in men and methods. Rhodes, reputed to have sneered 'who cares for honesty nowadays', offered members blocks of shares in the Chartered Company at par. Election expenses rose from £40 to £1,500, and the House was electrified as the old issues, which had turned on railway sidings, police stations and sheep scab, were illuminated by the purposefulness of imperialism. There was money and opportunity in a house in which Rhodes and Barney Barnato sat. The Bond, building its membership on skilled lobbying to get its constituents the public works they wanted, could now bargain for even more important issues of principle, notably the progressive raising of franchise qualifications against the coloured voter. This, to Rhodes, was a cheap price to pay for the golden vistas opening to his Progressive Party in the north. He offered the Cape a new vision, as well as unrelenting opposition to Colonial Office laggardliness and sentimentality. Out of the representative institutions that the settlers had produced, had sprung the man of destiny, who perfectly fitted their ideas, who led, bullied, jollied and dominated them, and who by-passed the rules of the game.

The fiasco of the Jameson Raid to seize the Transvaal cost Rhodes office, but not popularity. He lost, it was true, Hofmeyr and the Bond party. The old Anglo-Dutch Cape society, people like the Cronwrights and Merrimans, who had trusted him to work in a gradual way for a United States of South Africa that would give them the educated leadership, broke with him, and later broke up entirely. But the hero image is the natural one for a colonial society in Africa, and later 'the son of the boss', Jameson himself, took advantage of it to float to power, largely on trade union anger at Milner's introduction of Chinese labour to get the mines working again.

But Jameson came to power when power had already fallen from the Cape parliament, much as Blundell later failed to master the situation in Kenya. Suddenly the British wanted to think only about business, and Jameson gave them that urbane reassurance which a British electorate so frequently needs. He soothed their doubts, lamented the dullness of parliaments, would not let public affairs interfere with his golf and bridge, electioneered in an expensive motor-car, loathed the 'menagerie' of Groot Schuur entertaining, loved society nonetheless, and left the big decisions to others.

In tropical Africa newspapers were far slower in creating effective politics and politicians. 'One of the objects of this sheet,' editorialized the first issue of the *Bathurst Observer and West African Gazette*, in January 1833,

is to rectify the existing evils which parade and exist in nearly every institution and department under the present administration. For the last six years we have seen every institution and department tottering for want of common support . . . we have seen the hospital neglected; schools little cared for; government buildings out of repair; the police and convicts badly clad; streets and roads unmended and the colonial Church disregarded.

In 1892, the *Gold Coast Chronicle* ventured: 'Rumour is afloat that His Excellency Sir Brandforth Griffith will shortly be leaving these shores to enjoy a well-earned pension . . . he has worked very hard although some pessimists may be inclined to think that the results have not had much practical bearing on the material welfare of this country.' (He had a record tenure of office.)

Though the *New Era* in Freetown might promise to 'consult the welfare of the people', there were in fact no leaders to capitalize on the issues that the press raked up. A growl from Governor Macdonald in 1846 was enough to silence the *Dove*, even though it was printed by the missionaries. West African newspapers rose and fell, living briefly off advertisements for Holloway's Pills and mission society subventions. Nevertheless, a tradition of African journalism was planted, and it endured, even during the drought of high imperialism, when the flowery prose of Afro-English indignation merely produced laughter in the bomas. Journalism meant literacy, self-improvement, self-help, and out of these arose the black political philosophers, the Blydens and Caseley-Hayfords. The lesson of a free press and representative institutions in white Africa was not lost on them. Party organization, however, was more important than the press in making the black political leader a force that the British establishment had to reckon with. This was learned rather from Russia and Eastern Europe than from British democracy in Africa, where the settlers progressively destroyed what might have been a black liberal parliamentary tradition, beginning with the humble coloured voters who went at dawn to the polls in the Cape and helped to put a white man into parliament – no black candidate was even dreamed of.

8

WOMEN AND
DOMESTICITY

How women live, how they work, suffer and love, the conditions in which they serve and guide their menfolk, is the larger part of the social history of any society. Where women are reduced to chattels it becomes less possible to write social history. Political, military and economic history may be chronicles of men, inventions and ideas; legal and constitutional history impersonally documents institutional change; but social history may be said to be deeply feminine, directly and indirectly, for the best of reasons. It is possible to describe woman's place in tribal, or perhaps in ancient, society in an anthropological analysis. But unless women have the measure of freedom, literacy and personal choice accorded them in Western society, social history must be largely deductive, and even so, changes in fireplace design are a poor clue to changes in cuisine. The social history of the British in Africa is illuminated both by women's activities and reflections; that history sadly lacks, it may be added, the observations of the African women they lived with when deprived of the companionship of their country-women. Where British stalwarts explored, traded, ruled or hunted alone, the annals of their domestic arrangements soon pall. Accounts of escapades with animals or with natural hazards soon narrow into specialist studies. Social history is not adventure; it chronicles community life.

Social change is largely wrought by women working on technical innovation – and the Boers had little but family and dynastic chronicles till their women received the technology of the British. Englishwomen played, as we have seen, their role in settlement, trade and missionary endeavour to a varying but always substantial degree; in travel and even in exploration they played their distinctive part – as Samuel Baker said of his wife when success in finding Lake Albert had become a desperate throw: 'With the same self-sacrificing devotion that she had shown at every trial, she implored me not to think of any risks on her account but to push forward and discover the lake – that she had determined not to return until she herself had seen *M'wootan N'zige.*' Behind women's activity lay the texture of domestic life and experience which must now be sketched in their own words and impressions.

FIRST IMPRESSIONS

'. . . it is an unusual enterprise for an Englishwoman to visit the coast of Africa,' wrote Anna Falconbridge to a friend in 1791. This was certainly true. A number of ships' captains had brought their wives on trading ships to the Guinea Coast, and a few women had found themselves stranded by shipwreck, an experience they did not long survive. Mrs Falconbridge herself went to Africa because of a hasty marriage against the wishes of her family and friends; rather than endure their disapproval at home she resolved to go with her husband, who had official duties in the colony, 'even to the wilds of Africa . . . to meet such fate as awaits me . . .' The thought dampened her spirits.

She was, however, only the first of a long line of wives who braved African dangers in the course of duty, and reported their experiences to friends at home. Among them were women who went out married or unmarried as missionaries; the wives and daughters of those who settled in the more temperate zones, of officials and of soldiers; the travellers in sun-bonnets and skirts who showed that there was nowhere a Victorian lady would not go; the career women who followed later, ranging from nurses and governesses to farmers and traders, and finally fortune- and husband-hunters.

In West Africa Anna Falconbridge was the pioneer. She was perhaps happily unaware of just how ill-equipped she was to cope with the climate, but the social difficulties arose at once. On Bance Island her delicacy was offended by the islanders' curiosity, especially the scrutiny of dark-skinned women who transpired, to her embarrassment, to be mistresses of the English inhabitants. Thus she immediately encountered what was to become a fruitful theme in Englishwomen's experience in West Africa.

For the first few weeks she stayed aboard the cutter *Lapwing* in which she made the voyage out, because her husband, whose mission was to establish on behalf of the St George's Bay Company a new settlement for liberated slaves, preferred that to accepting hospitality on shore from men of 'diabolical sentiments' who supported the slave trade. The cutter was like a 'hog-trough'.

Conceive yourself pent up in a floating cage, without room to walk about, stand erect, or even lay at length; exposed to the inclemency of the weather, having your eyes and ears momently offended by acts of indecency and language too horrible to relate – add to this a complication of filth, the stench from which was continually assailing your nose, and then you will have a faint notion of the *Lapwing* cutter.

M

At last Anna was able to come ashore and pick out one of the best huts in the new settlement for her own residence. She had space, but little else: 'I had a kind of bedstead, not unlike a hospital cradle, erected in my hovel; but the want of a door was some inconvenience, and as no deal or other boards could be procured for the purpose, I made a country mat supply the place.' She was only the first Englishwoman to decide ' 'tis necessary to accommodate myself to whatever I meet with, there being few conveniences or accommodating things to be met with in this part of Africa.' The description fits the makeshift quarters many women were to meet when they ventured into Africa before settlement had developed.

Among the 'inconveniences' was a very high death rate. During the first nine or ten months of 1792, about three-quarters of the Europeans who went out that year died of fever. 'Musquettos are growing so troublesome, as to oblige us to keep continued smokes in and about the house,' wrote Anna plaintively to her friend, but this simple palliative failed to save her brother-in-law William or the master of the *Lapwing*. Eventually provisions ran low and the Falconbridges went home to report their first tour's progress.

Anna had seen Africa with a white woman's eyes, and concluded that 'if I had a little agreeable society, a few comforts, and could ensure the same good health I have hitherto enjoyed, I should not be against spending some of the years of my life in Africa; but wanting those sweeteners of life, I certainly wish to return to where they may be had.' She was the first to feel the magnetism which Africa was to exert upon so many British women, and which was ever to conflict with its hardships.

Forty years later there were still less than a hundred white people in Sierra Leone, of whom only thirteen were women, though Freetown never lacked one or two. In 1834 F. H. Rankin wrote:

The white men are chiefly bachelors. Of those who are married, all do not desire to expose their ladies to the chances of the climate, or the tedium of a small and dispersed community; but leaving them at home in Britain, live as bachelors ... During my continuance in Freetown, I never on any occasion had the happiness of meeting so many ladies as four, even at parties at Government-house; and one unmarried white lady only existed throughout Sierra Leone.

Even seventy years after this a similar situation obtained. Mary Gaunt asked a District Commissioner 'if he did not think of bringing out his wife. He looked at me a moment, seeking words to show his opinion of a woman who insisted upon going where he thought no white woman was needed. "My wife," he said, with emphasis that marked his surprise. "My wife? Why, my wife has such a delicate complexion that she has to wash her face always in distilled water".'

Very different was to be the environment of women in South Africa where, six years after Mrs Falconbridge arrived in Sierra Leone, Lady

Anne Barnard arrived in Cape Town. The things Anna lacked – pleasant society, comfort as the eighteenth century knew it, and good health – all awaited Lady Anne in a colony which had been settled by the Dutch and Huguenots for over a hundred years. As wife of the Secretary of the colony she was, in the absence of the Governor's wife, the first lady in Cape Town, taking precedence over the burghers' wives, with whom, however, she got on very well. '. . . Mr Barnard and I are very great favourites of the Dutch inhabitants. We are both very civil, and never despise anybody, which I can perceive has been one great error in some of the English.' Sarah Eaton, too, who arrived in 1818, was on visiting terms with local families, and found herself returning calls on 'the families of Twycross, Bailey, Menger, Christian, Schultz, Cadogan, Bergh, De Wet, des Escotais, Ross, Voget, Lowdem etc.' Their homes were spacious and often luxurious but she found that her eyes and nose suffered because of the shuttering off of light in order to keep out flies, dust and heat, 'by which means, the rooms have a faint close smell, increased by using much oil and turpentine on their furniture . . .'

During the first British occupation of the Cape, and the early years of the second, Englishwomen there were mainly the wives of soldiers or officials. It was not until 1820 that they began to arrive as settlers. A community then developed rapidly. They met with fewer hardships than ladies who went to West Africa, but they had the usual experience of women who helped pioneer new colonies. The voyage out was both dangerous and comfortless, especially as they spent most of their time below decks tending fractious children and cooking for the men. The reception camps at Algoa Bay, the journey inland to the locations by ox-wagon, and the prospect of building a home from a tent must have daunted many of the 659 women of the party of 3,736 original Albany settlers. Most of them were, however, educated to the job. They were farmers' or mechanics' wives, familiar with farm routines of the early nineteenth century; they were trained domestics who could also milk a cow, groom a horse, and even cut their own umbilical cord when giving birth without medical aid. In the settlement of Natal thirty years later, Robert Mann pointed out that

wives cannot too soon be aware that in all young hard-working, colonial communities, there is very little room for the display of drawing-room graces and accomplishments. The wife in Natal is either a 'help-meet' in the fullest and strongest sense of the term, or a hindrance and draw-back to her husband. The Colonial wife commonly needs to be, as well as companion and adviser, the instructor of children, the cook, baker, laundress, gardener, farming bailiff and often tailor. For these duties, solid and sterling qualities are required, rather than refinements and elegancies.

The British women who took part in the early settlement of Rhodesia in the 1890s and early 1900s, were somewhat removed from these do-it-yourself conditions, and in Etta Close's view Kenya was a country 'to which no man need hesitate to bring out a lady'.

By the 1840s, as British power began to creep inland through Africa from the Cape and the West Coast settlements, women's role for the next century emerged. It was threefold: pioneering with the men, who entered one new territory after another; maintaining houses and amenities in the growing coastal cities; and developing the sort of inland settlement life already being lived in Australia and New Zealand. Compared with these colonies, however, there were two differences. On the one hand, Africa provided a growing abundance of cheap domestic servants; on the other, there was the risk of encounter with the embattled border natives struggling against the stronger culture, faced not only with the political power of the rifle, but, after a time, with the psychological power of the crinoline and bustle.

Crinoline and bustle were going out of fashion by the time women began to take up residence in East Africa and Rhodesia. Annie Hore was an early visitor in the East; in 1877 her husband was appointed Scientific Officer of an expedition to Tanganyika to examine prospects for missionary and agricultural settlement. With her baby son she walked, or was carried in a modified bath-chair, to Lake Tanganyika, and found when she started up a home that missionary life afforded scope for 'every energy and accomplishment in all the various auxiliary work of house-building, social economy, conveyance, preservation and maintenance of people, goods and mails, and the problem of existence apart from the aids of civilization'.

The settlement of Mashonaland and Matabeleland involved pioneering, but, as in Kenya, the railways and the aids of technical advance followed hard on the heels of the pioneers. Women were not allowed to go up with the first column into Matabeleland, so the Marquise de la Panouse, who was by origin an English servant girl, disguised herself as a boy to accompany her husband. She was followed by Mother Patrick and her Dominican nursing sisters, whose services were needed in the military campaigns. Nurses Rose Blennerhassett and Lucy Sleeman were among the first white women in Mashonaland, arriving by steamer from Beira up the Pungwe River, and overland to Umtali where they set up a hospital. On their return home Rose records that 'in spite of all the joy of return, the warmth of home comfort, the pleasure of familiar ways, I cannot feel at all certain that either of us has looked her last on the Southern Cross.'

MISTRESS AND SERVANT

In Africa, as in India, the native servant was a major ingredient of social life. He was at once anthropological specimen, interpreter, comprador and general factotum for the white master. In colonies like Australia, servants had to be imported from the lower orders in England and Ireland, who very soon abandoned service to set up on their own account. The natural hazards of Africa could not have been overcome so quickly by Europeans without African servants, and white women would hardly have settled there in such numbers so early had it not been for local labour, nor would they so soon have begun to enjoy a standard of life higher than that of home. In 1929 Madeleine Alston recorded that 'South Africa, and perhaps Kenya, Nyasaland and Uganda are the only parts of the overseas empire where women do not grow old before their time with housework. Why? The answer is that, though they have enough domestic work to keep them occupied and healthy, the native servants are the making of them.' But it took time for this agreeable condition to become established.

Nevertheless, English servants could be found in South Africa, in ever decreasing numbers admittedly, throughout the nineteenth century. Some were brought out under the patronage of middle-class emigrants, others were forced into service when their fortunes were not realized. They presented problems in a country where social distinctions were drawn by colour rather than class. 'It is certainly demoralizing for English servants to come out to this country,' wrote Mrs Heckford in the 1880s.

They may begin fairly; but even serving under one whom they acknowledge as undeniably their social superior, their ideas of master and man are liable to become confused after a time . . . It is not easy to keep up the proper distance between master and servant when the very people he is called upon to bring coffee to whilst they sit on a visit to his master . . . are ready to drop into familiar conversation with him the next moment . . .

Joanna Gog, a faithful white servant of Helen Prichard, was dismissed, in spite of her good qualities, for forgetting 'her place'. Fortunately for her she did not need a reference for she married a wealthy trader. An effort was sometimes made by the lady of the house to maintain class distinction while recognizing that white servants needed in their turn to occupy a position above black servants. This was done by grading the work, the most menial chores being reserved to the natives. Even so, a good working arrangement was difficult to achieve as Mrs Alston found out. 'I tried two English "ladies", a mother and daughter, as cook and housemaid, giving them two coloured people to help them with the rough work. We never had less to eat, and the house was never kept so badly as under their regime, for there was too much "lady" and not enough cook and housemaid about them.' This pair told their employer that they had understood that they would only be called upon to supervise the blacks. This feeling led to the belief inherent in South African life now that the white should never be seen in a menial position, or do 'kaffir' work. Nevertheless, the use of English servants in senior positions survived into the 1920s.

As soon as she arrived the Englishwoman began to train Africans to service, as her husband trained them to field and artisan labour. Complaints of their unteachability and recalcitrance were frequently recorded, and there was competition among the well-to-do to engage whatever trained help, white or black, was available. Coloureds and Hottentots were preferred to Kaffirs in the Cape until the mission stations turned out a class of Africans, male and female, relatively accustomed to European ways of living, and specifically indoctrinated with the concept of service. In Sierra Leone, Mrs Melville found she needed eight or nine servants, usually male, to do the work of three or four at home. She compared the ministrations of servants at home with the 'mercenary attendance of persons of another race, whose habits and manners are as strangely dissimilar to what you have been accustomed, as is their personal appearance; and who cannot be expected to care whether you live or die; to whom, indeed, you are nothing, except in how far you can remunerate their services'.

An attempt to train native girls to be ladies' maids or housemaids was one of the first tasks of the Englishwoman in Africa, and one in which she had little success. In West Africa it was first necessary to learn pidgin in order to communicate. This seemed as absurd to Mrs Melville as having to use brogue when training an Irish skivvy, but she found there was no help for it – she had to speak 'country fashion'. Her first maid was a little girl of eight whom she taught to dust the dressing-table, sew, and fasten hooks and eyes, but the child soon tired of this and was sent back to school. The next trainee made better progress: 'I never saw a better disposed negro child than my little handmaiden; so thoughtfully attentive when I am ill, and so contented with her situation.' But such satisfaction rarely lasted, and soon the servant problem developed to its acute stage: 'However philanthropically disposed you may be toward the negro on taking up your residence in Sierra Leone, so soon as the first novelty wears off, the indolence, stupidity and want of tidiness (to say nothing of graver faults) of the only persons you have to depend upon as domestic servants, throw you into a sort of actual despair.' Sentiments like these were doomed to rise in female breasts for almost the entire colonial period. During that time, of course, the Englishwoman's standards and expectations developed from eighteenth-century gentility to twentieth-century obsession with cleanliness and hygiene, while the African servant, all the time coming from much the same village background, had to be trained in ever more complicated household equipment and procedures. The mistress therefore had to supervise and teach technology, as well as cooking and deportment.

At times the African servant was rather free and easy, as English servants had been in the seventeenth century. Mary Church, another early visitor to Sierra Leone, and one who appeared to resist the appeal of Africa, was horrified at the manners of a liberated slave who applied to her for a post. 'She seemed not to consider herself at all inferior, for she walked across the room and took possession of the sofa with the greatest composure in the world and insisted on shaking hands with me.' Miss Church had to teach her the all-important 'gradations of society', 'for I do not see any reason for shaking hands with an African servant more than an English one'. The form of address used by servants to their mistresses was 'missus' or 'ma' in West Africa, 'madam' in South Africa, and 'memsahib' in the neo-Indian East.

While there is abundant evidence that the early settlers' wives were endowed with the qualities recommended by Robert Mann, they soon felt that to be served was their right. The emigration agents had used this idea as a selling point to attract them out. But good servants were often hard to find, and one English farmer is reported to have had to set up a separate home for his wife in Cape Town, as it was impossible to find a competent staff to run the farmhouse. 'I have never seen an Englishwoman in the colony,' wrote George Nicholson, 'at all raised above the very poorest, who did not complain bitterly of the inconvenience she endured when living on a farm.' When domestic slavery was abolished the Boers trekked away from British jurisdiction; the Englishwoman could see the point.

Just as the men chose their labour from tribes displaying suitable qualities, so did the women. In West Africa the Kroos, for example, were favoured because they were honest and willing, though according to Lady Hodgson '*bouquet d'Afrique* is one of his possessions which it seems impossible for him to part with'. The Fingoes made good servants in the Cape; '. . . a light-hearted merry sort of people,' said Lucy Grey, but 'their odour is shocking.'

What servants lacked in quality they made up in quantity because wages were so low. At first, in Sierra Leone Africans were prepared to work without wages for the sake of the experience they gained of European ways, and for the access to schooling for themselves or their children. Here they were organized, as in Britain, under a confidential major-domo who in the early nineteenth century could earn about forty pounds a year; his staff received much less, and some nothing except their board. But as the market for servants expanded wages slowly rose.

General house servants were not too difficult to find or to train, but cooks and ladies' maids were always in short supply. A cook 'lightened the work much, and gave us some leisure,' said the pioneer nurses in Mashonaland. Mrs Wilkinson, the wife of a missionary, referred to servant girls as the plague of her life in her letters home, until she learnt to speak Zulu, when she found them suddenly 'quite willing, cheerful and obedient', but it was conceded that she had a 'way' with natives. Not all the ladies had. One exasperated missionary husband in Kenya who always seemed to have incapable servants asked his Indian boy the reason. He replied, 'When master he say plenty d—m and missie she say plenty pig, then we very good servants.' Missionaries could not take such advice literally, but the laity could and did, and largely master-servant relations were conducted for a century on a basis of abuse, sometimes, but not always, well intentioned. Mrs Wilkinson said that her untrained servants watched her as closely as animals, and seemed to know by instinct 'whom to obey and serve, and whom to disobey and despise'.

Working with 'boys' was an important part of the Englishwoman's life, and as the experience grew it produced a psychological lore and even literature of its own. On the whole, a half authoritarian, half indulgent attitude developed, and the African servant was at first an amusing subject for letters home. An essential quality of the Englishwoman was the ability to manage servants, and to teach them to respect her, even if they were, as Eve Bache found when she started a farm in Kenya, 'a pack of savages with not the slightest intention of obeying the orders of a woman unless it suits them'.

A typical nineteenth-century portrait of 'my boy' epitomizes the relationship:

Boxer is our general servant indoor and out. More out than in, because Boxer has a mousy-like odour pervading him, in common with his kind, for which he is not to blame, and by which it is easy to discover when he is trying to sneak noiselessly by the window on some private frolic of his own, leaving me and my household work to take care of ourselves ... Boxer may be aged anywhere between ten and twelve ... his wool set thick and close to his round bullet of a head; his eyeballs are, if such an anomaly can be, whiter than white, and his teeth almost glisten as his wide mouth opens for a broad grin ... Set Boxer down in a London thoroughfare with a white skin instead of a black one ... and none of our street gamins could hold a candle to him ... Not that he is ever impudent to us ... Boxing Boxer's ears was a trial to me, I confess, but I came to that at last, and repeated the dose when I once discovered its efficacy. I had been before but a poor thing in his estimation.

Through their contact with their servants, Englishwomen got to 'know' Africa. Through the door of the servants' quarters they had a glimpse at tribal family relationships, marriage ceremonies, witch-doctors, and pagan rites.

As the servant situation settled comfortably down in one colony after another, the Englishwoman could count on a smooth-running establishment, superior to anything available at home. With her retinue of servants, which was much larger in tropical than in southern Africa, she became a chatelaine who looked after their wants, involved herself in their family affairs, and always had a perfect excuse for interference, which was often kindly intended. Lady Barker was so worried about the way in which her boys' relatives fleeced them 'that I shall find it very difficult to stop any threepenny pieces out of their wages in future'. They tried to rid their servants of superstition as well as parasites. 'Take my present Nandi boy,' remarked Marguerite Mallett in Kenya. 'Again and again I have questioned him regarding the devil *Chemosit*, laughed at him, reasoned with him, all to no purpose. *Chemosit* is as real to him as if he had seen it ... and yet this boy lives among civilized people, a civilized life, but nothing will shake his belief.'

In the 1880s a servant was paid about one pound a month, clothes and food provided – about as much as an Irish skivvy in London; by 1910 it was a little more; in Nigeria you could have a staff of seven for £100 per year. One perplexity for the white woman was the native's extraordinary desire to return at intervals to his kraal or shamba. To want to break with the joys of service was quite incomprehensible to the Englishwoman, and is to her descendants. 'Often and often by the time you have taught them with infinite pains and trouble to do their work, they depart, and you have to begin all over again.' Lady Barker replaced three English servants with Zulus, whose only serious fault, she said, was 'an ineradicable tendency to return periodically to their kraals – not from family affection but the desire to get back to the savage life, freedom from clothes, and native beer'. Mrs Alston complained that she was being used as an unpaid teacher of cookery after two cooks she had trained left her farm to seek work in Cape Town 'where they can display their *crêpe de Chine* frocks and silk stockings'.

Nevertheless, as the Empire broke up, many English families were prepared to settle anywhere in the 'servant belt' rather than return home and toil unaided. The truth is that in a high standard of living, a house-servant is a very important ingredient, and affluence is a misused word when it does not assume this. Once accustomed to African servants, many white women cannot live without them.

HOMEMAKERS

The introduction of domesticity to Africa proceeded at various levels. For the wives and womenfolk of settlers the home was to be a more or less final resting-place, where children and grandchildren would be bred and reared. No ready-made homes awaited the earliest arrivals; they had to transform and extend the primitive huts that their men had erected. They soon formed a solid opinion against anything which detracted from the possession of land, wealth and the houses built with their own hands which could be passed on; hence the women as much as the men became expansionists, then imperialists. They did not live in wagons, or tents, or official residences or huts; they were in their homes to stay.

There are some records of the unpromising material with which they started. One of them, from the Cape, reads:

A mud and stone cabin, with bare rafters and thatch showing overhead, its one long room divided into three by rude canvas partitions, without a trace of paper on the walls, and with planks supported on the rafters doing duty as shelves. Outside a straw house did duty as an outhouse, stable, cowhouse or anything else; a conical straw hut with a hole in the top did duty as kitchen, and another small straw structure close to the sheep kraal served for a fowl house . . . there were no windows, only square holes in the wall with movable frames stretched over with calico fitted to them, and there was no chimney.

Lady Barker, settling in the more developed colony of Natal in the 1870s, had a worthier residence, though aesthetically not up to her aristocratic taste: '. . . architecture, so far as my observation extends, is almost at its lowest ebb in South Africa. I have hardly seen a single pretty building of any sort or kind since I arrived, although in these small houses it would be so easy to break, by gable and porch, the severe simplicity in which they are built. Whitewashed outer walls with a zinc roof are not uncommon; and the combination is a bald and hideous one, until kindly, luxuriant Nature has had time to step in and cover up man's ugly handiwork with her festoons of roses and passion-flower. Most of the houses have fortunately red-tiled roofs, which are not so ugly, and mine is among the number.'

Goatskin rugs and antimacassars went some way to brightening up stark surroundings. Bare walls were partially covered by guns, native spears, hunting trophies and pelts, stirrups and horse-brasses, warming-pans, pictures and china plaques.

Even with servants, the settler's wife often had to work harder than her husband. 'Dressmaking, mending, dusting, copying Samuel's sermons and studying the Dutch language or Grecian history left little time for recreation or social calls,' said Lucy Grey plaintively. Soap and candle-making, dairying and poultry-keeping, teaching children and supervising the servants kept the country housewife busy.

The homes of early settlers in the new more northerly colonies were almost as simple. Eve Bache, writing about Kenya in the 1920s, pointed out that the first settlers there put all their surplus cash into farm improvements rather than permanent houses, and lived in 'glorified native huts' until their land was really productive. Since they had no transport she did not leave her farm for two years, and spent a monotonous but busy time clearing the ground and planting coffee and maize. Her house 'consisted of bedroom, dressing-room and store, and a very comfortable abode it was, except, perhaps, when an extra heavy storm found out a weak place in the thatch. There were no windows because glass was unprocurable, so neat square openings in the walls took their place to let in light and air, and were covered with wire netting to keep out leopards. The doors were made of packing-case wood – the tables were the lids of cases on four short poles sunk into the earth floor. Locally made furniture being an appalling price, we contrived our own from odd boxes and bits of timber at first . . .'

Most officials, on the other hand, were provided with some sort of housing, though the furnishing and fitting still usually depended on their wives. The standard varied tremendously. The Melvilles were entertained in comfort, even opulence, in an official residence when they were first posted to Sierra Leone in the 1840s.

An avenue, bordered by beautiful trees and plants, brought us across a green lawn in front of a large white house, whose exterior of painted wooden boards, and casements of latticed trellis work, gave an idea of coolness and shade, which was not dispelled on entering its lofty and spacious apartments. The airy piazzas, entirely surrounding the house, are merely constructed of planks on the outside, those on the entrance floor being lighted and ventilated by jalousied windows, those on the upper floor by glass. Large folding doors, with Venetian-blind panels, lead through the inner wall of solid mason-work that separates these verandahs from the interior rooms, the darkness of which immediately struck me. But this want of light is connected with shutting out the fiery sun, and all the floors, with the exception of the drawing room, being uncovered, the general appearance is that of coolness.

Their own residence was in the upper part, which was considered healthier, of a two-storey building in Freetown. Later they moved outside the city into a large house designed to afford as much coolness as possible. 'In this there are nine large doors in one of the inner rooms, six in another, with two windows opening into a verandah, or piazza as it is frequently termed, and, none of these being shut during the day, a free current of air is always admitted.' Mrs Melville passed her day in a variety of domestic pursuits. She made marmalade, supervised the tending of cows and milch goats, riding-horses and poultry, sifted rice, and took care to keep her house clean and insect-free. 'Every drawer and wardrobe shelf has to be emptied and dusted out oftener than one would deem at all necessary in England. Heavy pieces of furniture against the walls have to be moved very often to prevent an accumulation of these spiders, with cockroaches and moths; the species of the latter we have here being of all other insects the most difficult to extirpate.'

The diaries, published and unpublished, of wives of officials record the simplicity of junior official accommodation. Jean Kennedy described a residence in Uganda in 1920 which consisted of three rooms in a row, of sundried bricks with a thatched roof and verandah, with cane furniture and iron beds; on one occasion a woman friend went out to the privy, failed to notice that the floor had been eaten overnight by white ants, and fell into the cesspit. A service wife in Nigeria recounted how she nearly wept when she saw the first house the Colonial Office had prepared for her and her husband in 1910 – two rooms with mud walls and a small verandah; however, one consolation was a contraption like a huge meat safe for dining in, to keep the insects out of their food.

Housekeeping was made easier as labour-saving devices were introduced. By the mid-nineteenth century a meat chopper, a small patent mangle and what the author euphemistically described as a washing-machine (a tub with a hand-operated dolly), were recommended by Robert Mann. At the same time enamelled crockery was being used instead of china ware, which was short-lived in the hands of servants. Ice boxes and ice-cream freezers, thermos flasks and sparklet syphons contributed to the comfort of home by the turn of the century.

No English household was complete without its domestic pets. Women as well as men were great tamers of African fauna for this purpose. At first English dogs did not survive long, especially in West Africa, even when the natives did not eat them; so animals like meerkats, serval cats and lion cubs were popular; baboons were common pets in the Cape (the Cronwrights had one called Adonis) and chimpanzees in West Africa; parrots, crested cranes and ostriches were common too; indeed, reminiscences suggest that almost any animal that was not too messy, dangerous or large, the English tried out as house pets.

SICKBED AND KITCHEN

Bad as the West African climate was for men, it was a greater barrier to white family settlement. Mary Kingsley observes that 'there is no other region in the world that can match West Africa for the steady kill, kill, kill that its malaria works on the white men who come under its influence. The man who will make West Africa pay will be the scientific man who gives us something more powerful against malaria than quinine'.

Mrs Melville first thought that the air of Sierra Leone 'possessed a sanatory influence, and that to the envy of those dwelling under less glowing skies might be ascribed the invention of all those appalling histories of the deadliness of its climate'. But she was soon undeceived. First she herself, then her young son took fever, as she described in a letter home:

Upon the very day that my last letter to you was ended, I was seized with country fever, which confined me to bed for twenty days, and I had scarcely gained strength enough to move from one room to another, when my little boy was taken ill of ague, from which most enfeebling malady he has suffered severely, poor child! But as he is now recovering, and I, although still weak and unfit for much exertion, have, at last, safely got over the *seasoning* fever, you have no reason to feel uneasy on our account.

Ill health became a recurring theme in her correspondence until it forced her to go home for good.

Such experiences coloured the Victorian view of the coast, where the British certainly had little wish to extend imperium into the interior; only the missionary families persevered. Even when Mary Gaunt visited the area in the early 1900s she found that Englishwomen who accompanied their husbands there were still regarded as heroines and martyrs, but she herself rejected the view that the climate was too much for women. However, in 1898 Harold Bindloss noticed that 'where it is dry and free from malaria, you may see Englishmen thrive and grow bronzed, broad-shouldered and wiry; but their wives and daughters almost invariably weaken and wither or drag out their lives in chronic listlessness.'

By contrast, the suitability of the Cape for the delicate of health and sex quickly became renowned. Before the opening of the Suez Canal, Cape

Town was the resort of Indian civil and military personnel and their ladies for recruiting their health between tours of duty. Lady Duff Gordon, a noted and literate traveller, describing herself as a *poitrinaire*, visited the Cape for health reasons, and noted in her letters home the beneficial effects she felt from the bracing air outside the city. Natal, 'notwithstanding its almost tropical position on the earth, and its frequent vicissitude of temperature . . . is remarkably free from the more grave forms of disease,' wrote Robert Mann.

Among minor domestic duties was the collection and processing of herbs for medicines. Besides those used in Britain – rhubarb pill and powder, calomel, tartar emetic, laudanum and quinine, which settlers were enjoined to bring out with them – native herbal remedies were tested and occasionally adopted. Marina King, reminiscing after a long residence in southern Africa, remembers as a child helping her mother to search in aun-bear holes for the male ferns used to alleviate stomach upsets; 'for fever we collected willow leaves, which when boiled made a dreaded bitter medicine rather like quinine; for making poultices we used the leaves of the blue gum tree, and for dysentery . . . the wild geranium root.'

'Let no-one go to the colonies without some idea of treating simple complaints,' warned Miss Lowndes, who went to South Africa in the 1890s as a governess. 'The nearest doctor was 40 miles off, and as visits are charged according to distance, that would cost £5 each.'

The white woman had also to tend her servants, as much to protect her own family as for altruistic reasons. 'Miss R and I have not had our clothes off for ten nights keeping little Pulu alive,' wrote Mrs Wilkinson. 'She would have died without Liebig's extract of meat.' Mrs Bache in Kenya claims to have saved the lives of several black babies by the medicinal use of ipecacuanha wine, without which, she thought, no properly constituted household should be.

Mortality among white children was naturally high, both in tropical and temperate regions, but the robust view of the time that families would survive prevailed. Mrs Hore took her small son with her on the long journey from the coast to Lake Tanganyika. He fell ill on the way, and 'we were indeed in bad case and I think poor Jack must have perished, but for the ample supplies of food and medicine we carried, and the various conveniences afforded by the organization of our system.' It was obviously necessary for the Victorian woman pioneer or settler to know her midwifery, as trained medical aid was rarely available, but black female servants were also called in to assist at deliveries.

For women on long treks with their husbands, or living alone in the early settlements or on remote farms, it was quite usual to have accouchement sets, which were no doubt a revelation to any native woman called in to assist at the birth of a Briton. One popular brand claimed that 'The risk of puerperal septicaemia is reduced to a minimum by using Hartmann's complete guinea outfit'. In towns and cities women were content with the services of coloured midwives and nurses, with or without the assistance of a doctor, whose fee in Cape Town was £2 in 1823 and £5 in 1830. Melina Rorke recalled that when her first baby was born she had too much milk and offered the surplus to a black baby, but her coloured attendant was horrified at the idea and scoured the town till she found a needy white one.

Diet in Africa varied from the coast inwards according to the availability of fresh food, and the supply of imported foods. The development of food preservation methods throughout the nineteenth century ensured that much European food could be widely distributed. British residents in Africa would not eat local dishes, as those in India did, apart from the aromatic stews of the West Coast. Generally the basis of their diet was meat where game was plentiful – almost everywhere except West Africa – and local fruit and vegetables; everything else had either to be introduced and grown, or imported in can and keg. Mrs Melville's market report is typical for her part of the continent:

Fruit is cheap and abundant. Eight to a dozen fine oranges for a penny. Pine-apples for ½d. to 1d. each. The vegetables are really excellent. All native productions are cheap, but whatever comes from England is proportionately dear . . . African mutton is about the size of the lamb you have at home, usually lean and dry, and 6d. or 7d. a lb, though a sheep may be had for two dollars. Geese and ducks are very large, common fowls remarkably small, fish is plentiful and good. Bread is high-priced and so bad that we use English biscuit instead. A wine-glassful of milk costs a penny and there is no such thing as cream in the country. Butter is brought from America, is excessively salt and melts into oil on the cask being opened. Bountiful as the climate is it does not afford one half of the common articles of food which one is accustomed to at home.

Gradually the housewife learned to come to terms with the dietary situation. She kept a garden for herbs and fresh vegetables, including many European varieties, some of which thrived in the unaccustomed climate. She discovered how to tenderize meat by wrapping it in pawpaw leaves, and used spices to enliven insipid dishes. She also learned how to protect food from the ravages of insects. 'I find, to my cordial satisfaction,' wrote Mrs Melville, 'that there is a way of keeping ants from sugar and sweet things, by placing the prohibited article upon a plate of lime-juice, all acids being carefully eschewed by the *formicae* in general. Sperm-oil, also, these insects shun.'

For the wealthy, meals were lush: 'You sit down to a table set forth with highly seasoned dishes (smoking under covers) of meat, fish, fowl and vegetables; pickles and sauces are handed round as at dinner, and the wine decanter stands vis-à-vis to the water jug; claret and ale are in readiness, being merely cooling in the shade; tea, coffee or chocolate follow, with bread, biscuit, boiled eggs, fruit and sweetmeats . . .' And this was only breakfast!

Miss Lowndes, however, endured a plain and monotonous diet in the up-country Cape household where she was employed as a governess. Midday dinner consisted of mutton, the only meat available, with rice and occasionally mealies or potatoes, and the cold leftovers were served for evening tea. Puddings were rare, and fruit was scarce. To cite an extreme example of dietary variation, Mary Kingsley and her Fan porters once ate a viper for supper.

FASHIONS

Writers like Bird, Mann and Irons who encouraged emigration to the new South African colonies were careful to include in their books a list of effects that intending settlers should bring out with them. The list naturally included clothing, and since they were usually compiled by men (Mann in fact got a lady to write his section on hints to wives), women readers often found themselves grossly misled. One lady even brought out a fur jacket and muff, which she found not only useless, but 'a great anxiety to me, on account of the swarms of fish-tail moths . . .' In fact, she moaned: 'The only things I can venture to recommend as necessaries, are the things which no one advised me to bring . . . One was a light waterproof Ulster . . .'

When the ladies had gained some experience of colonial life they were able to give newcomers more reliable advice. 'The colonial rule for clothing,' stated the governess Miss Lowndes, 'is only to wear thin garments such as are right for the middle of the day, wearing an extra wrap if chilly.'

In his *The Colony of Natal*, published in 1859, Mann intimated that ready-made clothing suitable for the climate was abundant locally, but in the very early days this was not the case, so when settlers' clothes wore out, they had to be hand made. The first sewing-machines are recorded in Cape Town in 1860 and in Pietermaritzburg in 1863, and some years later a ship wrecked on the Natal Coast threw up seven sewing-machines which were sold by auction. There was plenty of work for dressmakers in the Cape in the 1850s, and although wages were low, they compared favourably with London rates, and hours were shorter. Emma Rutherfoord spoke of a visit to the dressmaker as a great event in her fashion-conscious life. A Victorian dress with its boning, padding and flounces was a work of art, and the invention of paper patterns enabled South Africans to import the latest fashions from London and Paris and run them up locally. A wide variety of materials came from the East as well as from Europe. These included silk muslins, striped Orleans, printed corahs and surahs, sarsnet and cassimere. More serviceable fabrics were preferred in the country districts, where the dusty paths made skirts filthy and laundering methods were still primitive. One lady was disconcerted at the loss of her store of cotton gowns. 'For a day or two each gown in turn looked charming; then came a flounce or bordering of bright red earth on the lower skirt . . . still I felt no uneasiness. What are gowns for if not to be washed?' But they were all destroyed in the native washing process and she resorted to 'some old yachting dresses of ticking', and advised others to stick to serge, tussores and foulard. Tulle, frilling, and other 'pretty adjuncts' to Victorian attire she wrote off as useless. Washing was done by natives in a river or stream. A good substitute for ironing was 'to fold smoothly all the house linen and plain garments, pack them in a flat bundle, wrap it up tightly and fasten it securely. The package was then laid on the floor, and on it a native man danced to the music of his own song, with the result that the contents became as smooth as if ironed.'

Trousers for women were almost unheard of in the nineteenth century, but Georgina Lister, the wife of a forestry officer in South Africa, remembers her horror when the daughter of the Governor, Sir Humphry Barkly, lifted her habit to mount her horse and disclosed a pair of breeches. Mary Kingsley took an old pair of her brother's with her on her exploration of the Ogowe River in West Africa, but she does not appear to have worn them. In fact, she was grateful for the protecting folds of her thick skirt when she fell into a spiked animal trap, and expressed thanks that she had not taken the advice of friends who had pressed her to wear masculine garments. Bloomer suits enjoyed a brief vogue in the 1890s, but despite their obvious convenience on trek never attained popularity.

Shoes were always difficult to get. Mrs Melville, disappointed when successive ships failed to bring any, had to make shoes for her little son from the uppers of her own.

In the temperate zones, and in high altitudes in equatorial regions, ladies were reminded that the evenings might be cool. Laura Jackson, sister of the Governor of Uganda, paid him a visit in 1915 and found that 'Wraps are nearly always required while sitting in the garden after six o'clock, light blanket coats and golf jerseys being always useful. Sometimes a good thick one is required when motoring late. The nights at Entebbe are rarely oppressively hot, not like they are in Mombasa and one generally required a blanket.' Miss Lowndes also emphasized this, and Constance Larymore suggested a light cloth coat for Nigerian evenings.

Sunbonnets were the usual head-dress of southern settlers, but for the ladies of West, Central and East Africa the pith helmet, or terai, was de rigueur.

Lady Cranworth's recommended outfit for the Kenya settler's wife in 1910 included 'plenty of muslin and cotton frocks, two khaki-coloured coats and skirts, a divided skirt, a thin riding habit for the races, and riding boots, tweed suits, a large double terai helmet, and two or three crepe de chine evening dresses, with a few smart hats to wear after 4 p.m.'

Social Life

Lady Anne Barnard, first lady of the Cape of Good Hope, 1796–1802, whose writings described early Cape social life. Engraving from a miniature by Cosway.

Early social life at the Cape was heavily military and official. Its formality and suffocating boredom is here caught by Sir Charles D'Oyly in his Personages at the Cape.

The Sunday concert was an amenity of British life in Africa , wherever a military band could be provided. The Sunday Concert at Cape Town, by T. W. Bowler, an early Victorian water-colorist.

The Victorian colonials tried to repeat in their African homes the cosiness of the well-upholstered interior in Britain. Mrs Annabella Harkness's sitting room at Fort Murray.

At the Club in Port Elizabeth in 1867.

Playing tennis in full Victorian dress must have been extremely difficult, but the
game nevertheless flourished in the African heat. Tennis courts at Simonstown in 1885.

Hunting the local substitute for the fox was started at the Cape in the early nineteenth century, and was a permanent British institution along with horse-racing in Africa. The Salisbury meet in 1902.

Polo was imported into Africa from India, as the sport of cavalry regiments and local chiefs or emirs with stables outside the tse-tse belt. A match at Maseru, Basutoland; a similar scene could have been sketched in Northern Nigeria by 1898.

MARRYING AND GROWING UP

Many of the 1820 settlers came out in family groups, so there was some scope for their children to intermarry; nevertheless there was an inevitable shortage of women for many years. Relations between Boers and British at the Cape were a mixture of warmth and hostility. For Englishwomen it meant that there were from the start white women to meet, occasionally to lean on and learn from, frequently to dislike. The Boer girls were often rivals. Many Englishmen who failed to make their fortunes as they hoped, married Boer ladies with land and cattle, as a last resort, and felt they were conferring an honour. When an English lady married a Boer it was usually a case for adverse comment, but Bird wrote in 1823:

> Only one British lady has as yet honoured a Cape-Dutch gentleman with her hand. From his European and professional education, and the consequence and habits of his family, attached to English manners, customs and society, he can hardly be considered in any other light but that of an Englishman. Very frequent marriages take place between English gentlemen and Cape ladies.

Mrs Heckford employed a gentleman in low water, who became the butt of other white artisans '. . . after his many struggles he had quite made up his mind to the advisability of marrying a rich Boeress if he could; he told me so, in fact, more than once, candidly admitting that all he should absolutely require, money, youth and beauty, he should like if they could be got . . .' To this end he became a tutor in a Boer family.

There was a constant demand for wives and governesses. Even the plainest girls were courted. Walter Derham, visiting the Cape in the 1870s, described fellow guests in Rathfelder's Hotel, among whom was a girl who 'being the only young lady here, carries off the palm of beauty; but she has a large nose and rather a heavy figure, and has about five stock pieces for the piano, which she plays in succession like a street organ'.

The Female Middle Class Emigration Society was founded in London in 1862 by Maria Rye, who was advised to 'teach your protégées to emigrate; send them where the men want wives, the mothers want governesses, where the shopkeepers, the schools and the sick will thoroughly appreciate your exertions and heartily welcome your women'. There were agents of the Society in the Cape and Natal who helped sponsored immigrants to find suitable posts. There was a rapid turnover of governesses as those with any pretensions to beauty were snapped up as wives. The nursing profession also provided wives for many early residents and continued to do so throughout the British occupation. Nurse Welby, who worked in Umtali with sisters Blennerhasset and Sleeman married Dr Lichfield, the medical officer, in a simple but dignified ceremony:

> The marriage took place at four in the afternoon in a hut which we had draped with blue and white limbo for the occasion. Mr Sewell officiated; the

Resident Magistrate gave the bride away. Dr Lichfield looked quite smart in a new Karkee suit, and Mrs Lichfield extremely nice in a white serge uniform frock . . . After the ceremony the party adjourned to another hut and partook of tea in tin mugs . . . Then the Doctor and his bride walked across to the township, where he had put up a few picturesque huts, which Mrs Lichfield decorated very prettily.

Georgina Lister's sister, who married before her, in the 1880s, had seventy-two guests at her expensive wedding breakfast of turkey, chicken, ham, fruit and jellies. Her dress cost £22 – 'an unheard of price for us in those days'. Georgina herself was privately engaged for some time before her fiancé's salary was large enough to support her and a household boasting an English gardener, a French groom and cook, and later a French nursery-maid.

Babies were frequently placed under the care of native servants, girls or young boys, but they had to be watched as Lady Barker found when she caught her nurse boy 'stuffing a half-fledged bird into baby's mouth "to make the little chieftain brave".' In early Umtali, it was reported that baboons were trained as baby-minders in preference to Africans.

There were schools in the main towns of South Africa from an early date. Thomas Pringle opened a private academy in Cape Town, much welcomed by English families, in the early 1820s. Outside the towns, education was in the hands of mothers, but it was widely agreed that children learned little until a governess arrived or a school was opened. Emigrants bound for Natal were advised to bring school books for their children. A Superintendent of Education was appointed in that Colony in 1859, and both primary and high schools were opened. Itinerant teachers toured the remote districts holding brief sessions for isolated groups. There were also private schools, some only short-lived, run by individuals or missionary societies. These were often preferred to Government schools which some thought 'rough'.

In East and Central Africa it was usual to send children home after the age of six or so to be educated in England, but Joyce Boyd in Tanganyika early in the twentieth century decided that as the climate on her farm was so good her children could stay out all the year round. She and her husband taught them until they were old enough to board in a convent in Nairobi.

In the early nineteenth century the English arriving in the Cape thought it natural to learn Dutch, as it was essential on trek, and only unnecessary in the towns. Emma Rutherfoord took lessons as a matter of course in 1852. The Taal, however, was considered to be a limited language, 'quaint' like the Boers themselves, unsuited to the making of any but general statements, and unbacked by any 'great literature'. Mrs Alston thought it a positive hindrance to education: 'The South African child is, I consider, two years, if not more, behind the English child of the same age in general knowledge of nature and literature and history and geography – that is, *in culture* . . . it is this bilingualism that keeps the South African child back . . .'

Outside school, children could often find much to amuse and interest them. Barbara Buchanan, writing of early Natal, said that children had to make their own amusements. 'Balls, tops, tin soldiers, inartistic dolls, and Noah's arks with grotesquely unnatural inhabitants were practically all the toys manufactured, and, as we had no money for these toys we did without them and never missed them.' Instead, she and her brothers fashioned wagons and oxen from clay, did carpentry in their play-room which had a bench and tool chest, climbed trees and played 'tom boy' games like mock battles between Zulus and whites. They were encouraged by their parents to read – Livingstone's travels was a favourite book – and to ride, swim and shoot, even the girls, though public opinion was generally against girls doing the latter. She and one or two little girl companions rode to school on the back of an old mare led by a servant, while her brothers rode on oxen.

Because of the exigencies of settler life, children were sometimes called upon to perform dangerous tasks. Barbara Buchanan's brother once carried £300 for four hundred miles when there was no postal service. However, as Georgina Lister recorded, 'There was never anything to fear in those days . . .' Marina King had to help with the chores – candlemaking for example: 'We melted [the fat] down in a great cauldron; then it was purified and run into moulds. That was mother's job. I had the wicks to make, by plaiting together rags which were put in position in the moulds before the fat set hard . . . For hours I used to sit in the big kitchen, a heap of rags on the floor beside me and very few wicks completed on the table. I hated candlemaking days.' When it was not candles, it was soap, or something else. Georgina was given the daily job of cutting sandwiches for her brothers to take to school. She helped to make beds and tidy the house, and cut out her own patterns for suits and dresses for her younger siblings.

AMUSING ONESELF

The Englishwoman lacked the close-knit web of family relationships of the Boers – those that she had, she left behind in the mother country. The English therefore had to improvise their own social gatherings, from which cohesions and above all marriage and the founding of families could come. The Victorians carried to Africa their ability to amuse themselves at home. From picnics and walking tours to horse races and *conversaziones*, they transplanted home life. Croquet, archery and badminton came out successively. There are endless accounts of impromptu races, put on for holidays and to amuse troops, the evening often ending with bonfires, dances and songs 'comic and sentimental'. Mrs Cronwright, a relative of Olive Schreiner, was one of the many ladies at the Cape and in Durban who held dancing classes to instruct young ladies in the polka, waltz, mazurka and quadrille, as the older dances fell out of favour; this proved useful when Prince Alfred visited the Cape.

The bazaar to raise funds was another feature of small-town life. Lady Barker described one in Pietermaritzburg.

The things provided were selected with a view to the wants of a community that has not a large margin for luxuries, and although they were very pretty things there was a strong element of practical usefulness in everything. It must have been a perfect carnival for the little ones: such blowing of whistles and trumpets and tossing of gay balls in the air was to be seen all around. Little girls walked about hugging newly acquired dolls, whilst on every side you heard boys comparing notes on the prices of cricket bats . . .

In the towns, a decorous middle-class dullness soon asserted itself. 'Last night we gave what Frederic calls a tea fight,' wrote Emma Rutherfoord from genteel Cape Town on her social doings, 'and you cannot think what a pretty thing it was . . . At 7½ we had tea in the dining room, Ellen took the coffee, I the tea vis-à-vis; in the centre was a trifle, two very elegant dishes of fruit, peaches and grapes . . . These are the sort of things I pride myself in displaying good taste and Mr B[eaumont] tells me my arrangements are very elegant.' Visits, tea-parties, flower arrangement, the library, church, the newspaper, the mail steamer, and seasonal festivities made up the tenor of female life far removed from that of the women in the north, where, nevertheless, a distinct pattern of social behaviour was forming, as a pseudonymous writer from Uganda described in 1909:

I am well content to leave Society alone to its own devices, which here, in this remote townlet of Central Africa, follows with amusing fidelity the lines of Society at home. The microscopic Society of Entebbe (I am told there are about 500 English there) divides itself up into sets, dresses and dines, and, as far as the capabilities of the place allow, afflicts itself with all the conventionalities of Europe, which, to my mind, is a most unreasonable mode of life for the tropics, where, separated from all our home associates, denied such amusement as civilization affords, and living in a climate which most people denounce as unhealthy, we are surely entitled to such compensation as can be found in freedom from conventionality, and a general relaxing of those bonds of etiquette which are indispensable at home.

In the south there were balls, and the means for young girls to come out on the marriage market. Marina King records that at her first ball the dress she had made was too daring for her father's taste; she therefore presented herself to him in her underdress of white with a few ribbons added – and after he had approved its simplicity put the real dress on. Miss Rutherfoord noted that 'Wynberg is a terribly flirting, gossiping village. There are a number of gentlemen who hire and lend horses to the ladies and then go out in parties of eight or ten. There are a great number of idle young ladies and

gentlemen who have nothing better to do than amuse one another ...'
Melina Rorke was courted in 1885 in a teashop, induced to elope, and got
married at fourteen.

Pure romance of the Victorian sort was for the colonial upper class;
elsewhere Victorian rigour showed itself. In King Williamstown by 1850
there was an opera house and assembly room, a place of gaiety where the
troops were quartered and to which local wives repaired eagerly. Lucy
Grey attributed their infidelity to their husbands' neglect.

WOMEN ON THEIR OWN

But there were other fields for women than domesticity, and for a hundred
years Africa beckoned the unconventional and strong-minded woman who
did not fit into male-dominated Victorian family life. One such was Sarah
Heckford, who went out to the Transvaal in the 1870s, a widow with a
limp and a bank balance, who first acted as a governess, then took over a
farm, and finally set up with her own wagon and team to trade with
African tribes and Boer farmers, exchanging consumer goods like cloth
and tools for foodstuffs and pelts for resale in the towns. She lost her
little business when the Gladstone government abandoned the Transvaal.
Other examples were two women diggers, the Misses Russell, working a
paying claim in the Spitzkop fields during the gold rush. The so-called
Lady Avonmore followed the Empress Eugenie's entourage to the Prince
Imperial's grave in Zululand in an endeavour to report the pilgrimage for
the British press. Marguerite Mallet traded and hunted game among the
Masai in 1912, and the famed Dr James Barry, who introduced many
medical reforms in Cape Town between 1816 and 1825, was discovered
after death to be a woman. The ichthyological and anthropological studies
of Mary Kingsley in West Africa are widely known, but few will have
heard of Miss Gehrts who accompanied Major Schomburgk, FRGS, on
one of his filming expeditions to Togoland before the First World War, and
played the lead in such epics as *The White Goddess of the Wangora* and *The
Outlaw of the Sudu Mountains*.

Nursing drew more women to Africa, as to all the colonies, than any
other profession. By the time the British reoccupied the Cape in 1806,
some nursing services had already been set up by the Dutch, who had, for
example, appointed the first official midwife in 1687. The towns which
grew up in the Eastern Cape after 1820 needed hospitals as they needed
schools, and the Kaffir Wars provided plenty of patients, who were nursed
by military orderlies helped out by their wives. Successive wars in Zululand
and the Transvaal created a demand for trained nurses, which Miss Rye
was able in part to fill by the 1890s through her emigration scheme. The
Boer War brought out nurses in large numbers, many of whom stayed on
and settled. Miss Rye also helped to recruit women trained as farmers

and gardeners, shorthand writers and typists, governesses, dressmakers, shop assistants, and housekeepers for schools, hotels and boarding houses.

By the end of the Edwardian era, the professional woman had arrived. The 'mere wife' was beginning to be superseded. 'Where, before ... we dosed, and bandaged and diagnosed with anxious solicitude, and often remarkable success,' wrote a contributor to *Corona*, 'there are now baby clinics, Red Cross classes, St John workers ... trained and certificated Community Development workers ... – the "mem-sahib" is out of work.' She felt, however, that such specialization had reduced the sympathy and rapport of the earlier days.

NEW ATTITUDES

The arrival of white women in growing numbers in both tropical and temperate Africa, as the result of medical advance and economic development, produced new sexual attitudes. Hitherto the white women, because of her scarcity, had been, like technology, a component of white prestige. But more white women meant their accessibility to black men, who in turn were becoming educated. Assaults on white women in the streets of towns in Natal and the Cape began to cause concern, and people up-country noted with pride that it did not happen there. The reason was that the cultural gulf remained wide. By 1875 it was remarked that every white woman in South Africa should have a revolver and know how to use it – as a protection against black men; elsewhere women generally needed arms only against wild animals.

Even in West Africa, after so long a co-existence between the races, the marriage of a white girl to a black man was a stigma. One traveller, a mining engineer returning to the coast from leave in 1918, recorded sadly, 'We had as passenger, the only lady one, a young girl who seemed highly respectable, and who had kept much aloof. What was our horror to find as we ran up the Gambia, that she was coming out to marry a "Prince", really a shopkeeper in the Gambia, a negro she had met at home.' Mary Gaunt mentioned in 1912 that there were about half a dozen white women in Bathurst, including one who had ostracized herself by marrying a black man. She noted that 'even the missionaries who preach that the black man is a brother decline emphatically to receive him as a brother-in-law. That there should be any mingling of the races is unthinkable ... tall, stalwart, handsome as is many a negro, no white woman may take a black man for her husband and be respected by her own people.'

But since the white wives in West Africa could not have their children with them – or at least not after the age of about six – the official and commercial family with one home in Britain and another in Africa, with the wife shuttling to and fro in school holidays, or in alternate years, came into existence. This meant that the white husband often had a black mistress while his wife was at home with the children. Such hypocrisy was not lost on the Africans. As the entire white family eventually retired to Britain it did not matter, at least until black women could resent it as much as black men.

Where white people settled, however, there was the problem of sons and daughters. At first the white woman could be kept as a race apart. A turning point came with the arrival in South Africa during the war of 1899–1902 of loose English and European women who came to amuse and prey on the troops. White prostitution, though not hitherto unknown, now worried the authorities, because white womanhood was being brought into contempt in the estimation of native or coloured males who began to see that white women were attainable. At first it was a subject for cautioning: girls who marry black men, it was said, 'doom themselves to a life that no-one without knowledge of Africa can begin to picture'. One Kenyan author, without being explicit, told of a girl 'found by a military expedition living in an African village among her husband's black wives in a state, for a white woman, of the utmost misery and degradation'.

While the polygamous African lived in a hut and the Christian white girl in a house, the enormity of the misalliance was clear enough. But the mission of Western civilization, in which white women played such a part, was – in theory – to close that gap by Christianity, detribalization and economic development: the black man's home was to approximate to the white man's, and his wife was to have the rights, education and domestic conditioning of the white housewife. By 1900 people began to hope it would be a much harder job, and preferably an impossible one. Even in South Africa, the occasional black clergyman returned from ordination in England or Scotland with a British wife. But these were invisible to white society in the towns.

9

THE MILITARY LIFE

In the course of a hundred years the British conquered their segments of Africa at a relatively small cost in blood to themselves, though the Colonial Office and Treasury winced at the cost in money and kept the military establishments to the barest minimum. And the wars with 'kaffirs', Ashantis, Zulus, Dervishes, Boers, and with other strange tribes whose names became familiar to the newspaper reader at home, were punctuated with a series of resounding disasters to British arms and generalship. These seemed all the more disgraceful to the Victorian mind because they were incurred in campaigns against 'mere savages' or 'farmers on horseback'.

The truth is that, working in unfamiliar terrain with professional but inexperienced troops in limited numbers, some generals were lucky, and won the bubble reputation, others were not, and were duly torn to pieces in the reviews at home. There was a tendency to be grossly over-optimistic about the efficacy of white troops in small numbers against savages, whose military organization and valour were underestimated. From 1824 to about 1900 the skull, inlaid with gold, of Sir Charles McCarthy, sometime Governor of the British West African settlements, was paraded through the streets of Kumassi at the Feast of Yams after that commander had tried to teach the Ashanti army a lesson with a tiny Anglo-Fanti force unsupported by supplies. General Gordon, sent out by Gladstone to evacuate the inhabitants of Khartoum from the Dervishes, also paid with his life for deciding to challenge both the Dervishes to take the town and Gladstone to relieve it. The renowned Sir Garnet Wolseley failed to reach Gordon in time, partly owing to his mistaken conviction that he could treat the Nile as a supply-route, exactly as if it was one of the Canadian rivers with which he had had experience. Lord Chelmsford was lucky enough not to lose his life in 1879 at Isandhlwana, as he was not present when the Zulus overwhelmed his troops, following his refusal to heed the advice of the young Paul Kruger that one must always encamp at night in a laager of wagons.

Sir George Colley, however, did lose his life to the Boers at Majuba, in 1881 – also for ignoring the need to fortify one's positions. In the second Anglo-Boer War, the British commanders again threw troops against defended positions manned by sharpshooters and machine-guns, with about as much effect as the Africans had had against the British. Some British generals certainly tried to learn the principles of African warfare. Sir Garnet Wolseley showed how supplies could be organized in the Ashanti expedition of 1873 – but he was lucky not to be overwhelmed, and his retreat came near to being a defeat. Yet the autocratic Kitchener, sent out to rescue the defeated and discredited commanders in 1899, got his transport into such a mess by ignoring most of the experience of the Army Service Corps, set up in the course of the army reforms, that he prolonged the war for a year – at least in the Army Service Corps' judgement. He nearly missed King Edward's coronation, which he would indeed have thought a disaster, and one consequence was a less than satisfactory settlement at Vereeniging.

The British soldier paid most of the price. The fighting men did not feel the same as the armchair critics at home about African valour or tenacity, and gradually magnanimity spread. After the gatlings had dissolved the Fulani army at Sokoto, for the loss of one British officer from an arrow wound, the British told the surviving emirs that they had made a 'plucky stand' – which was said to have consoled them considerably. By the end of the century the British officer relied less on his sense of racial superiority and more on training; but it was the sheer professionalism of the engineers – who drew their strength from the potent Victorian engineering tradition – that underlay most of the British military achievement against African and Afrikaner.

CONQUEST AND CONTROL

In West Africa, as in South Africa and later elsewhere, the military problem was to prevail against a numerically vastly superior enemy by greater firepower, discipline and organization. The Africans had the advantage of numbers, knowledge of the terrain, and frequently of mobility. In tropical areas nature often also sided with them; they had the enlarged spleens, which the white troops had not, that enabled them to endure malaria. But they often suffered from other diseases, such as smallpox and dysentry, to as great a degree or greater. In West Africa the casualties from disease were so enormous that it was recognized by the early nineteenth century that British troops could not be used, or only for very short campaigns in small numbers. Officers might be expected to survive as long as traders on the coast, because of the greater comfort and better sanitation of their quarters. Defence of the coast settlements was handed over to the British-officered West India regiments, and later to the West African Frontier Force as it was ultimately called when it incorporated the Royal African Colonial Corps (formed 1816), the Sierra Leone Frontier Police (formed 1829), and the Hausa Constabulary ('Glover's Horse'), founded in 1865. It was at first a grisly service. Captain Napier described in 1862 the officers at Lagos 'with long beards and emaciated expressions, dull leaden eyes like boiled fish, hair shaved from fever, the remains of ague attacks that injure the brain', who 'bewailed their posts where there was neither society, amusements, books or even food, and where there was nothing to eat except poultry and no occupation except playing cards, quarrelling and drinking.' At first officers of the West India Regiment were employed in West Africa, where they served for one year, then had one year's posting in England to recruit their health before returning to their regiments in the West Indies.

Until malaria was conquered the occupation of inland areas was impossible. Military control of the coast was reinforced by naval patrolling; naval brigades were formed to fight inland when expeditions were undertaken.

In the south regulars could survive and indeed South Africa's reputation for healthiness made it an attractive station. But the problem there was to maintain enough regulars to deal with the hordes of Africans moving southwards, quite apart from the development of training and tactics to meet them. At first therefore local forces were raised, both white and coloured, with African auxiliaries levied from supposedly reliable tribes, like the Hottentots and Fingoes.

But there were two difficulties: the European volunteer and local forces could not keep the field for long because their farms or stores needed them, and for the same reason could only drill or exercise for short periods; on the other hand as settlers they were intensely uneasy at the arming of black 'sepoy' forces and increasingly opposed their use. Their anxieties found some justification by the number of times that they met deserters fighting with the marauding tribes against them, and by mutinies that bore some resemblance to the Indian experience. Meanwhile, the Government at home kept the imperial forces to a minimum on the grounds of the expense – they had to garrison a growing and periodically turbulent Empire with a standing army of 140,000 men. Wolseley and Frere thought Natal the most vulnerable colony in the Empire.

In South Africa, moreover, the settlers expected not only to be guarded from African incursions, which took place for ecological reasons beyond their ken, but also to add to their territory as their need or lust for land grew; land was taken when the Africans were thrust back, and the frontiers to be held as buffer zones continually expanded. There had therefore to be forts and patrols to show the flag along the frontier, and this was so weakly done that the Africans were frequently encouraged to attack when some injustice was done to them on an apparently ill-defended no-man's-land. Native war succeeded native war until the Africans were reduced to impotence and the white population was large enough to provide for its own defence.

TACTICS AND TRANSPORT

But for the redcoats, white settlement would have been reduced to an enclave round Cape Town. Soon after the British took control they clashed with the Xhosa who had driven the Boers from the Zuurveld, and in 1819 the Xhosa sought to retrieve it and were decisively defeated at Grahamstown, where Colonel Willshire with 45 men of the 38th, 80 Hottentots of the Cape Regiment, 39 men of the Cape Mounted Rifles and 135 of the Royal Africa Corps, with 30 civilians, held the town against 10,000 Africans; though the eastern Cape was to be overrun again and again, the Africans never had a chance of prevailing, as the base was secure and the white men's strength in population and firepower could be built up. The South African historian John Bond notes that this debt to the British regulars is grudgingly, if at all, remembered in modern South Africa.

The military problem in Africa soon emerged as the twin problems of mobility and transport. To hold fortified positions by superior firepower was not enough, whether troops were operating in the veld or the jungle: to bring the enemy to battle it was as necessary to advance against him as to lure him to attack forts or laagers. The Boers had long worked out a basic tactic which was to form laagers with their trek-wagons, perhaps reinforced with acacia, chained together by their disselbooms, in an unbreakable circle, from within which the defenders could fire without being overwhelmed by a press of black bodies or by showers of missiles. The Boers exploited two other advantages: their wagons, oxen, women and servants formed a slow-moving base of supplies, and their horses enabled them to mount commandos that could stay out of range of African spearmen and kill off stragglers or goad them to attack the laager. It was an effective military system – but it is doubtful if it could have sufficed to keep the Boers secure as African numbers and use of firearms built up, without the intervention of British arms.

The British infantry was much less mobile. With what they carried on their backs a British battalion could keep the field three days and fight one battle requiring 70 volleys; it had then to be withdrawn or supplied from base because it needed about a ton of supplies a day. As three days' campaigning was obviously insufficient, any large campaign required substantial organization. The Crimean War laid bare the scandalous insufficiency of army transport and supply, after the system built up in the Peninsular War by Wellington had been abandoned. It was largely in

Africa, where distances are immense, that the War Office relearnt the lessons of transport, mobility and supply. Africa was the nursery of the Army Service Corps. Two big campaigns pre-eminently showed that pre-planning could bring substantial British forces into the depths of Africa. In 1868 Napier brought an army of 3,800 British troops from the Red Sea to burn Magdala – the king killing himself in despair – by organizing a train of 41,000 pack animals ranging from elephants to mules, a specially built port and railway, a condensing plant to provide water in an arid area, and a road and telegraph line that went up to 10,000 feet. In 1873 Wolseley took a British army of three battalions through dense tropical forest to Kumassi from the coast, organized and supplied by Commissary-General O'Connor with forty non-commissioned officers of the Service Corps, fighting a pitched battle and burning the town. These feats were based entirely on human porterage once the attempt to use traction engines and light railways in place of pack animals had proved premature. Both commanders, however, were lucky; both had to retreat rapidly – Napier from gathering Ethiopian forces, and Wolseley from the onset of rains and malaria, as well as fresh Ashanti armies.

When the British adopted laager tactics, as at Kambula and Inyanzane River, after the bitter lesson of Isandhlwana and the demonstration in fighting Zulus from fortifications subsequently given at Rorke's Drift by Chard and Bromhead, everything went well. Thus the British force dined comfortably in the laager before the attack, and, well-fed, in four hours decimated a hungry Zulu army of 20,000 which attacked the wagons in waves. The British lost twenty-five dead, and fifty-nine wounded, largely by African snipers using captured British rifles. After the Zulus withdrew, exhausted, the British cavalry and the native levies cut them up further. In 1901, long after laagering had ceased to be necessary against Africans in the south, Captain McNeill formed a zariba for the precise purpose of luring the forces of the rebel leader, the 'Mad Mullah', to attack it, baiting the trap with camels stolen from his followers by mounted patrols. The Sudanese led by only two white officers and backed by a single maxim manned by Indian soldiers devastatingly defeated it.

When the British had adequate forces and firepower, they used effectively their Peninsular War formation of the square; against an African *impi* or a Dervish horde it had to be strengthened with artillery and machine guns, and used in conjunction with cavalry. Even so, squares in the Sudan were broken by Dervishes attacking in vastly superior numbers. Chelmsford at Ulundi drew up his army in square formation, not in a laager, because he said 'We must show them that we can beat them in fair fight'. Rather than lose the king's kraal, the Zulus dutifully attacked the square, but never even got within range of the men's bayonets, so tremendous was the out-pouring of lead from rifles, gatlings and howitzers.

Even when Africans were unwilling to attack white troops, they usually had no alternative because the British, on expeditions or punitive raids, if unopposed systematically destroyed their livelihood, driving off cattle and burning crops and kraals. As one officer put it, 'We destroyed every green thing we could see'. It was a form of scorched-earth policy. The Boers, in addition, carried off the Africans' women and children; when putting down the Herero or the Maji-Maji revolt, the Germans killed everything that moved.

In West Africa similar principles were observed. If the Africans would not attack *en masse*, the British forces destroyed their economy until they did. The Africans adopted such tactics as were open to them, particularly constructing ambuscades and stockades in wooded or mountainous country, and frequently inflicted heavy losses upon the British, because of the carelessness of commanders who thought them a rabble. Captain King, 74th Highlanders, who fought through the war with Kreli in 1850 finally admitted that they were 'a most formidable foe even to the flower of the British army'.

FIREPOWER

The British trusted particularly to the weight of their firepower in disciplined formations, which accorded with their parade ground training at home. Their 'firelocks' were often little better than the Africans', purchased from traders. Armed with the Brown Bess, a .75 calibre flint-lock smooth bore, the troops had to let the Africans get within one hundred yards and then could supposedly fire and reload at fifteen-second intervals. Such an armament in small units soon involved hand-to-hand fighting, in which the bayonet seems to have been fairly effective in trained hands against spears. In 1842, the troops' flint locks were replaced by cap or percussion firing. This did not add to rapidity of fire but made it easier to fire in adverse conditions.

Rifles were much more accurate weapons, but until the principle of the hollow conical shot was introduced with the Minié during the Crimean War, rifles were too slow to load and fire for line troops, since the ball had to be forced hard down the grooving. The conical bullet could be dropped in without a ramrod and on discharge spread to make a tight fit. It was usual for officers to have rifles, while other ranks only had smooth bores; these rifles were used for sharpshooting and skirmishing, and according to a regimental doctor, Captain Black, 'They astonished the Caffirs when they got a pop at them up in some crag or kranz across a valley.' The advantages of accuracy at long range quickly became apparent to officers in Africa, even if Boer prowess did not impress them. Captain King of the 74th noted in 1850 that 'Scarcely a mail steamer arrived from England without bringing some new improvement in firearms; smooth bore, four groove and polygroove, half- and quarter-twist, rifle barrels; conical bullets, plain and winged, sharp pointed and rounded, with wooden plugs or iron cups, concave and convex based were each in turn tested, advocated or rejected.'

Breech loaders could not be successful until precision-turned light-weight brass cartridges could be supplied; and this innovation was also the precondition of a successful machine gun. The gatling, invented during the American Civil War, spelt the doom of mass attacks by savages, capable as it was even by a hand-turned crank of 500 rounds a minute. Wolseley tried to deter the Ashanti chiefs from opposing his advance in 1873 by demonstrating an early model of a British-made gatling, but it jammed and moved them to anything but the 'superstitious dread' that Wolseley subsequently told his soldiers these weapons would inspire. The naval brigade was at first often made responsible for operating gatlings and maxims as it proved to be handier when the mechanism failed. By 1880 the gatling was a prerequisite of any native expedition, and even the police acquired them.

Before gatlings were available the British had to rely on artillery to provide dense firepower. At Grahamstown in 1819, two small brass cannon charged with grapeshot saved the day. Artillery, loaded with shell, could be used to dislodge Africans from their ambuscades on hill tops, or to sweep charging masses with cannister. 'I ploughed streets through them,' remarked an artilleryman at the battle of Berea, when Moshesh, who had pony-mounted cavalry, tried conclusions with a British force under Cathcart in 1852. The British also used the Congreve rocket extensively in Africa; it was supposed to do the work of artillery where guns could not be manhandled. The tripod and metal trough from which it was launched were light to carry, but there is little evidence that it was ever a decisive weapon in any engagement.

Only in West Africa did the Africans employ their own artillery: in 1861 at Lagos the defenders fired on the British warships with fifty-two well-emplaced guns which were described as 'admirably served', though, at the cost of an officer and thirteen ratings killed, a naval landing party disposed of them. In the south the Zulus tried in vain to master the intricacies of the six-pounders they captured from the Royal Horse Artillery at Isandhlwana. Nor were machine guns, even in the skilled hands of mutineers, as in the Uganda revolt in 1890, effectively used. The most impressive example of African firepower was shown by the Ashanti army, which fired and retired by command as in the British army.

In general both Boers and British troops were heartened by the ineffective use that Africans made of such firearms as they bought or captured. The British soldiers noted that the Africans could not measure the charges for their muskets correctly, either overdoing it and injuring themselves, or the reverse, when the balls fell short or struck with no penetrative force. Even when the Africans had bullet moulds they failed to cast the bullets correctly and fired them with the nipples untrimmed at the expense of accuracy, and when they ran out of bullets they were prone to fire stones, links from chains, flattened tins, even sections of their ramrods.

The inability of the Africans greatly to profit from their military experiences was, however, fully paralleled by the inability of the British commanders to learn the lessons taught them. They attacked the Boers, who were among the best marksmen in the world and generally had better rifles than the British, in much the same massed formations that the Africans vainly threw against the British firepower. Yet in the second Boer War the British generals merely thought it necessary to employ larger forces to make a success of the tactics that cost so much blood and humiliation in the first – quite oblivious of the fact that, in the meantime, the Boers had acquired magazine rifles, maxims, artillery, barbed wire (which had been used for cattle fencing since the 1880s), and foreign experts; against such defensive weaponry they threw their troops.

OFFICERS AND GENTLEMEN

Between 1834 and 1906, seventy campaigns were fought in Africa for which medals and campaign ribbons were awarded.* Service in Africa thus offered the career soldier more possibility of distinguishing himself than any theatre of empire except perhaps India. Apart from the second Boer War a very high proportion of the regiments of the British army saw some service in some part of Africa. But there were, as we have seen, many other opportunities in Africa for an officer to make a career, notably in exploration and in colonial administration. The great majority did not; they were content with garrison life. Exceptional leaders rose rapidly. Many made fortunes in imperial business in the heyday of chartered companies, though the directors of De Beers treated army commanders almost like cabmen.

Until Cardwell's reforms in the 1870s the army was little more than a collection of regiments, and these so few for the maintainance of the *Pax Britannica* that they were much overworked. They were not trained for this task; insofar as they were trained at all, it was for a European war, at which, when it came in 1853, they showed little proficiency. Even parade ground efficiency sometimes left much to be desired. Officers were amateurs who purchased their commissions much as doctors bought practices, until Cardwell abolished the system; it never applied, fortunately, to the engineers or artillery for which examinations were needed, as in the Navy.

* Regiments involved were the 1st, 2nd, 3rd, 4th, 6th, 8th, 9th, 12th, 17th, 18th, 24th, 27th, 42nd, 43rd, 45th, 57th, 58th, 67th, 72nd, 73rd, 74th, 75th, 76th, 80th, 85th, 88th, 89th, 90th, 91st, 94th, 99th, 100th and 102nd Foot; 60th (Rifle Brigade); 1st, 3rd, 7th Dragoons; 12th, 17th Lancers, 7th Hussars; Royal Artillery; Royal Engineers, Royal Army Service Corps, etc., and Royal Navy. In addition to the West Indian, African and settler regiments deployed in Africa, the Bombay Regiment, the Sikhs and Punjabis served in Ethiopia, Somalia and Nyasaland (units in 1899-1901 not included).

Nor did it apply to commissions in the Indian Army or in the Colonial Corps or militia; or of course in the volunteer regiments. Lord Kimberley wearily described British officers as 'ignorant, idle and prejudiced'. They came mainly from county families with money in land. These were not entirely barbaric, and a knowledge of agriculture and hunting, as well as public school discipline and vice, equipped them with two essentials of the infantry officer: leadership and horsemanship. Gallantry and 'dash' were considered to be the equivalent of professional skill. Colley's aide-de-camp fell at Majuba shouting '*floreat Etona*'. Such attitudes led to disaster in Africa and to service there being regarded by some as 'one of the worst risks to a professional officer's reputation' Those who did well, like the Wolseley 'ring', had correspondingly little competition to meet; and as promotion in the field was not subject to purchase, Africa could be a lucrative opening for the professional soldier who knew, or learnt, the job to be done there.

The unreformed system had some advantages. Purchase of commissions permitted men of means to move in and out of the army and to follow their hobbies: a surprising number had a scientific bent. Men of unusual talent, like Lugard, carved solid careers for themselves, following the example of the many half-pay officers who had turned to Africa after the Napoleonic Wars. For those who wanted social success, South Africa had not much to offer, except a good climate and good hunting. For this reason it was favoured, while many half-pay officers, both naval and military retired there because the cost of living was low. Indian army officers knew the Cape as a port of call, and many took their leave there to recuperate from the Indian climate – long leave was granted without forfeiture of pay and allowances. The idleness and profligacy of Indian army officers were a byword; their wealth earned them obsequious service. The custom of the officers of all regiments kept inn-keepers, lodging-house keepers and shopkeepers prosperous; at one time every house in Cape Town took lodgers. The richer officers kept race-horses and foxhounds. They set up hunts at the garrison towns, notably Fort Beaufort, where Lt Robert Arkwright (7th Dragoons) was riding master, and forty-six and a half brace of jackal were killed in 1842–3. Their quest for amusement stimulated the provision of theatres for both amateur and touring professional performers.

The main garrison towns were Cape Town, Pietermaritzburg, Grahamstown, Kingwilliamstown and Fort Beaufort. The last was jokingly described in the Cape newspaper *Sam Sly's Journal* as having 'four 2-storey high 'uns, a mail coach, a theatre Royal, a Hotel, a Hospital, barracks and stables for the dragoons and the foot soldiers, a Martello tower, bombproof, an elegant stone bridge, a race course, a new doctors shop, a Wesleyan chapel, a pack of foxhounds, a newsroom for the information of the people . . .' When in 1880 the garrison from Grahamstown

Government and Army

In the south, Governors were frequently unpopular with the settlers, who wanted
their own representative government. Early Cape cartoon by Frederick I'ons,
lampooning the entry of the 'Governor', Sir Andries Stockenström, to Grahamstown
garrison station.

The old slave forts provided bases from which British power extended into the 'white man's grave'. Sir Garnet Wolseley received with pomp at Cape Coast Castle in 1873, and by the Africans in their own style.

The famous 'Westminster model' for the Cape settlers: opening the first Cape Parliament in the state room, Cape Town, in 1854. Erskine May was closely followed in its procedures, but Rhodes came to dominate it.

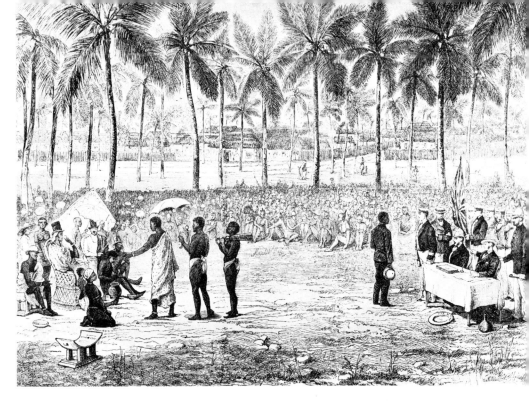

British power was extended by 'palavers' with local chiefs, who signed treaties accepting protection and suzerainty. A meeting with a local Gold Coast chief after the successful expedition to Kumassi, 1874.

The arrival of the first District Commissioner, Captain Ambrose, in southern Nigeria in 1895. This encounter between British government and the local ruler is commemorated in a carved wooden panel on the palace doors of the Ogogo of Ikere Ekiti, carved by the Yoruba people.

The heads of society in any colony were the Governor and his lady. They set the tone in deportment, dress and demeanour, and everyone's pecking order was observed rigorously. *Above* a group at Government House, Entebbe. *Below* Garden party on the occasion of the visit of the Duke and Duchess of Connaught to Freetown in 1911.

The Governors were fathers of their people, and could rely on a good send-off as well as a welcome on installation – and bitter newspaper criticism of their failures in between. Sir Leslie Probyn leaves Freetown in 1900.

Only the Sovereign took precedence over the Governor – but Royalty vastly reinforced His Excellency's prestige, enhanced careers and impressed Africans, or so it was thought. Between the wars the Prince of Wales was a keen colonial visitor. Lagos, 1925.

Africa was the scene of many British military disasters – but they were all duly revenged. After Sir Charles McCarthy lost his head to the Ashantis, Col Sutherland restored British prestige in 1824. Painting by D. Dighton.

Vigorous defence with a musket against a party of Kaffirs during the 1846–8 Wars. Painting by C. D. Bell.

The Kaffirs fought vigorous bush warfare against the British in the south, proving sound tacticians and brave warriors, but they were worn down by the tattered redcoats' superior firepower and discipline. The Africans' women ran their commissariat and even screened their retreats

The Ashanti expedition (1873–4) showed what skilled planning achieved against thick bush, a bad climate and a well-entrenched enemy. Troops were landed on the Gold Coast to a time-table to minimize sickness.

The discovery of sites of African horrors deepened the Victorian conviction that white rule would be for the good of the natives, as soon as climate and resistance could be overcome. An impression of the Asantehene's slaughtering place at Kumassi.

Even when outnumbered, British calm prevailed – especially after the disaster at Isandhlwana had taught the British to fight Zulus from behind sound defences. Greytown, 1879, while awaiting the impis.

Garrison life was enlivened by occasional forays against recalcitrant African rulers. British troops bringing Chief Sekukuni and his seven wives into Pretoria in 1879.

The Victorians were deeply convinced that their very uniforms would overawe the Africans – besides being more economical than sending the overworked troops. The Queen's envoys to Lobengula, however, did not convince the Matabele.

When the Matabele rose against Rhodes' pioneers in 1895, the settlers learned to use the ox-wagons for laagers, exactly as the Dutch had done a century earlier.

Seven pounders and barbed wire were used to reinforce laagers during the Matabele Wars.

The British beseiged by the Boers during the second Boer War, 1899–1902. At first the British thought war was a game, the Boers mere farmers on horseback. A sketch by the defender of Mafeking, Col Baden-Powell.

Even in the Boer War, medical conditions were still primitive, and dysentery killed more British troops than Boer bullets. Field hospital at Paareberg Drift, 1900.

In the end the British overwhelmed the Boers by sheer numbers rather than generalship, though they found they could only end the guerilla war that followed by a generous peace. The first Welsh regiment arrives in camp.

was withdrawn the town declined and became a nonentity socially. The reputation of Wynberg for smartness was based on its patronage by the officers. They gave society its *ton*; and they looked down on the colonial townsfolk. Officers could challenge an advocate of the colonial bar. Those of the Pietermaritzburg garrison tried to tar and feather the editor of the *Times of Natal*, William Watson, for an alleged aspersion on one of their number, when they invaded his house at dinner and demanded an apology which was refused. Dragoons rode their horses into the Black Horse Tavern. They were by turns detested and lionized.

Colonial women were naturally dazzled by them. The feeling was not reciprocated, however. Sir Garnet Wolseley when Governor of Natal delighted the ladies with his receptions, his insistence on ceremonial dress, his champagne (of a brand inferior to that which he drank himself). He sneered at their 'yellow-green complexions' and described them as 'a collection of housemaids with their greengrocer admirers in attendance on them. Only fancy having to make love to such a set for months to come.' This, however, his staff proceeded to do: according to Butler the colonial wives and daughters fell totally in love 'with the dashing officers of the Governor's staff. Brackenbury was carrying on half a dozen love affairs simultaneously, Lord Gifford was proposing to a Jewish girl; Major Buller had another affair; I might have had a rare time of it.'

Hunting antelope and jackal with foxhounds was no doubt the main sport, but officers also went out increasingly after big game, when Gordon Cumming showed there was both kudos and a fortune in it. He was a jest as an officer, hardly capable of getting on parade in time properly dressed. Lion hunting, both at the Cape and in Somaliland became an important diversion for Indian army officers who had bagged tigers in India; and on campaign everyone was ready to take time off for hunting when possible, both for the pot and for trophies. They have left many expressions of regret at having to abandon a promising lion or kudu to return to their duties of hunting African raiders. It was sometimes easy to confuse the two. 'The war was at best a hunt,' commented Major Fenn, an officer of the Frontier Force when campaigning against Sekukuni in 1878, and an officer in the West African Frontier Force during the Hut War in Sierra Leone in 1898 described the shooting of Africans through the head as they swam across the Mafwe River in retreat as 'grand sport'.

To see 'the party' or 'the fun' when fighting lay ahead, some of Wolseley's officers, left at base in 1873, offered to go as non-commissioned officers. They were sometimes undeceived about what awaited them. 'Several officers of the distinguished regiment to which I had the honour of belonging,' remarked Trooper Adams of the 7th Dragoons in 1845, 'looked on the commencement of the war as the beginning of a glorious succession of picnic parties' – only to lose all their mess plate, their wines and other delicacies – even their swords – in a well-laid ambush which lost the regiment its entire wagon train. They lived hard thereafter. 'We lay under the shade of a spreading mimosa,' wrote Captain King of the 74th, 'a merry party, little dreaming that this would be the last time we should all be together: some sketching, some sweeping the vast panorama with their field glasses, others practising long ranges with their rifles.' Eagerness to see the 'sport' grew through the century, and some titled officers were astonished to be *paid* by the War Office while campaigning with Kitchener.

Officers were a tight-knit club in each regiment, often having little contact with outsiders. They were intensely proprietorial to their men and their regiments. When Colonel Fordyce fell in a skirmish with Kaffirs, he abjured his officers 'Take care of my regiment, poor boys'. When men could no longer keep up with the column in West Africa, whether in the 1873 or 1895 campaign, observers noted that the officers, glittering-eyed with fever, were nonetheless carrying their men's rifles and packs. 'It is by such acts of devotion and self-sacrifice as these that have ever made the British officer stand pre-eminent in the annals of civilization,' declared George Musgrave, the journalist who accompanied them. Officers had the grace to blame themselves, or each other, when the men failed to carry the day. Colley called the remains of the 58th together after Laing's Nek, where every officer, except a subaltern who took command, was killed by the Boers, and apologized for 'making such a mess of it'. It was Buller who blamed Colley for the mess, just as it was Wolseley who blamed Wilson for the failure to reach Gordon in time; everybody blamed Buller for Spion Kop. But it was noted that the men tended to pity their humiliated generals. Grant, after the defeats of 1899, noted that the men were saying 'poor old chaps' of the generals while the generals were saying 'poor boys, poor boys' of the men. 'Are we not fortunate in our anachronistic old army?' he asked. 'One could not help thinking so, when there lay in front of Magersfontein, Stormberg and Colenso the fine English armies, led by three fine old English gentlemen and generals with the bubble of their generalship burst in the tremendous hand-clap of war.' For he noted that these defeats produced no despondency. Buller was admired by his men through every disaster, because he *looked* like a soldier – in fact as the regimental officer he was.

An avalanche of military incompetence [sighed Milner over] good lives . . . thrown away by idiotic leadership. Splendid men, splendid officers, and so many things – commissariat, mobilisation, sea and railway transport – admirably done. It is as if the thing were altogether rotten . . . the most ridiculous fetich worship of seniority and positive pusillanimity about the removal of admitted failures . . . What between the stupidity of our generals and the frivollings of fashionable females I often feel desperately ashamed of my country.

It was not only the females who frivolled: Dan Owain, a private in the Dragoons, tells with a ranker's sarcasm how Kitchener found officers sliding down the banisters and giving parties in Cape Town hotels, and gave them the choice of the next train to the front or the next mailboat back to England. It tended to be other officers who thought officers were always heroes to their men. The colonial volunteers were searching critics. Baden-Powell during the Mashonaland rebellion quoted an offer from a group of settlers which read: 'We will consider it an honour to serve under you, sir, but object to eye-glasses and kid-gloves otherwise.' He warned that 'the slightest show of domineering, letter-of-the-regulations discipline is apt to turn [colonial troops] crusty and irresponsible'. His advice was sometimes taken. Sir John Willoughby officered the Rhodesian pioneers in 'a gaudy red field cap, a khaki jacket, a pair of baggy blue trousers with broad red stripes, while his seat on his horse was ugly in the extreme'. But many Imperial officers were up to Baden-Powell's worst specifications.

In the end the Engineers left the most indelible mark on Africa. Sir Benjamin d'Urban built the military roads in the Cape and the bridges over the rivers which enabled troops to concentrate, and artillery, as well as trade, to move freely. The Engineers laid out Grahamstown and Bloem-fontein, built Port Elizabeth, made topographical surveys, and erected churches and schools as well as fortifications. The testimony to their labours was the railways and public works that opened up the country; Bain, a leading roadmaker, was attached to the Engineers, for example, while Robert Hart of the 91st started the first experimental farm at Somerset. They laid the telegraph lines along the railways and first used cameras and balloons for reconnaissance and intelligence. 'If the first white men had gone up in one of those,' said a Tswana chief, 'we should have worshipped them as gods.'

RED COATS AND KHAKI

The use of British troops had to be abandoned in West Africa for reasons of mortality, but the conditions that Florence Nightingale found in barracks at home also existed in South Africa. It was considered a healthy station for troops, yet disease claimed far more victims than assegais, and regiments were always needing fresh drafts to keep up to strength. Soldiers did not hesitate, since there were no instructions to the contrary, to drink from stagnant pools when well water or running water was unavailable. It was common in barracks for a single slop pail to serve all purposes, and Adams of the 7th Dragoons reported how twenty men would wash themselves in one half gallon of water; he mentioned casually how rotten their teeth had become, though all must have been in their twenties and thirties. One symptom of insanitary conditions in camps and barracks was the periodic epidemics of ophthalmia (trachoma and conjunctivitis), for which fumiga-tion was the supposed cure. Adams said that at one time one-third of the regiment was down with it, many so badly that they had to be discharged. Once they moved to a river site the contagion cleared up. The flies were sometimes so bad that they could kill them with bait and gunpowder. The killer diseases were typhoid (enteric) and dysentery, and not even the advance of medical knowledge could control them. A doctor in the second Boer War noted that 'The amount of sickness is terrible ... our water supply is a difficulty as probably the camp sewage system connects by surface flushing with the wells from which we draw our water'.

Rations were poor, though they improved as the Army Service Corps took over. In the 1840s and 1850s the commissariat provided 6 oz of salt junk a day with biscuit, meal, sometimes vegetables, and tea or coffee, but Adams recalled the day when 'for the first and last time in the whole war' they received their full ration. As the cost of victuals was stopped out of their pay, but no back rations were allowed, the men felt that they were being cheated, and Adams, something of a barracks lawyer, calculated that the War Office had made over £13,000 out of the troops in 1847. Sergeant McKay of the 74th wrote that, when 5d. a day was stopped from pay for rations in South Africa after the Horse Guards had reduced the amount to 3½d., it was calculated that the colonial government had made £3,000 out of the regiment, and he added, 'What misery, hunger, cursing and discontent did the extraction of that sum from the soldiers' small pay create among all ranks ... how many expressions of contempt and ill-feeling have I heard uttered by officers and men of different corps against the colony and its government.'

The troops could supplement their rations by slaughtering some of the African cattle that it was often their task to capture, but without salt or vegetables the meat was sadly unpalatable; yet Adams saw animals 'within an hour alive, slaughtered, frizzled and eaten', often raw and with the blood running. When the commissariat, whose stuff was described as usually rotten, failed to keep up, then men became so hungry as even to turn to the leaves on trees. On campaign cavalry carried their rations in mess tins in the horses' nosebags, which were often fouled, while the infantry carried theirs rolled in their greatcoats. Meat was boiled in camp kettles and 'had the appearance of pieces of thick leather very much shrivelled up, and the soup put me in mind of water that greasy dishes had been washed in'. The officers ate more daintily than their men, though they too often had to subsist on 8 oz of dirty meal a day and a herring or two, or simply on biscuit and coffee; much depended on how ingenious was the cooking of their batmen, who were paid largely from an officer's private rations – and stores of brandy. 'I always allow you ten bottles out of the dozen, sir,' said one of them to his officer. The colour sergeants sometimes cheated the men of their rations, and if they did not the storekeepers who followed the troops in their winkel-wagons usually did. Nothing was sold, the soldiers all noticed, for less than a threepenny piece.

Until after the first Boer War uniforms were red jackets and blue trousers for the infantry, and up to 1850, on ceremonial occasions and at one time in battle, the men wore stocks which held their heads as though in a vice. Stocks were cut to a standard size no matter whether a man had a long or short neck; it was a crime to cut them down; men fainted at Sunday service in the African heat. The men were 'loaded like a donkey' with a heavy shako, knapsack, straps, cross-belts, packs and ammunition containers. 'The advantage the kaffir has over regular troops is immense,' mused an infantry officer in 1850.

Armed only with his gun or assegais, free and unencumbered by pack or clothing, his naked body covered with grease, he climbs the tracks and works through the familiar bush with the stealth and agility of a tiger, while the infantry soldier, in European clothing, loaded with three days' rations, sixty rounds of ball cartridge, water canteen, bayonet and heavy musket, labours after him with a pluck and perseverance which none but British soldiers possess and which somehow or other wins its way in the end.

Even an army wife, Mrs Hutchinson, felt foreboding at the advantage of the Zulu over the 'heavily encumbered' British soldier in 1877. The red showed up splendidly for marksmen like the Boers; an officer as early as 1835 said, 'It is a pity that the red jacket is so easily seen at a distance; still it has its *effect* after a short experience of the gallant breast it covers.'

However, the infantry uniform ceased to be so distinctively red in the course of a campaign of any length, for it was soon in a condition which must at times have amounted to an early form of camouflage, albeit an uncomfortable one. The troops made a fine show when they marched out, as the journalists noted: 'The soldiers of the line in scarlet coats, artillerymen in neat blue tunics, mounted policemen in sombre-coloured shell jacket and jaunty little forage cap, frontier light horsemen in cord suits with puggaree carelessly twisted round their wide-awakes.' After a few days in the bush, Adams reported, 'Our uniform like Joseph's coat was of many colours all more or less patched with pieces of sheepskin. Our headgear was equally of as great variety from the regimental forage caps to the blue or red nightcap, and one or two black pots slung to every saddle.' The men were as dark in skin from exposure as Kaffirs. Captain King wrote how the 31st, 'literally in rags, marched steadily through the camp, many with bare feet, and their thin and scanty clothes so tattered as to be barely decent'. He subsequently saw that the 6th were as bad, 'Their coats patched with leather, canvas and cloth of all colours with straw hats and wideawakes, long beards, tattered trousers and broken boots revealing stockingless feet'. After seventeen days never removed, the tartan trousers of the 74th were tormentingly verminous.

Such was the inevitable result of jungle warfare – 'the laborious progress through all but impenetrable forest, overgrown with wild vines, while the hooked thorns clinging to our arms and legs, snatching the caps off our heads, and tearing flesh and clothes, impeded our every step.' Wolseley saw how unsuitable Horse Guards ideas were and insisted on a special jungle uniform of loose grey serge, worn with a cork helmet. This became the forerunner of operational khaki after the moral of how the Boers had picked off the red-jacketed 58th at Laing's Nek in 1880 had sunk in; but another ranker who has left memoirs of African service, Dan Owain of the Dragoons, noted that 'the Boers spied us just the same . . . our regiments of infantry would rush forward only to be sent trickling down in bloody heaps like ninepins'.

In the nineteenth century the plight of the wounded was, of course, pitiable. Small expeditions took no surgeon, and if they did there was little such men could or would do beyond amputations. Exposure and starvation undermined resistance and there was often no transport to take sick men to the rear, although a terrible fate at the hands of the Africans awaited them if they were abandoned. If they were moved the journey in a spring-less ox-wagon was too appalling to describe. Asked to relieve the sufferings of the groaning men a doctor told his colonel, 'I have only got my instruments case, a few small pieces of rag, a piece of plaster, my pipe and tobacco pouch.' Lt Gordon of the 74th preferred death to amputation, saying to the surgeon, 'Begone, you butcher! When you are so unkind to the men, how can I expect you to be humane to me?' Soldiers were sickened by the way Kaffirs dug up the bodies of their comrades and mutilated the corpses. In the Anglo-Boer War there were doctors, ambulances and nurses in the field; but the War Office sent out only one quarter of the Royal Army Medical Corps personnel actually needed after Boer bombardments, while Kitchener cut down on the ambulances so that the stretcher case in 1900 experienced the same miseries in unsprung ox-wagons as in Adams' day. 'It is not the fighting we mind, sir,' remarked a Tommy to a saddened civilian doctor. 'It's the 'ardships.'

Soldiers, as opposed to officers, had few amusements. After Omdurman Owain wrote that the officers had 'hunting, games and a damn fine swing; then we underscrub officers had a lesser share, with the privates always on duty and having to keep alive with mouth organs and an occasional game of football'. Trooper Adams was more versatile, and was noted in the Dragoons for his *extempore* versification on current events which served 'to pass a pleasant hour'; the officers called on him and other men with good voices to sing on mess nights, for which they received a guinea and a glass or two of wine. Soldiers also sometimes put on private theatricals, which were acceptable in the little dorps. Writing of one of these, Utrecht, Mrs Wilkinson remarked, 'Penal servitude at Dartmoor would be the wildest dissipation compared with being quartered here.' The officers preferred the stages of the town theatres; some of the officers of the 24th played in Sheridan's *A School for Scandal* at the Pietermaritzburg Theatre Royal the night before they marched to Zululand in 1879. The troops were unpopular with the settlers both socially and militarily, and Adams described how during a storm a 'specimen of the English settler actually refused us shelter and said he would as soon have a lot of kaffirs in his house as soldiers'. The bitterness of the troops was increased by the knowledge that the settlers waxed fat on the gunpowder they sold the Africans and on the disposal of army stores. Chelmsford bought oxen and wagons from the Natal farmers for three million pounds which he sold back to them for one million pounds or less. 'What with disobliging commissariat issuers, saucy waggoners and money-grabbing colonists, kaffirs were not the only enemies we had to deal with,' Adams said.

For many men, drink was the only way to deaden their cares, but this was often forbidden to them, certainly when on campaign. 'Heavy punishment was the due of any NCO or private who dared to bring a single glass of liquor within the camp,' wrote Sergeant McKay. 'While in the tents of the officers, which were ranged behind those of the men, nightly carousing and jollity were carried on, the sleep of the men being disturbed of course ... but such nightly sprees were strictly forbidden the plebeian soldiers.' Some men disobeyed, and loss of stripes was a frequent punishment. Punishment was even exacted for mistakes made when under fire. For worse crimes there was flogging, to the disgust of decent soldiers and colonists alike. One colonial volunteer was flogged under martial law. Soldiers were glad to be invalided out by disease or small wounds. It is hardly a wonder that, in a new country where others were making good livings in freedom, soldiers deserted.

Deserters, being men on the run, were often exploited by their white employers. Many defected to the Dutch republics, others joined the coloured community. The shortage of white skilled labour made it worthwhile for employers to tempt discontented soldiers in grog shops while plying them with drink. On a hunt for deserters, Adams described how he found men living in log huts with Hottentot women and noted that 'their children were the most repulsive creatures I ever saw. I have been told that the children of mixed race of pure Hottentot and English are so'. Deserters were even found fighting with the Boers against British forces; Adams reported how the Dragoons captured two of them and were disgusted when a humane colonel reprieved their formal sentence of death by firing squad.

Others took their discharge in South Africa; they were settled in military villages, the soldiers receiving twelve acres (officers got one hundred), a span of oxen to every twelve farmers and a wagon to every twenty. The villages, located on the frontier, were destroyed in some cases by Kaffir attacks; the settlers' bones littered the streets for a year in 1851. A few soldiers were able to bring out their wives, but the number entitled to passages and married quarters was strictly rationed by the colonel of the regiment; those who married without his consent, on 1s. a day before stoppages, often had to see their wives go on the streets. Some soldiers married

197

into settler families, but women were hard to find. Adams tells, with some delicacy, how he rested a horse for three days at a Boer farm where the youngest daughter fell helplessly in love with the red-coated stranger; his bearing so impressed her elders that they offered to buy his discharge if he would join them. Though he had been happier there in three days than in the three years of his service, he decided not to do so.

THE COLONIAL FORCES

It was the defeats, rather than the successes, of the imperial forces which impressed the settlers in Africa. They formed auxiliary units, learned Boer tactics, and considered in general that, but for their scouting and cavalry role, the red-coats would have suffered even more. They complained of the inefficiency and even cowardice of the regulars, and that the Governor kept too many troops for ceremonial purposes and provided too few for patrolling. Local forces were raised in the Cape for defence in 1806, and in Natal even before the Byrne settlers arrived; but the most famous regiment, the Carbineers, was formed in 1855, and the Natal Mounted Police soon afterwards. By 1850 the Cape Mounted Police was eight hundred strong, composed of twelve troops, eight white and four coloured. Many of the Europeans were recruited from men of the imperial army, and conditions in the regular colonial forces were at first not much better. A man began his service with a debt of £50 because he had to buy everything, including his horse, saddlery and uniform; only his carbine and ammunition were supplied. His horse was insured for 2s. 6d. a month, which hardly covered replacements, and Trooper Owain, who transferred to the Mounted Police in 1890 in operations to 'nip risings in the bud', reported that on the Modder River the horses were so sick that they 'would suddenly drop down, throw their tongues right out of their heads and, while our eyes popped out of ours, the poor beasts would sicken and die'. The role of the Natal and Cape Police was to hold down the natives once they had been (often to local disgust) forcibly enrolled as citizens of the expanding Empire by dint of imperial expeditions, conquest and annexation. In Rhodesia this role was taken over by the British South Africa Police.

The colonial volunteers in mid-century regarded their military as an extension of their social life. Gentlemen joined the Carbineers, and sometimes the Mounted Police; others joined the Volunteer town guards and burgher forces. The Carbineers elected their officers, who had generally had a military career. Their first commander, Sir Theophilus St George, was formerly commissioned in the 12th Lancers; other officers – Proudfoot, Sutherland and Barter – had seen much service overseas and were 'well versed in Bantu and Bushman wiles'. They called Parkinson 'the Garibaldi of Natal'.

Raids against bushmen were like picnic parties, as much part of the social scene as the dances and mess dinners they gave. The Carbineers and the Mounted Police under Major Darnell, 'the hero of Jhansi', were an indispensable adjunct to British governors and commanders, notably Shepstone, Lanyon, Chelmsford and Evelyn Wood, who might have been captured by the Boers in 1881 but for their work.

Rhodes, like other settlers, had small opinion of the British army, though he had faith in selected officers, like Colonel Pennefather of the 6th Dragoons who commanded the Chartered Company's forces in the Queen's name. When Lobengula asked the Colonel his intentions on his march through Mashonaland, the latter replied, 'I am an officer of the Queen of England, and my orders are to go to Mashonaland, and there I am going. We don't want to fight, we only want to dig for gold, and we are taking this road to avoid your young men, but if they attack us we know how to defend ourselves.' The well-planned expedition got through without fighting. When the column dispersed and when the Matabele and Mashona later rose against the settlers, and tried to exterminate this new menace to their tribal life, the imperial forces showed that they had at least learned the lessons of preceding African wars. They formed squares or laagers and mowed down the blacks with machine-guns.

It seemed rather a pitiful thing [wrote Owain]. The Great Imperial Army mounted outside those caves [in the Matoppos] and a bunch of niggers and their women lying up terrified inside and we trampling and bivouacking in their little gardens outside . . . we traced the living quarters of the blacks, working in the ground overhead of their caves, which ran for a quarter of a mile underground. Our blacks dug a huge hole, we put down six cases of dynamite, laid the detonators and stood clear. There was a horrible bang and out shot the Matabele.

The soldiers threw the bodies of the black warriors into rivers after cutting off their limbs to dispossess them of the valuable pure gold bangles they wore. The bones of others littered the veld, where the Administrator's wife, Lady Grey, and her friends went to view them.

It was not quite so easy for the great imperial army to deal with the Boers, as Owain found from the vantage point of the ranks when he rode out with Dr Jameson two years later. 'We fought till our ammunition was done and all our horses killed. There were only 300 surviving at dusk . . . our arms thrown down we were marched all night to Krugersdorp. Of course we lower ranks were kept in the dark about the whole business . . . we thought it was a punitive expedition against some murdering niggers.'

By the turn of the century Africa had largely become an area where Mounted Police, and the British-officered East and West African frontier forces could keep law and order. The Africans made a few last struggles. The Basuto and Griquas rose in 1897, there was unrest in Bechuanaland in 1898, and the same year the Mende rose in Sierra Leone; the Ashanti were finally crushed in 1900, and in the same year a British square shot to pieces the forces of Sokoto and completed the conquest of Nigeria. The Zulus were again put down by the police in 1906, and the Nyasas under John Chipembe in 1916. The job of the British officer was now to create native forces that would ensure law and order and defend larger imperial interests when needed.

IO

DECOLONIZATION
AND DEPARTURE

Historians are now examining the process by which the colonial Briton in Africa became conscious that Empire, racial superiority, even mission and purpose were ebbing: that he could no longer gaze into blue smoky distances with the eye of overlord or proprietor; that the 'dear old flag' stood for no abiding authority. In Africa, as in India, the timetable for departure was in preparation long before the farmer, the businessman or the district commissioner realized that the carpet was sliding from under his feet. One community refused to accept their fate, and finally balked at London's plan. How long the Rhodesian republic will last is a contemporary issue.

When India became independent in 1947, an opinion developed among the British in Africa, and in the City of London, that post-war Africa, sometimes called Eurafrica, would move into a new frontier of development in the second half of this century in a way that would recoup any losses (psychological and racial as much as economic) incurred from Asian nationalism. In 1955 Britain and South Africa concluded the Simonstown agreement to hold the gates of Africa militarily against communist aggression; it contained no provision for termination by either party. In 1956 Nasserism triumphed at Suez. In 1957 Nkrumahism triumphed in the Gold Coast.

Thereafter the divergence in the ways of the British north and south of the Zambesi River widened steadily. North of the Zambesi events moved to a new, strange and accelerating rhythm, to the throbbing of militant, bullying African voices, towards that moment when the British would gather to see the flag pulled down at midnight and sing 'God save the Queen' for the last time. South of the Zambesi events moved in counterpoint. The British began to undergo a conversion from love, allegiance and confidence of the weight of the motherland at their backs, to contempt and hatred for the British in retreat, as they found themselves joining in the laager of the people their imperial forebears had defeated or despised. The British found their mentality changing uncontrollably into something new, un-British and alienated, as Dr Jekyll swelled up into Mr Hyde.

THE LOSS OF FAITH

The African Empire was put together no more durably than the Indian Empire. Its temporariness was concealed for perhaps half a century by the tide of national self-confidence which had blossomed into territorial empire, dominion over palm and pine. Alexander Stewart, passing through Portuguese waters on Livingstone's steamboat *Pioneer* in 1865, noted after an encounter with a sodden *intendente*, 'I don't wonder, though, that we as a people are the envy and astonishment of other nations. Here, in this particular case, we come leaping ashore with as much energy and activity as would almost eat them up.' No matter how fevered the Briton, no matter how feeble his steamboat, he felt he was the future, the driving force of history. The peak of such ebullience, it has been suggested, was reached at the Diamond Jubilee of 1897; if so, it was drained on the Somme.

In Africa, nevertheless, through the theme of success and progress runs a sense of the precarious, a precariousness that was psychological as well as a matter of the hostile climate and African superiority in numbers and in fecundity. Modern medicine, modern transport, could not wholly dispel it; it can be traced in a wide variety of African writings. The missionaries expressed at first a genuine sense of mere trusteeship, of being *in loco parentis* to peoples who would not yield and lose heart as had the Red Indians, the Aborigines, the Polynesians. This sentiment found a certain political recognition in indirect rule through chiefs (to a greater degree in practice than is always realized), Lugard's much-praised 'dual mandate'. The sense of impermanence, however, was held in check by the spectacle of material progress at the end of the century. The visible spread of European technology, the vast distances remaining for it to penetrate and to transform, the apparently slow adaptation of the African personality to this change – so that the gap between European leadership and African tutelage seemed rather to widen than to shrink – all combined to convince the ordinary British resident or visitor that the passing of white rule lay far in the future whatever might befall elsewhere.

Of African nationalism, the meetings of African intellectuals in London and Paris from 1905 onwards, of the writings of Marcus Garvey and W. E. du Bois, hardly a whisper reached white – or even black – society. The eclipse of the black intellectual on the West Coast in the 1890s was noted, and seemed, like the wretched defeat of the Griquas, merely to show that the black man had no real staying power, whatever education he was given. Far-seeing men could scent trouble ahead. Milner, even, could remark in the Boer War that the 'native question' would diminish the Anglo-Dutch quarrel to its true, limited, dimensions. The stereotyped reaction remained in South and Central Africa that the mission-educated boy was a spoilt boy. 'Never trust a native who speaks English and wears trousers,' a remark made by Charles Payton in 1872 in the diamond fields, was a fairly standard attitude. Slightly more sensitive people saw in African aspirations a theme for tragi-comedy, for they considered that the fully-educated native existed in numbers too small to leaven the mass of savagery; the man of two worlds was therefore introduced not as a forerunner but as a freak capable of more mischief to himself and his tribe than good.

As early as 1910 Cullen Goulsbury wrote a novel to consider what would be the effect of a British public school education on a chief's son, if some sentimentalist about African potentialities should make such a guinea-pig of him (he seemed unaware that English education had been given to a number of Africans since early in the nineteenth century, and that men like John T. Jabavu could run newspapers). He took leave of his unhappy hero, rejected by his tribe, doing a vaudeville act on the London music hall stage, with revengefulness in his heart.

AFRIKANERIZATION

It was in South Africa that the decline of British supremacy began. The Boers converted their military defeat into a political triumph. The British victory turned to ashes in the mouth. The concentration camps where 20,000 Boer women and children died from disease while their menfolk prolonged a guerrilla warfare to achieve, in the end, tolerable terms while still in arms, were unveiled by Emily Hobhouse, defying the jingoes, to the British puritan conscience.

'Sympathy shown to anyone of Dutch blood is the one unpardonable sin in South Africa,' she told a nation sick of war and ashamed of mafficking. The reaction against imperialism helped to create the Liberal landslide victory of 1906, and Milner grimly despaired of bringing fickle democracy and great imperial purposes together. To his horror, and to that of many British in South Africa, the high festival of embracing one's dour and contemptuous enemies, of sportsmanlike patting the good loser on the back, was prolonged into a negotiation which opened to the Afrikaners an early comeback and dominance through the ballot-box (which was also, at their behest, denied to the coloureds, however educated). When Botha and Smuts were weaned over to the British side it was hailed by London news-papers as a stroke of British imperial genius. The logic of the Act of Union in 1910 depended on the belief that the British victors would imperialize, anglicize, absorb and liberalize the Afrikaner majority, and out-populate them; a feat of which the British had proved incapable in the preceding century. The reverse process began.

The co-operation of Botha and Smuts split the Afrikaners politically for a time, but did not halt the cultural processes which were making them more powerful than the British minority. The British fancied that the Transvaalers, the platteland Boers, would follow the Cape Dutch, but thoughtful observers in Cape Town were not deceived. It was the Transvaalers who absorbed the Cape Dutch. The latter had been exposed to European civilization from overseas, had proved apt pupils in parliament, in the courts, in the professions; but their sense of unity with Afrikanerdom was not impaired. In the Cape it had long been said that they had never really changed their opinion that a British colonial government was scarcely better than government by Kaffirs.

After the war the local British saw the Afrikander Bond transformed from a Cape political party rather like the Irish at Westminster, into a semi-secret society, dominated from the Transvaal, for the purpose of reversing the decision of Vereeniging. Stafford Ransome, an engineer of imperial cut, was typical of the colonial doubters when he wrote in 1903 that 'history all over the world has shown that Britons cannot live under Dutch rule', and lamented the bitter fruit soon to be eaten as the result of a policy 'in which we treat the Dutch well and the English badly . . . Only if English labourers come out could we snap our fingers at the Africander Bond.' But he voiced profound doubts about British capacity even to maintain their export trade, so slack and self-indulgent did he find Edwardian Britain. He was only one of the Cassandras who saw the British abandoning their high destiny for the fleshpots. Sir Percy Fitzpatrick wrote his story *Jock of the Bushveld* to rally the race. If Jock, an imperial dog of the highest ideals, could not do this – and the book was a best-seller – what hope could there be?

Twenty years later, Sarah Gertrude Millin, noting the British decline, said that before the war the Dutchman had hated the Englishman but stood in awe of him; after the war, he merely hated him. 'The Englishman, uneasily conscious of having lost something which, however little he may have appreciated it, was still a spiritual possession, was humanly anxious to be considered a fine fellow. As the Dutchman stepped back, he stepped forward.' Psychologically, the British were thereby softened for the suppliant, subordinate role.

The British saw the strength of the Bond, which Whitehall did not see; but even the British in South Africa did not see what underlay that strength. This was the work of men like Hofmeyr (and, earlier, the Englishman L. H. Meurant) in creating a national language, and the use made of British institutions in 1880–1900. Politics, a Dutch writer noted, became the centre of discussion on every *stoep*. English achievement created Dutch determination to master the art of power. By 1910 they were fully capable of producing political adepts.

From the first, the Union was controlled by Afrikaner politicians; the British political tradition atrophied. Sir Starr Jameson was, indeed, the last considerable English figure in politics. J.X.Merriman was passed over in favour of Botha to lead the Union. The price of appeasing Afrikaner resentment, and of splitting Afrikaner leadership, was that henceforth the British were never ruled by one of themselves, or even had much representation in the cabinet. In 1949 Dr Jansen, the minister of native affairs could tell a Nationalist party congress with deadly truth: 'It is now almost forty years since Union, and the English-speaking section of this country have not produced one leader of consequence in the political sphere . . . Never so far have the majority of them been inspired by a true and pure South African spirit, and yet it has suited them to make use of Afrikaans-speaking leaders to carry out their imperialistic colour policy.' If that had been their game, it was in 1949 certainly played out.

British readiness to leave politics to the Afrikaner was excused on many grounds, one of them being that the two European stocks had in any case merged into one South African nation, a nation as distinctive as the Australian nation. 'Union,' enthused Violet Markham in 1913, 'has wrought a revolution in the whole habit of thought and outlook in the land . . . strong men on both sides have shaken hands, and have settled down to a common task.' The temperament of the British was partly responsible. Politics is rarely popular in Britain itself until issues are acute, and, except under Rhodes, and in occasional crises before him, politics had been secondary to other interests. Sir Percy Fitzgerald, who had been one of the uitlanders' toughest fighters against Kruger's refusal to grant them political rights, recorded his dismay when, trying to do political business at the Cape, he found the British apathetic. Simply for a game of golf a local M.P. broke his promise to take Fitzgerald to see an area in Sundays Valley, thought to be suitable for settlement by British immigrants; it was an ominous sign.

The case for specialization between the two language groups, the Dutch doing the political and administrative chores, the British (or Jewish-British) doing the profitable business, was complacently accepted. The language settlement (which gave Afrikaans equality with English) helped. Afrikaans became the effective medium of politics and administration. In the Cape parliament, when members had spoken in Afrikaans, the English had strolled out. The English had in fact largely run the Orange Free State as paid officials. Now the tables were turned. 'It is a simple matter to say,' remarked Hamilton Fyfe in 1911, 'why do not Englishmen learn Dutch? Languages do not come easily to our race. It takes us a long time to talk fluently in a tongue not our own. And why in any case should one waste one's time in learning a language like the Taal when it is not really required?'

The equality given to Afrikaans ensured, as Milner warned, that after the war the Dutch would move into all forms of government service, railways and posts; and that, once ensconced, they would methodically increase their community's grip on avenues of promotion. Milner, however, hardly encouraged the British in South Africa to take public affairs seriously by confiding most of the top jobs during the reconstruction period (1902–9) to his kindergarten of intellectual young ambitious Englishmen, largely from Oxford, who had great ideas and absolutely no understanding of grass-roots Africa, and all of whom returned home to plummier posts, having failed (it may be added) to discover how a central imperial government could be reconciled with colonial self-assertion. Milner virtually ignored the uit-landers, and their leaders, for whose sake the war had ostensibly been fought.

British emigration to South Africa increased after the war, but the Boer community had become too firmly established for it ever to be reduced to such a minority as the French in Canada. Milner saw the point. 'A great deal will depend,' he wrote, 'on settlers of the right type. Artisans and miners will come out of their own accord, but we want a leaven of British settlers . . . to make a success of agriculture.' And of course to provide a rural electorate. But as Afrikaners flowed into the cities after the war, and the competition of the coloureds in menial tasks grew, vacancies in mining, services and on the land became scarce. Prices were high against the artisan, and the prospects for gentlemen, whom Milner most wanted to see, were poor, according to Ransome who had studied the problem: 'Class distinctions, though there is but little excuse for the fact in this sort of community, are very marked. For this reason the poorer gentleman, who would live as such, is much worse off than the highly-paid artisan who need not keep up appearances. A fitter or smith saves more than the highly-paid engineer for whom he is working.' Capetown was a graveyard of hopes, where the British were fleeced and rooked; and, Ransome noted, 'a visitor may see white men kneeling in the muddy streets cleaning the boots of the coloured population. This is a humiliating sight.' He concluded that only English capitalists had much prospect.

Almost as soon as the British began to establish themselves the war of 1914–18 called them back to the colours to fight in France and against the Germans in Africa. In 1913 the leaders of the strike against the mine owners on the Rand were all English (many were Cornish) and were suppressed with relish by Boer commandos who felt the British needed to be reminded of the *sjambok*. In the Rand strike of 1922 the leaders were Afrikaners.

SOUTH AFRICA FOR SUNSHINE

The English-speaking community had more interesting pursuits than leadership. The English, together with the Scots and the Jews, dominated big business, with the Randlords living palatially between Parktown West and Park Lane at the top of the heap. The commercial British generally enjoyed a standard of life superior to that available at home. The wealthier families, and those who in Natal considered themselves the squirearchy, maintained links with England, giving their sons a public school and Oxbridge education and their daughters a London season for coming out, and they noticed nothing irreconcilable in South African politics and British culture under MacDonald and Baldwin. This custom was criticized in South Africa, where a public school education was held to 'denature' the colonial character. It certainly did not eradicate his racial exclusiveness. The British were far more anti-semitic than the Boers, in spite of the example set by Rhodes. They were anti-Indian; indeed, during the Durban riots in 1948 Englishwomen were reported to have danced in the streets in sheer delight at the mishandling of the Indians by Africans. It was necessary to urge English parents to enjoin their children to be courteous to black servants.

After business came pleasure. Even when the English worked hard in the office their African servants freed them, men and women alike, from the ordinary chores of daily domestic life so that they could put great energy into cultivating leisure. In this pursuit of fitness they became – or so it was said – physically larger and lustier, a better breed, than their kin at home. From the 1890s onwards, the British turned South Africa into a playground for themselves. The number and variety of their amusements were a revelation to the Dutch, who at least did them the compliment of taking up racing and rugby football with enthusiasm.

The first British thoroughbreds arrived in the Cape in 1792, and the first race meeting was held six years later 'attended by all the fashion of Africa', including members of military personnel who were stationed there. The Turf Club was established in Hottentot Square, and in 1814 Lord Charles Somerset drew up rules for the Jockey Club. Racing developed slowly but steadily as the two colonies spread; by 1885 the Port Elizabeth Turf Club held the first South African Derby, with a totalisator that took £70. In 1887, the Transvaal Government graciously provided the uitlanders with facilities for sport, and a three-day meeting, presided over by Sir Abe Bailey, was held in Johannesburg, whereat 'centuries' were wagered like sovereigns in England. Racing on this scale of magnificence spread to every city thereafter; a race meeting caused the postponement of the Jameson Raid.

Cricket was played in Africa wherever the English could muster teams, including blacks, to make up a side. It was widely played after 1840, became an inter-province contest during the 1850s; and in 1862 the first match took place between a team from England and a colonial team at the Rondebosch barracks. In 1888 the first Cape team visited England. In 1896, to general rapture, Natal beat Lord Hawke's touring team, and after the Anglo-Boer War South African cricket flowered when tests began with both the Marylebone Cricket Club and Australia. Cricket remained a game for city clubs; English village cricket found no counterpart in the veld.

Rugby began in the missionary colleges and seminaries, imported by public school clergy practising muscular Christianity. It developed naturally into the major university game; and within twenty years won a large Afrikaner following which tended to run in families. The first 'tournament' was organized in 1884, the colonial style featuring a strong forward line; after 1902 tours by the English clubs began. For the Springboks it became a game of almost religious significance such as soccer never achieved.

Soccer, tennis (on hard courts), hockey, basketball and – above all – golf were introduced into South Africa in the last quarter of the Victorian era, and became widely played as the new century opened. They flourished in a climate of sunshine, leisure and affluence. Indeed, other British crazes were taken up quickly; for example, roller skating in 1909 and the 'bioscope' (movies) even earlier.

In the early years of the century, South Africa's beaches were discovered. Hitherto they had been places where invalids recuperated in sea air, occasionally bathing in voluminous costumes from tents. South African Railways put up posters depicting the carefree joys of Durban, East London and Algoa Bay. By 1910 the area of Durban beach, roped and netted safely against sharks, was overfilled with holiday-makers. The coast holiday had become a new institution for those wealthy enough to escape the altitude and heat of the Rand summer. Swimming pools began to be built in private houses at the same period. (Electric kettles, heaters and cookers were more common in Johannesburg than in London in 1910.) The life of sport, parties and comfort became the English goal, and its symbol was the luxury hotel. In 1912 the Automobile Association was founded and the provinces began to harden their dirt roads as the motoring age opened. The trek-wagon abdicated or withdrew to remote bush or volk museums.

THE POOR WHITES

Not all the British lived in suburbia or surveyed the broad acres of their patrician veld farms from gabled manors. Urban poverty from the first disfigured the British-built cities, which were often jerry-built in parts. After 1902 the 'poor white' became first a social, then a political problem, on which heavy reports were written. Afrikaners predominated in the white lower class, flooding into the cities as the farms were subdivided to a point at which the eroded pastures could no longer support large families; the process began with the extinction of the herds of game with which trek boers, like bushmen, were essentially symbiotic. Poverty mattered less in the nineteenth century, when the African, like the white man, was rural, and life was simple, and lived in the open air, with a horizon of twenty miles. It became a different condition when Africans, Indians, Chinese, coloureds and whites lived cheek by jowl in Johannesburg. In Westrupp's novel, *The Toll*, the shift-boss warned his fiancée of life in the mine quarters: 'Haven't you seen the dust and sordidness of everything? Often I am on nightshift and then you will be all alone here after dark with nobody to protect you ... [from Africans and Chinese] mad with drink, likely as not. And there will be slights to be endured, for a shift-boss is a nobody and social distinctions on the mine are very sharply defined.'

For the British trade unionists it seemed for some years to be a situation made to order for a cloth-cap Labour Party. Organizers like Tommy Boydell began with Keir Hardie ideas before 1913, and after 1917 injected Marxist ideology. Trade unions had been formed by white miners from the early days of the Rand, but their idea of defending their members' interest was as much to fight the aspirations of the black miners, and keep their wages down, as to extract better conditions from the mining companies. In Kimberley the white miner struck against having his rectum examined, like an African worker, every time he went off shift, and won the right to mere random sampling for that essential employers' safeguard. In the main, white workers' unions fought for skilled status, and for safer conditions, which the capitalists strongly rebutted on lines familiar to British workmen, and sacked miners' leaders: both miners and employers regarded the Africans as so much equivalent in horsepower. There was therefore a strong working-class interest – but it was wholly white and hardly provided a basis for a British-type Labour Party.

The South African Labour Party became a rather regional party defending white skilled labour from African or coloured competition, no matter what obeisances its manifestos might make towards Moscow. A convinced socialist like Wilfred Harrison could fulminate against the monarchy and the mine owners but declare that 'in all the centuries of tribal life of the South African native they have not got much further than an assegai and a reed hut.' It was natural that such a group in the 1920s should ally itself with Hertzog's Nationalists, just as trade unionists had been sympathetic to Oom Paul, simply because the Afrikaners were poor, were urban voters, and were against the 'Smuts imperialists'; they were deeply interested in anti-native regulation. The communist party learned by bitter experience that it was, in fact, anti-white and pro-black; its destiny was to become an underground resistance movement for the blacks against white South Africa as a whole: a long march which it duly undertook. The artisans and poor whites, British and Afrikaners, were far keener on job reservation than the industrial managers, after it was discovered, or rediscovered, upon the expulsion of the Chinese, that the blacks and coloureds were readily trainable to skilled work. They talked, far more than did the British businessmen, of 'the need to raise white prestige', talked of the black peril (i.e. miscegenation) and complained of the growing threat to their women in urban areas from Africans (who were largely deprived of their wives and families by the mine regulations). 'Little girls are not safe from these monsters,' cried Mrs Lionel Philips in 1899; in 1912 there were 648 charges of rape and sexual assault.

Sarah Gertrude Millin, writing in 1925, expressed the view that the poor whites were largely Englishmen who had emigrated some years earlier for the wrong reasons and had degenerated into slum dwellers living on charity and relief. This judgment of shiftlessness was the general one of white suburbia, and of the English on their farms and plantations. Georgina Lister recalled that in her childhood 'the "poor whites" round us were a great source of worry to mother. Whole families of them would arrive and demand supplies of coffee, sugar and clothing, with tales of bitter want. This went on for some time in father's absence, but he soon found out that they were not really in need of food, and were just too lazy to do anything for themselves.' Ethelreda Lewis described them as degenerates 'who felt no hurt in being neighbour to a family that is not quite white – to a Chinaman, to an Indian laundryman who hides illicit liquor under the snowy linen in his ironing room; who smiles knowingly at the night-long lights over the tumbledown, blistered balcony opposite, the gentle opening and shutting of doors in a house up the street.' Such folk had

flat-chested, hollow-cheeked, sharp-featured lanky children, neither fair nor dark. Their eyes were small and shifty . . . Most of them were miserably dressed and told lies with natural ease. They were idle with an idleness that ate like a disease into the bone . . . descendants of settlers, Dutch or English, or Dutch and English, who had sat dreaming too long in one spot, hypnotized by the enormous forbidding spaces and by the unceasing sun into believing that all was well so long as they sat still, said their prayers, and had the natives fetch and carry. The men lost imperceptibly the vigour of pioneer grandfathers. The women forgot the industrious skill in cooking, sewing and in the management of a small farm that had been their grandmother's dowry. Even marriages became idle affairs of promiscuity. Few men saddled a horse and rode far for a wife. So that in two or three generations the illegitimate, the imbecile, and the slightly foolish were many among them; and dark children were not rare.

Poverty tended to Afrikanerize the British faster than politics did the richer. At Knysna, in 1947, H. V. Morton noted that the poor whites had British names though they could only speak Afrikaans. They were the descendants of the servants and grooms of the squires who settled in the eastern Cape in the 1820s and 1830s; and he found them reduced to shacks far worse than native huts. Among them he described a seventy-year-old woodcutter of English descent living with a half-English, half-Afrikaans wife in a quasi-English cottage garden redolent of the rural indigence described by Richard Jeffries; the house filled with worn-out furniture, broken chairs and tables and faded family photographs. Poverty was even grimmer in the Rand slums and mine locations than in the countryside.

To British as well as Afrikaner leaders miscegenation – the creation of the Eurafrican 'in whose veins run the corruption of black and white' –

became a growing worry. Until the Nationalists took power in 1949, and passed the Mixed Marriages Act, and later the Immorality Act, colour remained a matter of class; and the comfortably-placed English held aloof. For they felt that mixing was essentially a matter of fitness; only those who 'let themselves go' became involved with black or coloured women. To moralists like Mrs Millin, the coloured race was a standing reminder of the supposedly dysgenic effects of mixing the chromosomes that carry racial features: the standing argument, never examined by those who advanced it, was the failure of the Griqua and Bastaard Republics. In the 1920s English people, not Afrikaners, even began to leave South Africa for Rhodesia or Canada because of the growing difficulty, as Colonel Silburn put it, 'of rearing a pure-blooded, self reliant and hardy family. Many depraved half-caste degenerates are to be found in South Africa today bearing the names of some of Britain's most noble families.'

Great was the sensation in 1926 when a South African, William Plomer, until then little known, published a novel in which he proclaimed that a new and coloured South Africa was emerging from the decadence of the poor white in the towns and the mentally degenerate settler in the ruinous veld farm: that the only sensible policy was to assist in the birth of this new nation by painfully reconsidering all the ideas of race and by breaking down current social inhibitions by a new love that would find its full expression in sex. 'I believe,' said the eccentric missionary in *Turbott Wolfe*, 'that the white man's day is over. Anyone can plainly see that the world is quickly and inevitably becoming a coloured world. I do not yet assert that miscegenation should be actively encouraged, but I believe it is the missionary's work now, and the work of any white man in Africa worth his salt, to prepare the way for the ultimate end.' Prophetic as the novel was about race relations, it disgusted British suburbia, press and society. It determined the Afrikaner establishment to bridle a civilization and a culture that Plomer himself described as 'obscene'.

CULTURAL ROOTS

Yet it was the inflow of this civilization which had sustained the English strain against Afrikanerization. After one hundred and fifty years of British endeavour and settlement in Africa, local culture was colonial. It was a matter of suburbs, commerce, public works, organized sport, universities, and journalism. The Boers had built an indigenous culture more sedulously than the British, who were receiving the latest from New York, London and Paris with every mailboat, ever could. Smuts admitted cheerfully that 'the genius of South Africa has shown itself in action rather than in the domain of art. Neither in painting nor in sculpture have we anything yet to compare with the performance of other countries.'

Thomas Pringle wrote a poetic evocation of Africa that Coleridge thought lyric perfection; but upon this foundation little was built until Olive Schreiner's *Story of an African Farm* delighted everyone from Gladstone downwards. It painted the veld in its true and severe colours, and laid bare the plight of colonial womenkind, of spirit fighting African aridity, that singled it out from all the journalese junglese, and caused it to be acclaimed as a great novel. But it produced no immediate results. Africa inspired British writers like Rider Haggard, one of the first novelists to attempt to see the black man as anything but a depraved savage, as, indeed, the expression of the European's own anarchic libido. South Africa's literary flowering came late and sparse with William Plomer and Roy Campbell (who frankly declared there was no South African poetry). The writers that followed them and received serious recognition, like Nadine Gordimer, Doris Lessing and Alan Paton, were stimulated precisely by the failure of the white conscience to meet the challenge of race and by the crassness of white leadership. They were fated mostly to become exiles, along with the political liberals and journalists who fled Afrikaner repression to impart a South African accent to the left-wing protest in British society.

British impotence to produce a school of South African painting must seem even more significant considering the potentialities of African (not to mention bushman) art. There was, of course, a long and respectable history of sketching, especially for purposes of record, beginning with Lady Anne Barnard. The demand by British publishers for illustrative material for the lithographer and engraver at home, in service of the illustrated magazines especially, was a continuing one. Gordon Brown, the art critic, lists four hundred illustrators and painters in his *Pictorial Art in South Africa* published in 1875: it shows that British men and women took their pencils, paintboxes and pads everywhere with them on their travels to catch the scene. The camera naturally diminished this great and valuable industry, stimulating to the historian and essential to the naturalist. Leaders in this genre were Thomas Baines (Official Artist during the Kaffir War of 1850–2), T. W. Bowler and Lang Schmidt. A new burst of creativity may now be expected as art becomes one of the few South African media left for social criticism, but it will be strictly post-imperial, post-British.

The experts' judgment on British art in South Africa is that it was not deeply rooted in African soil. And what is true of a people's art is related to their other achievements. The dearth of artists and the failure to produce political leadership are not unrelated. The British were in Africa but not of it. They built public works for Africa; they did not build a home in Africa for themselves. They could not become, any more than the French, an African tribe. Their monuments are economic and therefore less durable than a school of great art would be. Yet one outstanding cultural achievement of the British should not be overlooked. Willy-nilly, they created the Afrikaner nation. The determination of successive Afrikaner administrations from Hertzog onwards to belittle and if possible obliterate the trace and influence of British culture, to rewrite the school history books, to treat English-speaking South Africans as aliens until they become Afrikaans speakers and Nationalists, the re-education of Englishwomen who became the wives of Afrikaners, the exclusion of English from the Voortrekker memorial celebrations in 1949; all such reactions paid unconscious tribute to the fact that the British presence had provided the nursery and the schoolroom of Afrikanerdom.

In the early nineteenth century the Afrikaners would have had to be rescued by some European nation if they were not to die out gradually, submerged in a black sea, whose oncoming tides of Bantu were barely apprehended in the Cape during the Napoleonic Wars. The most that would have survived would have been a mixed race – perhaps a talented race – with its own tribal or cultural ambience like the Liberians and the Freetown Creoles. An immense process of cultural absorption through a British filter went on from the 1850s, even in the Transvaal, where the predikants fought all foreign corruption with zeal. The Afrikaners were in a real sense parasitic on the British Empire. Sucked slowly dry, the South African British became a semi-digested but affluent minority, providing specialist services but no longer influencing the course of events. Perhaps the last expression of British liberalism was the torch commando and the stiff rearguard action by English-speaking South Africans in defence of the freedom of the press, the inheritance of Thomas Pringle.

THE RHODESIAN DIVORCE

The Rhodesians, on the other hand, hung on to their British identity precisely because it was clear to them in the 1920s that the Afrikaners had won the day in South Africa. Offered a choice in 1922 between becoming a British colony or joining South Africa as a province, national pride and the sense of British self-confidence asserted itself. The Rhodesians thought upon their founder, Rhodes, and rejected the blandishments of Smuts (who wanted their votes in the coming tussle with Hertzog's Nationalists) and of the Foreign Office, which hoped that South Africa would take over all the liabilities incurred by the British South Africa Company. This decision is more indicative of Rhodesian psychology than has been realized. The quality of the late nineteenth century was embalmed there; the conviction that the Englishmen could meet any odds. The Conservative Government of the 1950s was quietly convinced that, as they had made the Kenyan settler come to terms with the Africans, the Rhodesians, who were socially inferior, would submit to the manipulations of a political master mind like Mr R. A. Butler without undue trouble. But Mr Butler, and subsequently Mr Harold Wilson, were fighting Cecil John Rhodes – a Victorian. The twentieth century, United Nations and all, has proved a poor match for the nineteenth.

Apartheid was better organized in Rhodesia than in South Africa. It became, from the first, the basis of social organization both in the cities and in the countryside. White and black farming areas were separated by the Land Apportionment Act, frequently amended. It was a basic article of belief that the white farmer had to have the best land, because he alone had the knowledge and the implements to get the best out of such land – the native would waste and spoil it as he visibly had in his South African reserves. It has been said that in parts of Rhodesia if white farmers had been prepared to work their own land as they do in Britain, white and black need never have met. The whole conception of Rhodesian farming was supervision of native labour. The Administrator Lord Grey noted grimly: 'The Jesuits, who work alongside their kaffirs, accomplish much. Of all the people in Rhodesia I respect them most. Also M. le Vicomte de la Panouse, ex-A.D.C. to General Macmahon, *sang bleu*, and a great gentleman – you may see him in his garden digging and trowelling and the kaffir boy holding the seed – but the Englishman, No! It is his business to hold the candle while the kaffir does the work and he knows his place right well.'

In the towns, municipal legislation enabled the councils to prescribe where and how Africans should live. They had no access to white clubs, cinemas, swimming pools, buses, hairdressers, doctors, schools, lifts or lavatories. They could have been kept entirely out, but servants were needed as well as labour in offices and workshops, so they were allowed to live in shanty-towns on locations outside the white man's town. In 1906 Bulawayo Council prohibited natives from walking on sidewalks, though this ban became a dead letter as African trade became important to the shops. Until the 1920s and even later African customers were served from hatches at the back of many shops.

There was thus brought into being a leisured, if not at first particularly affluent, English society, paternalist and landed, which created by hard work something of the casual yet purposeful eighteenth-century country-side after the enclosures. Until 1931, when Rhodesian tobacco received imperial preference, the return from the land was modest. As late as the 1920s the image of the Rhodesian settler was still the bronzed pioneer for such women novelists as Gertrude Page:

Clever, handsome, debonair, well-read, he demonstrated unintentionally a healthy form of the simple life, absolutely free of asceticism, or any mawkish effeminacy . . . His farming . . . consisted largely of much prowling around with his gun; with occasional intervals of sowing seed, which invariably came up in the most annoying patches, superintending the curing of bacon and ham, and strolling round to yarn with other healthy young demonstrators of the simple life . . . a good, all-round healthy, vigorous colonist . . .

By the end of World War II the infrastructure was laid and the country seemed ready to receive a fresh wave of white immigration. Visits by British airmen and others on training during the war had forged the necessary links with an otherwise somewhat closed society. These new immigrants came, it was said, for the sun and the servants, and to get away from the taxes and rationing of post-war Britain. They were mostly blue collar workers and lower middle class. British visitors often considered them poor material, and certainly inexpert, crude and offensive in their dealings with the Africans. It was a new experience for a British bricklayer to have an African menial handing him the bricks. Anthropologists diagnosed this new group of settlers as suffering from culture shock, the more severe perhaps in that post-war Britain was even more different from Africa than was Victorian Britain. Boris Gussman, the sociologist, considers that this shock produces 'regression' in the white man: 'There is a kind of honeymoon period when they stay in hotels, meet only the local residents who speak their own language ... They are pampered and petted wherever they go ...' Later the settler has to meet the problems of everyday life and exhibits the first shock symptom: hostility to the local people. Then comes such nostalgia for home ways that these become almost a form of religious observance. 'Social behaviour, language, beliefs are frozen at the level they had attained at the time the immigrants left their own country ... stereotyping follows from regression ...' The English visitor is amused at the way Rhodesians cling to the out-dated school and club blazer, *passé* in Britain except for special occasions.

Gussman noted that among shock symptoms was 'excessive washing of the hands, much concern over drinking water, food, dishes and bedding, fear of physical contact with attendants or servants, and absent-minded faraway stare that is sometimes called the tropical stare ... desire for dependence on longterm residents of the immigrant's own race or nationality; fits of anger over delays or other minor frustrations, and outright refusal to learn the language of the host country ...'

The Englishness of Rhodesia and the Kenya highlands was certainly calculated to minimize a shock that the Victorians seem not to have met; and the new wave of migrants helped each other in the building of villas, the creation of gardens, the running of services at the British welfare level. Every circumstance of a new immigrant's life was calculated to make him conform and to repress any 'liberalism' in his nature. One difference between Rhodesia and other white dominions was that it made 'Pommies' warmly welcome, so strong was the feeling that reinforcements were needed. But there was one other important pressure – the evident and vivid love of Rhodesians for their land. Yet Whitehall civil servants considered that when the crunch came they would quickly crack, faced with sanctions and the cutting of the umbilical cord with Britain. Organized by 'the old settlers', however, the Rhodesia Front party held, with considerable social skill, the whole white society together in a defiant Dunkirk spirit.

A factor in the transforming of British mentality in Rhodesia was the rise and fall of the Central African Federation between 1953 and 1962. It became clear to the old settlers that if Rhodesia was to take in more whites, expand and increase its standard of living, its economy needed a massive inflow of capital. The victory of Afrikanerdom in the election of 1948 made the time ripe to take up the earlier proposals for a tidy economic and political unit, white-ruled, in Central Africa. On the plea of building a barrier against Afrikanerdom (or a bridge between black and white Africa) the Federation of Rhodesia and Nyasaland was put together as a bargain between the white settlers and the Foreign Office, which wished to rid the British taxpayer of the cost of Nyasaland. Rhodesia tapped the copper wealth of the north and drew in massive investments.

Thus when the federation broke up the country was well-found to stand the siege, with good roads, defences and growing industries to take up the losses sustained by the vulnerable tobacco farmers. Between 1955 and 1960 the country went through a brief slightly liberal phase under Whitehead and Welensky, during which there were wider contacts between whites and educated blacks. A black minister sat in Welensky's cabinet; he had to live, however, in the black location. The Jamieson Hotel became non-racial, and African lawyers could have chambers in Harvest House. Probably it hardly affected the mass of Rhodesians who continued to think the Africans a different kind of human species – one that, in a series of local jokes, they compared unfavourably with baboons. Of the educated African they always said, 'They revert. When excited or drunk, they revert' (i.e. to native ways, such as squatting on the floor).

It proved therefore a false dawn as far as the liberal newspapers were concerned. The breakaway by Nyasaland and Northern Rhodesia, allied to the attack on whites in the Congo, returned Rhodesian opinion to its stereotype of African treachery and incompetence. The detention of black political leaders in remote camps again returned Europeans to the position in which the only Africans they saw were their servants. The break with Britain fostered the idea of a distinctively Rhodesian nation and culture. At U.D.I. in 1965 the Union Jack was kept flying, and only Britain was out of step; in 1970 the Rhodesians had a new flag flying over a Republic.

THE TRANSFORMATION OF THE TROPICS

Even in West Africa the proposition that Africans could quickly emulate Asians in taking over parliaments, governments and public services was dubiously received when the 1950s opened. The report of a United Nations commission that recommended that Tanganyika (a trust territory) should be given independence in a generation was read with incredulity, and the private lives of the commissioners from Latin America and elsewhere were the subject of ill-natured white gossip. When Whitehall began ordering the extension of African representation in colonial legislatures, white settlers began to emphasize the difference between West Africans ('in touch with Europe for 300 years') and East Africans ('in the Stone Age sixty years ago'). The Colonial Office was recruiting young men for colonial careers up to 1955, which often meant that those who entered young got out with compensation by way of capital bonus in time to embark on a new career. One or two got into Parliament. It was widely felt that a degree of uncertainty lowered the standard of material. Lower-deck promotions of black men to district officerships occurred.

The background to British life in the colonies was henceforth one of African politics, of growing black demands for an ever-increasing share of power, and often of African 'uppityness' in the office. Just as names like Gandhi, Nehru and Jinnah had been in the background to life in Indian bungalows, now in Africa the whites found themselves learning new names in the newspapers – Azikiwe, Nkrumah, Kenyatta, Nyerere, Mboya and others. Every colony soon had its African leader or agitator, its African nationalist party at grips with the British authorities and the C.I.D. Demonstrations, riots, imprisonments and even outright revolts became the hazard of the day, as the colonial government tested African pressure against its own powers of resistance – a balance not only of force, but of public opinion, both at home and at the United Nations. Newspapers in Africa proliferated, and the Africans produced their own, fiercely provocative, usually mendacious, as part of the battle. In 1956 the British Conservative Party made a new assessment of Africa: the position could not be held, the process of transferring power would have to be accelerated. In the South African parliament Mr Macmillan horrified his hosts and sent a thrill of premonition through the British everywhere, by announcing that the winds of change were blowing.

Settlers, farmers, businessmen in the tropical colonies concluded that the Tories were selling them out in a 'gutless surrender' to the bluster of agitators who had no backing from the chiefs and whose nationalist parties only mustered an appearance of support by intimidation. Intimidation became the theme of white newspapers, and servants told their *memsahibs* about it, afraid to take their afternoons off. But the educated African was arriving in ever greater numbers and expecting respect. By 1900 Bindloss had noted that on the West Coast 'when speaking to an educated man of colour it is always desirable to allude to his people as "Africans" – the word "Negro" is generally an affront.' By the 1950s the 'been to's' were returning with their English degrees and even with English wives. Such marriages proclaimed to the ordinary African that equality was dawning, even though the English *memsahib* (in Kenya at least) generally cut the white wives dead. In East and Central Africa the colour bar was less easily breached. Mr Attlee's government exiled Seretse Khama for allegedly upsetting his own Bechuana tribesfolk by taking an English wife; in 1962 the multi-racial university in Salisbury, at the height of the 'liberal' period, rejected a well-qualified African lecturer, Dr B. Chidzero, because he had a white wife. In West Africa such inhibitions were dissolving in the 1940s. Africans studying in England had long been emulating the English officials who familiarized themselves in bed with the psychology of the people with whom they had to deal; this work of mutual education of a generation of African leaders by Englishwomen is a social study in itself; its value was recognized on the Coast.

A factor for change in the British attitude to Africans had been operating years before educated Africans arrived on the scene. The work of the ethnologists was taken up in the early years of the new century and put on a more scientific basis by a new school of anthropologists, who began to find parallels between primitive societies and the conditions in classical times in the Mediterranean. The English in Africa who had found Darwin so acceptable were rather slower to correct their Eurocentric prejudices by reference to Sir James Frazer, Havelock Ellis, Margaret Mead, A. C. Haddon and R. R. Marett. The Colonial Office, however, began to think it ought to know more about African customs, even prior to 1914. In 1900 Sir Frederick Hodgson, Governor of the Gold Coast, nearly lost his life by assuming that the Asantehene actually sat on the Golden Stool. D.C.s were instructed to interrogate the natives and write reports for collation in London. The decision to ascertain, in Professor Forde's phrase 'the basic knowledge of habits of thought and pattern of behaviour among the people, which political leaders in autonomous responsible governments are presumed to have acquired', indicated that African customs were to be accorded some respect instead of being studied simply to change them into European ones.

Even before 1914 the idea that specialists should undertake such field studies was being absorbed, and the field anthropologists began to startle settlers and residents by 'going native' in the 1930s. 'Frankly,' remarked an editorial in a Northern Rhodesian newspaper, in 1934, 'we think that much of this anthropological or sociological study is hooey . . . it is not necessary to drop to the African level of village life in order to get Africans to unburden themselves . . . in the process they [the anthropologists] show Africans what they want to find, and the Africans naturally provide.' The leader argued that not only did the anthropologists get false information, but they brought Europeans into contempt with Africans. For Europeans to live with African women did not have this effect. But behaving as if they were Africans, and claiming to be scientific men, lowered all Europeans and their science in African eyes, it was argued.

District officers were disturbed, especially when the anthropologist turned out to be a woman. Nor were they always popular with African intellectuals who for a long time suspected that their work was part of white techniques for denigrating the African condition and exposing 'savagery'. Africanus Horton, indeed, had objected in 1870 to 'people who form themselves into an anthropological society to rake up old malice and encourage their agents to search out the worst possible characteristic of Africans.' Most white travellers, he thought, were anthropologists in that sense.

The Sudan government gave special facilities to Evans Pritchard, Nigeria to B. Northcote Thomas in 1915. Lugard gave his blessing to the formation of the International African Institute in 1926. As facts poured in, a feeling that Africans might be fitted for direct, as opposed to indirect rule, began to seep into official minds. Historians began to show that after all Africans had governed themselves before the European came. The idea that Britain had an educative mission in Africa began to take hold. This process met resistance. Sir Philip Mitchell, who failed to see the Mau Mau revolt stirring under his very eyes while Governor of Kenya, accused the anthropologists of 'asserting that they only were gifted with understanding, busied themselves with enthusiasm about all these minutiae of obscure tribal and personal practices which results in a large number of painstaking and often accurate records . . . of such length that nobody has any time to read them.' It had, he felt, little practical relevance. He and other Governors took more kindly to efforts to revive African crafts, to which Africans seemed better attuned than playing with machinery. But twenty-five anthropologists were delving away at government expense after World War II, filling questionnaires and taking long interviews with Africans in depth, finding out who had obligations to whom, why witchcraft mattered, and who owned land. When Kenyatta was judged organizer of Mau Mau the question might well have been asked whether his powers really did derive from witchcraft, or from his anthropological training at the London School of Economics.

The anthropologists did not deny the testimony of earlier visitors to rapine, famine, slavery and human sacrifice in the old Africa. But they found abundant merit in the texture of African family and village relationships, were tolerant of witchcraft, and responded sympathetically to a culture that was spontaneous, spiritual and ecologically sound compared to the tawdry materialism of the white civilization from whose crumbling edges they made their observations. African nationalists and some white Africanists quickly built up out of this changed perspective an African golden age which white (never or rarely Arab) slavers and soldiers had wrecked. This new appraisal of the African past percolated into British consciousness by various channels, gradually engaging the latent sense of guilt which underlies British philanthropic and political propensities.

Suddenly the professor was at large in British society in Africa. Whatever his speciality, he provided a new English voice in Africa. The result was that the settlers soon talked of the new universities in Africa as 'hotbeds', generally of communism. This dislike was reciprocated.

District Commissioners found themselves being told that not only had they no competence in law, engineering, agriculture, veterinary science, developmental planning, public works, and community development but also very little in administration, at least without an anthropologist to guide them. Despite this reduction in their responsibilities, they had more files than ever to get through. Sylvia Leith Ross, living in an African village and watching her local D.C., was 'struck by the paradox of the enormous increase in office routine work; of files and reports, and returns and forms, and the equal decrease in actual knowledge of the land and people. The letter is driving out the spirit and it's not even an efficient letter.' J.C. Cairns said, 'Thirty years ago [in 1919] a D.C. had leisure. He could be a friend and father to his people . . . now . . . paper work has grown to Frankenstein proportions, and there is no leisure. A D.C. works under more pressure than a businessman can imagine.' The introduction of the telephone in rural Africa in the 1950s added enormously to the D.C.'s problems. 'Well, anyway,' remarked a D.C. to one of the authors in his rather remote office in Sierra Leone, 'I am still chairman of the rural district council.'

THE TOURISTS

In the final stages of British rule, Africa became more and more accessible to Europe. Aircraft were being used for internal services before 1939, and afterwards flights from London to major centres became progressively shorter. Ministers and Members of Parliament were welcome in D.C.'s homes and the villas and *shambas* of settlers; Labour M.P.s were assumed to be as bad as the anthropologists, and Mr Stonehouse was even deported.

Travellers changed their fashions too. Though some still sought the remaining inaccessible places, most now explored the African community. It became the thing to travel on African buses or mammy-wagons, living in African homes or hotels, travelling third class, wearing short shorts or other modern leisure wear, and to come up with a fund of funny stories exactly as in Victorian times, but in a modern genre, recorded on tapes. Travellers were no longer amateur explorers in Livingstone's footsteps; they were amateur anthropologists. 'This is a book written after only six weeks of observation and thought in West Africa' was Naomi Mitchison's blithe preface to her book *Other Peoples' World*, an authoritative left-wing view of the region.

Travel in Africa lost most of its health risks after 1930. In that year atebrine and mepacrine were introduced as a prophylaxis against malaria. D.D.T. was discovered in 1939 and began to be used against most insect vectors of disease. Emetine, an alkaloid of ipecac was found in the 1930s to be effective against dysentery, and thereafter chemotherapy made rapid progress against human and animal sickness, though bilharzia until recently kept wise travellers out of lakes and rivers. Air-conditioning began to create a temperate climate within hotels and private residences from the 1950s. Roads and cars improved and aircraft could get one out of trouble in a matter of days. Food for Europeans was transformed by refrigeration and the deep freeze, though the British did not have almost their entire dietary flown out daily, as did French expatriates toiling in the white man's grave.

Africa thus became increasingly bearable for modern businessmen, sales representatives, civil engineers and every sort of expert. This produced a boom in hotel building even before tourism expanded. Chairmen of companies, who had thankfully left everything to the Coasters, began to travel out every year to inspect. Night clubs proliferated in West African cities. There were more British in Africa than ever; but more and more were clearly uncommitted to Africa. Nothing was more remarkable than the way in which Africa was the mecca for 'committed' journalists, especially from enlightened papers making their names in the 1950s; to be deserted as soon as the black-white conflict ended and African rule showed impatience of the criticism of left-wing journalists – who were suddenly reporting racial crises in the United States. Very bitter were the white settlers with such men; as one of them said to one of the authors: 'What has your editor ordered you to write about us?'

THE CHURCHES GO BLACK

African nationalism was, in a sense, the fulfilment of missionary hopes. In Sierra Leone the missions by the mid-nineteenth century were producing an African élite. Submerged under imperialism for decades, the mission-educated Sierra Leonian produced a yeast all down the coast. The same process occurred in varying degrees in other colonies from 1900 onwards. Mission schools usually did the bulk of African education for the first twenty-five years or so, because they did it cheaply and unobtrusively; then colonial revenues were put into both mission and secular schooling. No census has been taken of the British missionary lives spent in teaching Africans to read and write for a century or so in twenty colonies and probably three hundred mission stations and schools. At times settlers and officials realized that the power to read enabled Africans to study such downright communism as the New Testament, or such heady anti-establishment stuff as the history of England; but it was difficult to object, particularly when reading was combined with useful crafts like carpentry. A limited number of Africans read even more widely, although the missions relied heavily on a pabulum of pietism. 'Unless things are managed wisely and tactfully,' warned a prescient traveller, Captain Reynardson, motoring from the Cape to Kenya in 1933, 'we shall only educate Africans to antagonize them, losing all chance of their co-operation in a work for which such co-operation is essential – the development of the new Africa from within.'

Once the massive and dangerous work of setting up missions in savage Africa was completed, the dullness of missionary existence, except for the totally devoted, asserted itself. Missionaries found themselves affluent in farms and settlements which had reached maturity; they often became fractious and authoritarian, particularly as they sought to stem the temptations of imported Western life. Some spanked their pupils' bottoms. Others tried collectivism, with ill effects on farm routine. They were, however, often earlier in contact with African awakening from the shock of military and cultural conquest than were colonial officials. In Kenya, for example, there was a crisis in 1913 when the mission leaders notably ruled that female circumcision was incompatible with Christianity, just as polygamy had been. The immediate result was that one white evangelist lady was kidnapped and forcibly circumcized, from which operation she (like innumerable African girls before her) died, presumably a martyr. The longer term result was the turning away of a large part of the tribe from imported Christianity to new disciplines in which they judiciously added the gospel of Jesus the Communist to tribal customs. It was distressing to the missionaries as new Afro-Christian sects began to spring up all round them. Denunciation of Ethiopianism did little good when, for lack of larger worlds to conquer, the missionaries fought each other for converts.

As sects proliferated, and settler jests at African self-appointed bishops, eminences and even popes grew, the Churches took up their earlier decision to Africanize more seriously. Another return to tradition was the Churches' support for the African congregation against the white one in South, Central and East Africa. By the 1950s there was a new cause for the Churches, new possibilities of suffering and martyrdom in the name of Christ. In South Africa, men like Huddleston and de Blank fought the Afrikaner take-over of mission schools and universities, and the destruction of African rights by the Group Areas Act, and were gloriously deported. The price of not sympathizing with African nationalism was the loss of spiritual influence – and rightly, for missionaries otherwise found themselves in the position of arguing that Christianity had come to Africa to subordinate blacks to white government, instead of equipping them to govern themselves in a Christian polity.

The growing difficulty of recruiting white missionary labour encouraged rapid Africanization – and revealed to Africans that the white man was abandoning his own religion. African intellectual life and aspiration has been centred on the Church and missions, to the covert laughter of settlers or traders. Increasingly it was centred on the party, the secular university, and on the government department. The settler and trader found themselves facing the black man across the desk with themselves on the suppliant's side of it. North of the Zambesi the meek had inherited the earth.

THE FLAG CEREMONY

The ceremony of departure had a certain ritual and dignity. The British read of the results of the succession of constitutional conferences in London in which power was handed over piecemeal and African leaders demanded more and quickly. Those who were training Africans for top jobs in the civil service, army, police or otherwise received circulars urging them to redouble their efforts. Independence was announced. The programme of the Independence Celebrations was given out. Decorations went up in the capital. The name of the royalty to preside was announced. Committees prepared the details; there was even a British expert on independence protocol to arrange them, ensure no hitches and preserve the decencies. Routine became standardized. One quotation will stand for them all. 'During the last moments of British rule,' *The Times* wrote:

> The Union Jack will fly floodlit in the centre of a stadium seating 70,000, in front of the Duke of Edinburgh (who arrived today), Sir Richard Turnbull, the Governor, who at midnight becomes the country's first Governor-General, and Mr Julius Nyerere, the Prime Minister.
>
> There will be a few seconds of total darkness. Then, when the lights go on again, the Union Jack will have been hauled down and the new black, gold and green flag of Tanganyika will be seen slowly hoisted up the flagstaff.

And then there was little left but to wonder how the blacks would ever manage without us.

SELECT BIBLIOGRAPHY

Adams, W.J., *The Narrative of Private Buck Adams, 7th (Princess Royal's) Dragoon Guards on the Eastern Frontier of the Cape of Good Hope, 1843–1848*, Cape Town, 1941

Alston, Madeline, *From an old Cape Homestead*, London, 1929

Altrincham, Lord, *Kenya's Opportunity: memories, hopes and ideas*, London, 1955

Atcherley, Rowland J., *A Trip to Boerland, or a year's travel, sport, and gold-digging in the Transvaal and Colony of Natal*, London, 1879

Bache, Eve, *The Youngest Lion: early farming days in Kenya*, London, 1934

Baden-Powell, R.S.S., *The Matabele Campaign*, London, 1897

Baines, Thomas, *Journal of a Residence in Africa, 1841–1853*, 2 vols. Cape Town, 1961–4

Baker, Samuel White, *The Albert N'yanza, Great Basin of the Nile* . . 2 vols. London, 1866

Ballantyne, R.M., *Six Months at the Cape, or Letters to Periwinkle from South Africa*, London, 1879

Barbot, Jean, *A Description of the Coasts of North and South Guinea* . . 1732

Barker, Lady, *pseud.* (Broome, Lady M.A.), *A Year's Housekeeping in South Africa*, London, 1877

Barnard, Lady Anne, *South Africa a Century Ago: letters written from the Cape of Good Hope (1797–1801)*, London, 1901

Bell, Hesketh, *Glimpses of a governor's life, from diaries, letters and memoranda*, London, 1946

Benham, M.S. (ed.), *Henry Callaway, first bishop for Kaffraria, his life history and work*, London, 1896

Bindloss, Harold, *In the Niger Country*, Edinburgh, 1898

Bird, W.W., *State of the Cape of Good Hope in 1822*, London, 1823

Blennerhassct, Rose, and Sleeman, Lucy, *Adventures in Mashonaland*, London, 1893

Blundell, Michael, *So Rough a Wind: Kenya Memoirs*, London, 1964

Boyd, Joyce, *My Farm in Lion Country*, London, 1933

Boydell, Thomas, *My Beloved Country*, Cape Town, 1959

Bradley, E.G., *A Household Book for Africa*, London, 1939
Bradley, Kenneth, *Once a District Officer*, London, 1966
Bryce, J., *Impressions of South Africa*, London, 1899
Buchanan, Barbara I., *Pioneer Days in Natal*, Pietermaritzburg, 1934
Burns, Alan C.M., *Colonial Civil Servant*, London, 1949
Burton, Richard, *First Footsteps in East Africa*, (First publ. 1856), London, 1966

Cairns, John C., *Bush and Boma*, London, 1959
Carnegie Commission of Investigation on the Poor White Question in South Africa, Report, 5 vols., Stellenbosch, 1932
Catling, R.C., *The Kenya Police*, London, 1962
Cattrick, Alan, *Spoor of Blood*, London, 1959
Church, Mary, *Sierra Leone: or the liberated Africans, in a series of letters from a young lady to her sister*, London, 1835
Clapperton, Hugh, *Journal of a Second Expedition into the Interior of Africa .. to which is added the Journal of Richard Lander* .. London, 1829
Cloudsley-Thompson, John L., *Animal Twilight: man and game in Eastern Africa*, London, 1967
Coaster, *pseud.* (J.M. Stuart-Young), *Coast and Bush Life in West Africa: a book for the potential coaster*, London, 1924
Cobbold, Lady Evelyn, *Kenya: the Land of Illusion*, London, 1935
Cranworth, Lord Bertram F.G., *A Colony in the Making: or sport and profit in British East Africa*, London, 1912
Cranworth, Lord Bertram F.G., *Kenya Chronicles*, London, 1939
Critolaos, *pseud.*, *Growls from Uganda*, London, 1909
Cumming, Roualeyn Gordon, *The Lion Hunter of South Africa: five years' adventures in the far interior of South Africa*, London, 1904
Cutten, T.E.G., *A History of the Press in South Africa*, Cape Town, 1935

Day, John R., *Railways of Northern Africa*, London, 1964
Day, John R., *Railways of Southern Africa*, London, 1963
Derham, Walter, *A Visit to Cape Colony and Natal in 1879*, Bristol, 1879
Duff-Gordon, Lady Lucy, *Letters from the Cape (1861-62)*, London, 1927
Dugmore, Henry H., *The Reminiscences of an Albany Settler*, Grahamstown, 1958

East African Women's League, *They Made It Their Home*, Nairobi, 1962
Emden, Paul, H., *Randlords*, London, 1935

Falconbridge, Anna M., *Two Voyages to Sierra Leone during the years 1791-2-3 in a series of letters*, London, 1794
Fenn, T.E., *How I volunteered for 'The Cape', and what I did there: being a short history of 8 month's service with the Frontier Light Horse* .., London, 1879
Findlay, Joan (ed.), *The Findlay Letters, 1806-1870*, Pretoria, 1954
Fitzpatrick, James Percy, *Jock of the Bushveld*, London, 1907
Fitzpatrick, James Percy, *Through Mashonaland with Pick and Pen*, Johannesburg, 1892
Fortescue, John, *The Royal Army Service Corps: a history of transport and supply in the British Army*, London, 1930
Freed, Louis F., *The Problem of European prostitution in Johannesburg: a sociological survey*, Cape Town, 1949

Fyfe, Christopher H., *A History of Sierra Leone*, London, 1962
Fyfe, H. Hamilton, *South Africa Today, with an Account of Modern Rhodesia*, London, 1911

Gardner, Brian, *Mafeking: a Victorian Legend*, London, 1966
Gardner, Brian, *The Quest for Timbuctoo*, London, 1968
Gaunt, Mary, *Alone in West Africa*, London, 1912
Gehrts, M., *A Cinema Actress in the Wilds of Togoland*, London, 1915
Gelfand, Michael, *Mother Patrick and her Nursing Sisters . . 1890–1901*, Cape Town, 1964
Gibbons, Alfred St H., *Exploration and Hunting in Central Africa*, London, 1898
Glover, Lady E.R., *Life of Sir John Hawley Glover*, London, 1897
Gordon, Lawrence L., *British Battles and Medals*, London, 1962
Gouldsbury, Cullen, *An African Year*, London, 1912
Grauman, Sir Harry, *Rand Riches and South Africa: a Pioneer's Searchlight*, London, 1936
Grogan, E.S., and Sharp, A.H., *From the Cape to Cairo*, London, 1902
Gussman, Boris, *Out in the Midday Sun*, London, 1962
Gutsche, Thelma, *No Ordinary Woman: the Life and Times of Florence Phillips*, Cape Town, 1966

Harding, Colin, *Frontier Patrols: a History of the British South Africa Police and other Rhodesian Forces*, London, 1937
Hardy, Ronald, *The Iron Snake*, London, 1965
Harris, William Cornwallis, *The Wild Sports of Southern Africa*, London, 1839
Harrison, J.W., *The Story of the Life of Mackay of Uganda*, London, 1891
Hattersley, Alan F., *Carbineer: the History of the Royal Natal Carbineers*, Aldershot, 1950
Hattersley, Alan F., *More Annals of Natal*, London, 1936
Hattersley, Alan F., *The Natalians: Further Annals of Natal*, Pietermaritzburg, 1940
Hattersley, Alan F., *Portrait of a Colony: the Story of Natal*, London, 1940
Hattersley, Alan F., *A Victorian Lady at the Cape, 1849–51*, Cape Town, 1951
Haywood, A., and Clarke, F.A.S., *The History of the Royal West African Frontier Force*, Aldershot, 1964
Heckford, Sarah, *A Lady Trader in the Transvaal*, 1882
Hickman, A.S., *Men who made Rhodesia: a register of those who served in the British South Africa Company's Police*, Salisbury, 1960
Heussler, Robert, *Yesterday's Rulers: the Making of the British Colonial Service*, London, 1963
Hindlip, Charles A., *British East Africa: Past, Present and Future*, London, 1905
Hoare, Rawdon, *Rhodesian Mosaic*, London, 1934
Hockly, H.E., *The Story of the British Settlers of 1820 in South Africa*, Cape Town, 1948
Hodgson, Mary Alice, *The Siege of Kumassi*, London, 1901
Hole, Hugh M., *Old Rhodesian Days*, (first published 1928), London, 1968
Holt, H.P., *The Mounted Police of Natal*, London, 1913
Holt, John, *The Diary of John Holt, with the Voyage of the 'Maria'*, Liverpool, 1948

Holt, John, *The Early Years of an African Trader*, London, 1962
Hore, Annie B., *To Lake Tanganyika in a Bath Chair*, London, 1889
Horton, James A.B., *West African Countries and Peoples, British and Native* ..
(first publ. 1868), Edinburgh, 1969
Hutchinson, Mrs., *In Tents in the Transvaal*, London, 1879
Huxley, Elspeth J., *The Flame Trees of Thika*, London, 1959
Huxley, Elspeth J., *The Mottled Lizard*, London, 1962
Huxley, Elspeth J., *Settlers of Kenya*, London, 1948
Huxley, Elspeth J., *White Man's Country: Lord Delamere and the Making of Kenya, 1870–1931*, 2 vols. London, 1935

Jackson, Albert, *Trader on the Veld*, Cape Town, 1958
Jackson, Laura M., 'A Trip to Uganda', *The Queen*, 24th April, 1915
Janzé, Frédéric de, *Vertical Land*, London, 1928
Jobson, Richard, *The Golden Trade: or, a Discovery of the River Gambia* ..
(first publ. 1623), London, 1968
Johnston, Harry H., *British Central Africa*, London, 1897

Kemp, Dennis, *Nine Years at the Gold Coast*, London, 1898
King, Marina, *Sunrise to Evening Star: my Seventy Years in South Africa*, London, 1935
King, W.R., *Campaigning in Kaffirland, or scenes and adventures in the Kaffir War of 1851-2*, London, 1853
Kingsley, Mary H., *Travels in West Africa*, London, 1897
Kingsley, Mary H., *West African Studies*, London, 1899
Kirk-Greene, A.H.M., 'Food for Thought', *Corona*, vol. 11, July 1959
Krapf, Johann, *Travels, researchers and missionary labours during an eighteen years residence in Eastern Africa*, London, 1860
Kuttel, M., *Quadrilles and konfyt: the life and journal of Hildagonda Duckitt*, Cape Town, 1954

Laing, Alexander Gordon, *Travels in the Timanee, Kooranko, and Soolima Countries in West Africa*, London, 1825
Laird, Macgregor, and Oldfield, R.A.K., *Narrative of an Expedition into the Interior of Africa, by the River Niger* .. 2 vols. London, 1837
Lander, Richard and John, *The Niger Journal of Richard and John Lander*, edited by Robin Hallett, London, 1965
Larymore, Constance, *A Resident's Wife in Nigeria*, London, 1908
Laurence, E.C., *A Nurse's Life in War and Peace*, London, 1912
Lewinsohn, Richard, *Barney Barnato: from Whitechapel Clown to Diamond King*, London, 1937
Leys, Norman N., *Kenya*, London, 1924
Lister, Georgina, *Reminiscences of Georgina Lister*, Johannesburg, 1960
Lloyd, Alan, *The Drums of Kumassi: the Story of the Ashanti Wars*, London, 1964
Lloyd, F.E., *Rhodesian Patrol*, Ilfracombe, 1965
Lockley, R.M., *A Pot of Smoke, Being the Adventures and Life of Dan Owain*, London, 1940
Lord, W.B., and Baines, T., *Shifts and expedients of camp life, travel and exploration*, London, 1876

Lowndes, E.E.K., *Everyday Life in South Africa*, London, 1900

Lugard, Frederick J.D., *The Diaries of Lord Lugard*, 3 vols. London, 1959

McCarthy, Edward T., *Incidents in the Life of a Mining Engineer*, London, 1918

McKay, James, *Reminiscences of the Last Kaffir War, illustrated with numerous anecdotes*, Grahamstown, 1871

Mackintosh, Catherine W., *Coillard of the Zambesi*, London, 1907

McNeill, Malcolm, *In Pursuit of the 'Mad' Mullah: service and sport in the Somaliland Protectorate*, London, 1902

Mallett, Marguerite, *A White Woman among the Masai*, London, 1923

Mann, Robert J., *The Colony of Natal: an account of the characteristics and capabilities of this British dependency*, London, 1859

Manson-Dahr, Sir Philip, *History of the School of Tropical Medicine in London (1899–1949)*, London, 1956

Martin, Henry, Unpublished ms., Rhodes House, Oxford

Mason, G.H., *Life with the Zulus of Natal, South Africa* (first published 1855), London, 1968

Maugham, R.C.F., *Nyasaland in the Nineties, and other recollections*, London, 1935

Melland, F.H. and Cholmondley, E.H., *Through the Heart of Africa .. a journey .. from Northern Rhodesia, past the Great Lakes, to Egypt*, London, 1912

Melville, Elizabeth H., *A Residence at Sierra Leone*, London, 1849

Mill, Hugh Robert, *Record of the Royal Geographical Society, 1830–1930*, London, 1930

Millin, Sarah L., *The South Africans*, London, 1926

Mitchison, Naomi, *Other People's Worlds*, London, 1958

Moffat, John S., *The Lives of Robert and Mary Moffat*, 3rd ed., London, 1855

Moodie, D.C.F., *The History of the Battles and Adventures of the British, the Boers and the Zulus in Southern Africa ..* Cape Town, 1879

Moodie, John W.D., *Ten Years in South Africa*, 2 vols. London, 1835

Moore, Decima, and Guggisberg, F.G., *We Two in West Africa*, London, 1909

Moore, Francis, *Travels into the Inland Parts of Africa .. to which is added Capt. Stibbs's Voyage up the Gambia ..* , London, 1738

Morris, Donald R., *The Washing of the Spears: a history of the rise of the Zulu nation under Shaka ..* , London, 1966

Morton, H.V., *In Search of South Africa*, London, 1948

Moyse-Bartlett, H., *The King's African Rifles: a study in the military history of East and Central Africa, 1890–1945*, Aldershot, 1956

Murray, J., *How to Live in Tropical Africa: a guide to tropical hygiene*, London, 1895

Murray, Joyce, (ed.), *In mid-Victorian Cape Town: letters from Miss Rutherfoord*, Cape Town, 1953

Musgrave, George C., *To Kumassi with Scott*, 1896

Nicholson, George, *The Cape and its Colonists, with hints to settlers in 1848*, London, 1848

Page, Gertrude, *Edge o' Beyond*, London, c. 1911

Page, Gertrude, *Far from the Limelight*, London, 1918
Page, Gertrude, *Where the Strange Roads go Down*, London, 1913
Pascoe, C.F., *Two Hundred Years of the S.P.G.*, London, 1901
Perham, M. and Simmons J., *African Discovery*, London, 1953
Philipps, Thomas, *Philipps, 1820 settler: his letters*, edited by Anthony Keppel-Jones, Pietermaritzburg, 1960
Phillips, Florence, *Some South African Recollections*, London, 1899
Plomer, William C.F., *Turbott Wolfe*, London, 1926
Pope-Hennessey, James, *Sins of the Fathers: a study of the Atlantic slave traders, 1441–1807*, London, 1967
Pope-Hennessy, James, *Veranda: some episodes in the crown colonies, 1867–1889*, London, 1964
Popkess, A., *Sweat in my Eyes*, Leicester, 1952
Prichard, Helen M., *Friends and Foes in the Transkei: an Englishwoman's experiences during the Cape Frontier War of 1877–8*, London, 1880
Pringle, Thomas, *Narrative of a Residence in South Africa*, London, 1835

Rankin, F. Harrison, *The White Man's Grave: a visit to Sierra Leone in 1834*, 2 vols. London, 1836
Ransford, Oliver, *The Battle of Majuba Hill: the First Boer War*, London, 1967
Ransford, Oliver, *Livingstone's Lake: the Drama of Nyasa*, London, 1966
Ransome, Stafford, *The Engineer in South Africa*, London, 1903
Rivett, A.W.L., *Ten Years' Church Work in Natal*, London, 1890
Rivett-Carnac, Dorothy E., *Thus Came the English in 1820*, London, 1961
Robinson, Ronald, *and* Gallagher, John, *Africa and the Victorians: the official mind of imperialism*, London, 1961
Roberts, Brian, *Ladies in the Veld*, London, 1965
Roche, Harriet A., *On Trek in the Transvaal: or over berg and veldt in South Africa*, 2nd ed., London, 1878.
Rorke, Melina, *Melina Rorke, her Amazing Experiences in the Stormy Nineties of South Africa's Story*, London, 1939

Salmon, Edward, and Longden, A.A., *The Literature and Art of the Empire*, London, 1924
Scott, Harold H., *A History of Tropical Medicine*, London, 1939
Schreiner, Olive, *The Story of an African Farm*, London, 1883
Schreiner, Olive, *Trooper Peter Halket of Mashonaland*, London, 1897
Seaver, George, *David Livingstone: His Life and Letters*, London, 1957
Selous, F.C., *A Hunter's Wanderings in Africa .. *, London, 1890
Sharwood-Smith, Bryan E., *But Always as Friends: recollections of British administration in the Cameroons and Northern Nigeria, 1921–1957*, Durham, N. Carolina, 1969
Silburn, P.A., *South Africa—White and Black—or Brown*, London, 1927
Smith, William, *A New Voyage to Guinea .. *, London, 1745
Smithers, Elsa, *March Hare*, London, 1935
Speke, J.M., *Journal of the Discovery of the Source of the Nile*, London, 1863
Stanley, Henry M., *Through the Dark Continent*, 2 vols. London, 1878
Stewart, James, *The Zambesi Journal of James Stewart .. *, London, 1952
Struben, Charles, *Vein of Gold*, Cape Town, 1957

Swann, A.J., *Fighting the Slave-traders in Central Africa* .. , London, 1910

Swanzy, Henry, 'A Trading family in the nineteenth-century Gold Coast', *Transactions of the Historical Society of the Gold Coast*, vol. 2, 1956

Thomson, Joseph, *Through Masai Land*, 2nd ed., London, 1885

Trowell, Margaret, *African Tapestry*, London, 1957

Tylden, G., *The Armed Forces of South Africa*, Johannesburg, 1954

Varley, D.H., *A Short History of the Newspaper Press in South Africa, 1652–1952*, Cape Town, 1952

Ward, Harriet, (*ed.*), *Past and Future Emigration; or, the Book of the Cape*, London, 1849

Weinthal, Leo (ed.), *Memories, Mines and Millions, being the life of Sir Joseph B. Robinson, Bart.*, London, 1929

Whitehead, G.O., 'André Melly's visit to Khartoum, 1850.' *Sudan Notes and Records*, vol. 21, part 2, 1938

Whitford, John, *Trading Life in Western and Central Africa*, 2nd ed., London, 1967

Wilkinson, Anne M., *A Lady's Life and Travels in Zululand and the Transvaal during Cetewayo's Reign*, London, 1882

Women's Migration and Oversea Appointments Society, *New Horizons: a hundred years of women's migration*, London, 1963

Wymer, Norman, *The Man from the Cape*, London, 1959

Yesterday's Shopping: The Army and Navy Stores Catalogue, 1907, Newton Abbot, 1969

Young, P.J., *Boot and Saddle: a narrative record of the Cape Regiment* .. , Cape Town, 1955

INDEX